BASICS OF KEYBOARD THEORY

ANSWER BOOK

LEVELS PREPARATORY - 10

Seventh Edition

Julie McIntosh Johnson

J. Johnson Music Publications

(714) 961-0257
Fax: (714) 242-9350
www.bktmusic.com
info@bktmusic.com

Seventh Edition ©2020, Julie McIntosh Johnson
Previous Editions ©1993, 1997, 2004, 2007, 2012, 2014, Julie McIntosh Johnson

Basics of Keyboard Theory, Answer Book, Seventh Edition

Published by:

J. Johnson Music Publications
P.O. Box 230
Lockwood, CA 93932
(714) 961-0257
www.bktmusic.com

All rights reserved. No part of this book may be reproduced or transmitted in any form or by any means, electronic or mechanical, including photocopying, recording, or by any information storage and retrieval system without written permission from the author, except for the inclusion of brief quotations in a review.

©2020 by Julie McIntosh Johnson. Revised.
Previous editions ©1993, 1997, 2004, 2007, 2012, 2014, Julie McIntosh Johnson.
Printed in United States of America

Library of Congress Cataloging in Publication Data

Johnson, Julie Anne McIntosh
Basics of Keyboard Theory, Answer Book, Seventh Edition

ISBN 10: 1-891757-39-3
ISBN 13: 978-1-891757-39-6

LC TX 4-799-988

ABOUT BASICS OF KEYBOARD THEORY

Intended as a supplement to private or group music lessons, *Basics of Keyboard Theory* presents theory concepts to beginning through advanced music students. From note naming to advanced analysis, these workbooks provide a thorough theory education.

This answer book contains the answers for all levels of *Basics of Keyboard Theory,* from the Preparatory Level through Level Ten (Advanced Level).

Learning music theory can be a very rewarding experience for the student when carefully applied to lessons. *Basics of Keyboard Theory* is an important part of learning this valuable subject.

Basics of Keyboard Theory corresponds with the MTAC Certificate of Merit® Piano Syllabus. Certificate of Merit® is an evaluation program of the Music Teachers' Association of California. Reference to 'Certificate of Merit®' (CM) does not imply endorsement by MTAC of this product.

Ear Training Basics
Levels Preparatory through 10

by
Julie Johnson
Author of *Basics of Keyboard Theory*

- An innovative teaching approach helps minimize student guessing.
- Separate student and teacher books provide the framework for a collaborative learning experience.
- Teacher Books include activities to be completed at the lesson, teaching tips, and answers for the student home assignments.
- Student Books include worksheets and an MP3 CD.

www.bktmusic.com

J. Johnson Music Publications
info@bktmusic.com

Julie Johnson's Guide to AP* Music Theory, Second Edition

- Follows requirements of the College Board Advanced Placement* Music Theory exam
- Edited and expanded based on customer feedback
- More progressive sight-singing and ear-training
- New In-Class ear-training pages for instructor and student collaboration
- More "free response" assignments
- Practice test and grading guidelines
- Supplementary materials available online
- Downloadable audio files at www.juliejohnsontheory.com

*AP and Advanced Placement are trademarks registered and/or owned by the College Board, which was not involved in the production of, and does not endorse, this product.

TABLE OF CONTENTS

Preparatory Level……………………………………………………………………………..1

Level 1…………………………………………………………………………………....11

Level 2……………………………………………………………………………………..23

Level 3……………………………………………………………………………….…..33

Level 4……………………………………………………………………………………...47

Level 5……………………………………………………………………………………63

Level 6………………………………………………………………………..……………75

Level 7……………………………………………………………………………………..89

Level 8……………………………………………………………………………………105

Level 9…………………………………………………………………………………...127

Level 10 (Advanced Level)…………………………………………………………………..151

Basics of Keyboard Theory is dedicated to my husband Rob, without whose love, support, help, and incredible patience, this series would not have been possible.

PREPARATORY LEVEL

LESSON 1: THE GRAND STAFF (Pages 1-6)

Page 1

1.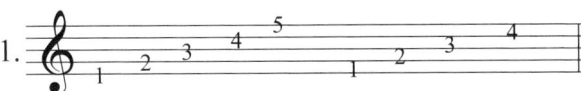

2.

Page 2

3.

4.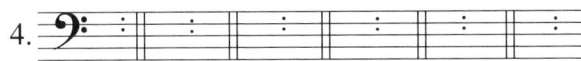

5.

Page 3

6.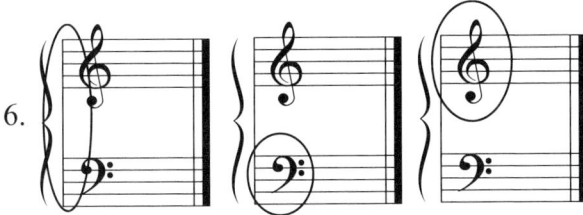

Page 4

7. 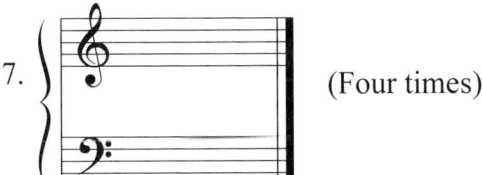 (Four times)

Page 5

8.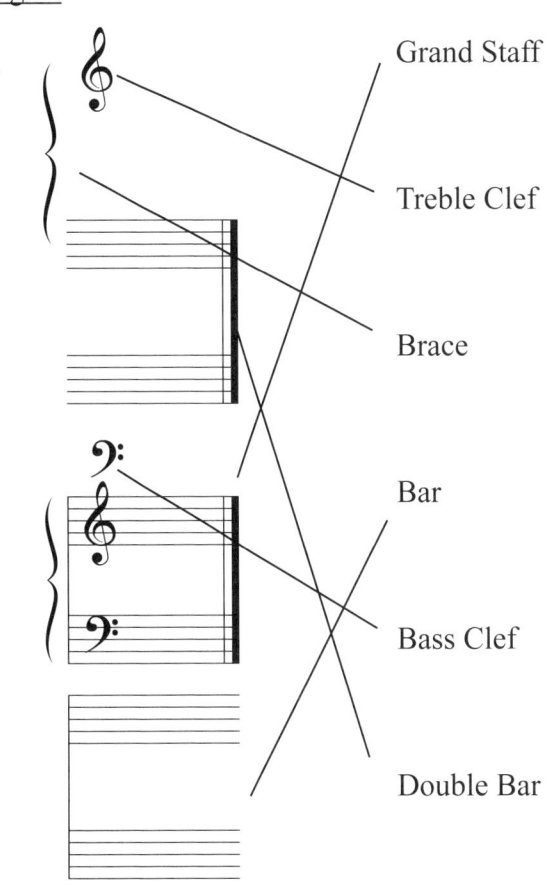

LESSON 2: LINE NOTES AND SPACE NOTES (Pages 7-8)

Page 8

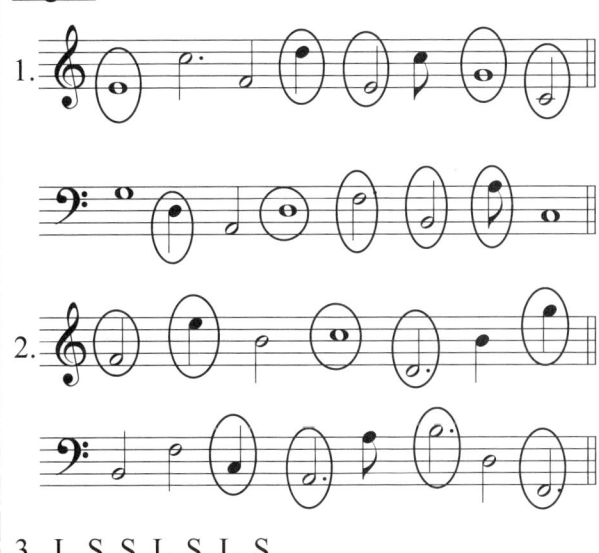

3. L, S, S, L, S, L, S

Page 8, cont.

4.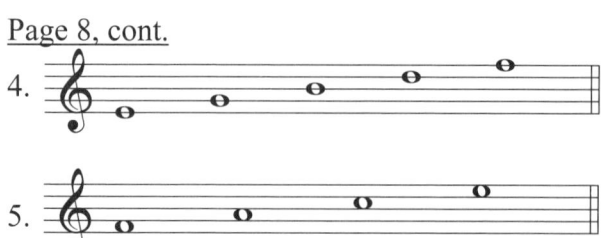

5.

LESSON 3: LETTER NAMES OF TREBLE CLEF NOTES (Pages 9-12)

Page 9

1. C, F, E, A, C, E, D, F, G
   A, G, C, D, C, F, E, A, D

Page 10

2.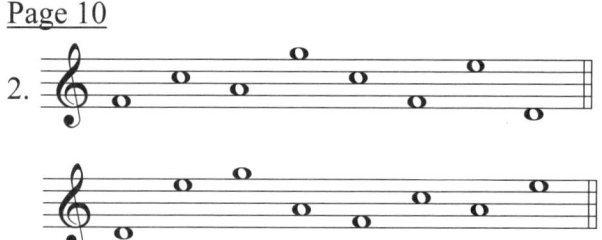

3. F, B, D, E, G, C, A, B
   B, F, E, C, D, E, G, A

Page 11

4.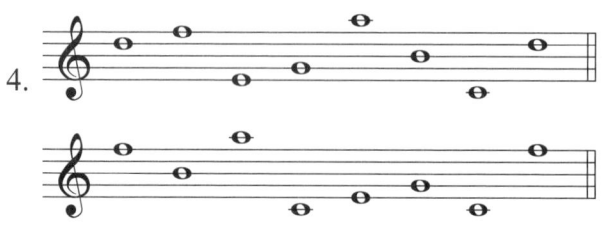

5. ACE   BEAD   FEED
   BAG   BEG   CAB

Page 12

6.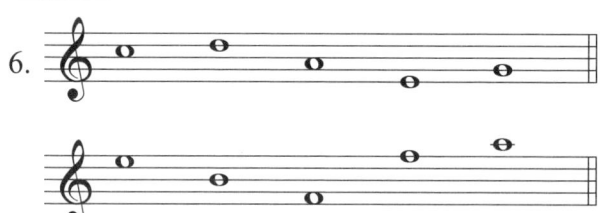

LESSON 4: LETTER NAMES OF BASS CLEF NOTES (Pages 13-16)

Page 13

1. G, C, E, A, E, B, C, E
   E, A, E, B, G, F, C, A

Page 14

2.

3. D, A, F, C, G, E, D, B
   F, G, A, B, E, D, G, C

Page 15

4.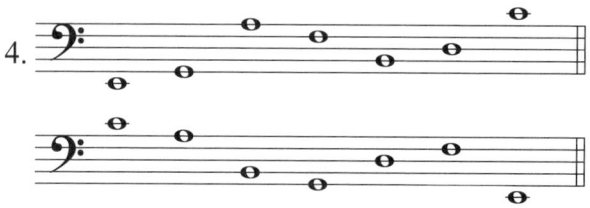

5. DAD   EDGE   DEED
   ADD   BAD   EGG

Page 16

6.

REVIEW: LETTER NAMES OF NOTES (Pages 17-18)

Page 17

1. F, A, F, E, C, A, C, B
   A, D, C, G, B, G, A, C

Page 18

2.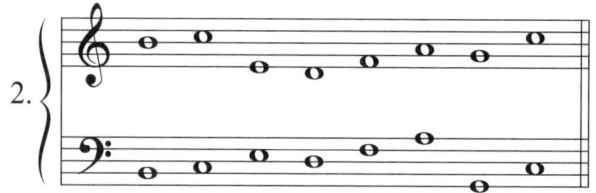

LESSON 5: SHARPS, FLATS, AND NATURALS (Pages 19-24)

Page 19

1.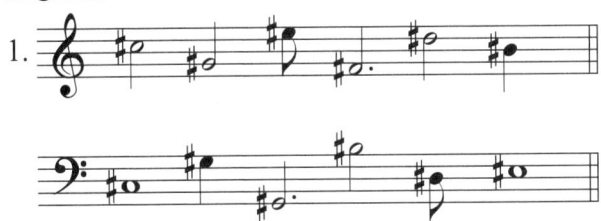

Page 20

2. A♯, C♯, G♯, F♯, D♯, G♯, F♯, B♯
   F♯, E♯, G♯, C♯, F♯, A♯, B♯, E♯

Page 21

3.

4. G♭, D♭, A♭, E♭, A♭, E♭, C♭, F♭
   E♭, E♭, B♭, G♭, A♭, D♭, F♭, C♭

Page 22

5.

Page 23

6. (Naturals are optional)

   E♮, G♮, B♮, F♮, D♮, A♮, E♮, A♮
   B♮, G♮, A♮, D♮, F♮, G♮, C♮, F♮

7. B♭, F♯, C♯, E♮, G♭, A♮, D♯, F♯
   E♭ A♯, F♮, C♯, G♭, D♮, E♭, D♭

Page 24

8.

LESSON 6: HALF STEPS AND WHOLE STEPS (Pages 25-26)

Page 25

1.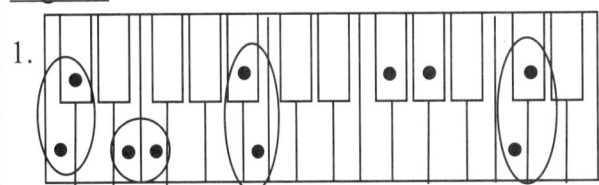

Page 26

2.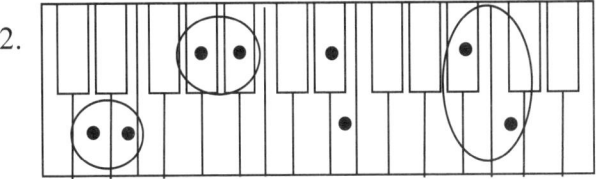

3. Whole   Whole
   Whole   Whole
   Half   Whole
   Whole   Half
   Half   Half
   Whole   Half

4. Whole, Half, Half, Whole, Whole, Whole
   Half, Whole, Whole, Half, Half, Whole

LESSON 7: INTERVALS (Pages 27-28)

Page 27

1. 4th, 3rd, 5th, 5th, 4th, 2nd
   5th, 4th, 2nd, 5th, 4th, 3rd

Page 28

2.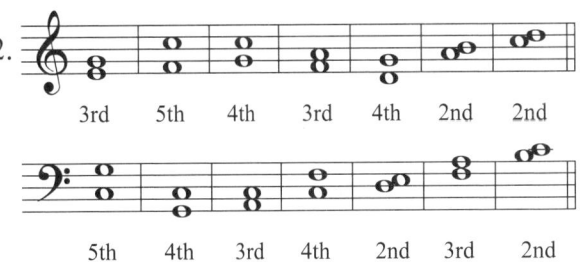

Page 28, cont.

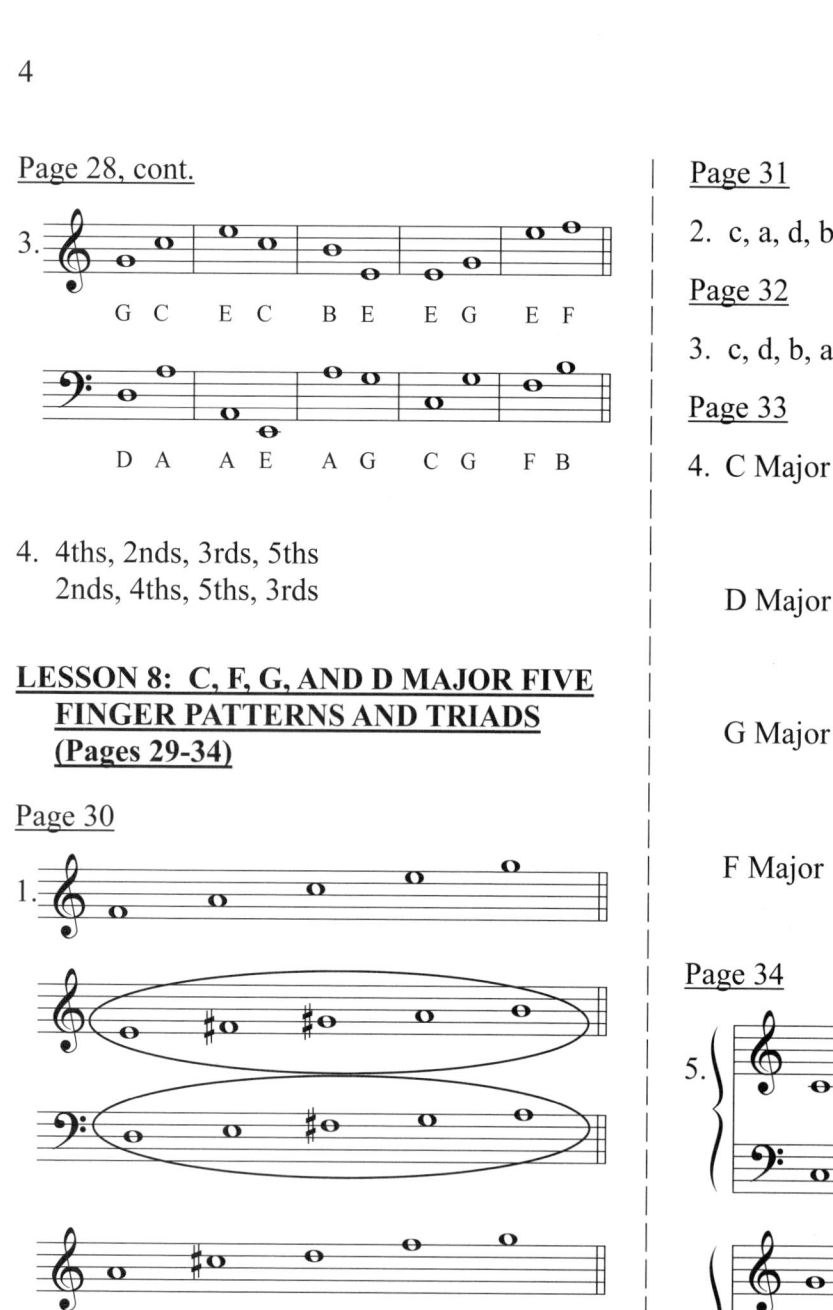

3. G C E C B E E G E F
   D A A E A G C G F B

4. 4ths, 2nds, 3rds, 5ths
   2nds, 4ths, 5ths, 3rds

LESSON 8: C, F, G, AND D MAJOR FIVE FINGER PATTERNS AND TRIADS
(Pages 29-34)

Page 30

1.

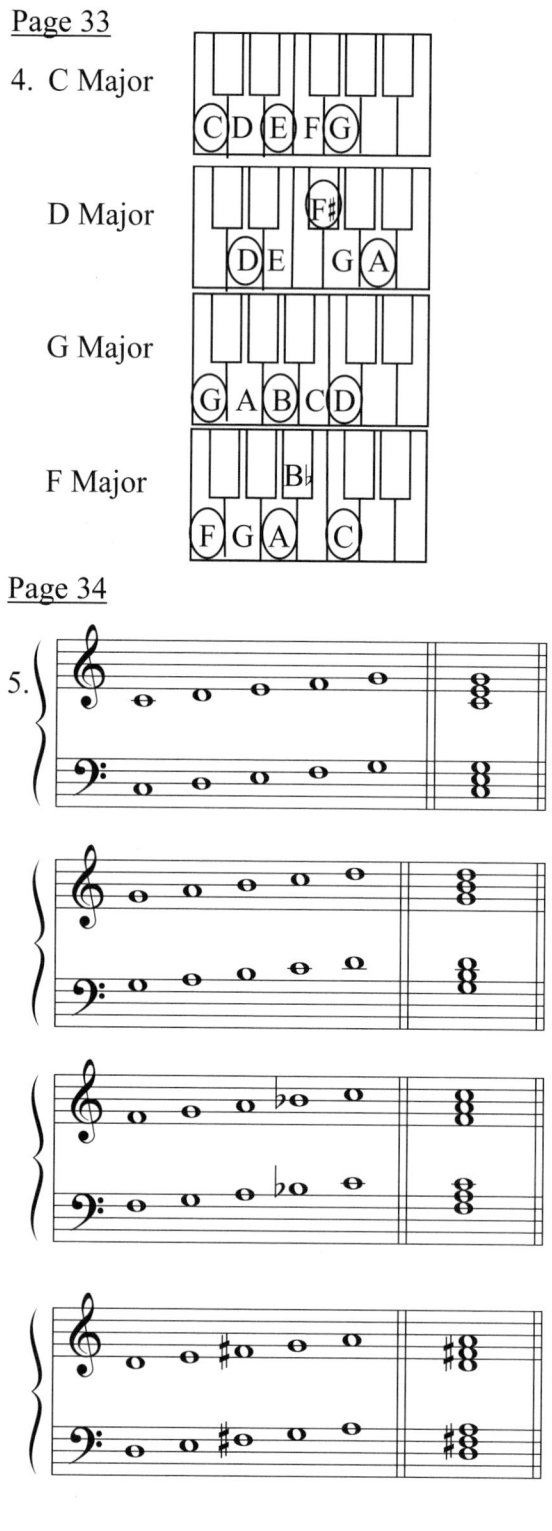

Page 31

2. c, a, d, b

Page 32

3. c, d, b, a

Page 33

4. C Major

D Major

G Major

F Major

Page 34

5.

Preparatory Level, Pages 28-34

LESSON 9: C, F, G, AND D MINOR FIVE FINGER PATTERNS AND TRIADS (Pages 35-38)

Page 35

1. d minor   f minor
   g minor   c minor

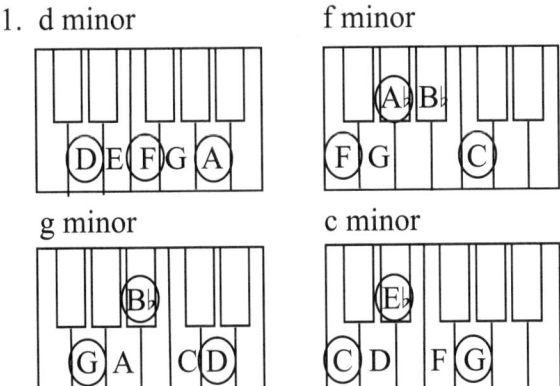

Page 36

2. d, a, b, c

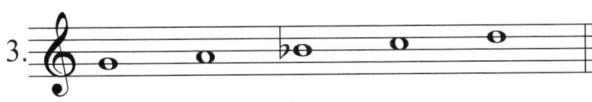

3.

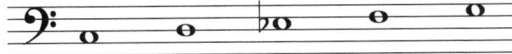

Page 37

4.

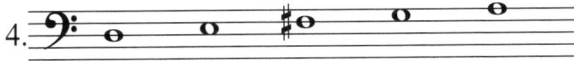

5. c, a, b, d

Page 38

6.

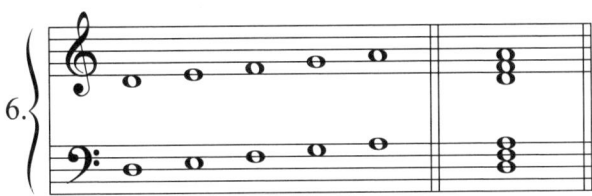

Page 38, No. 6, cont.

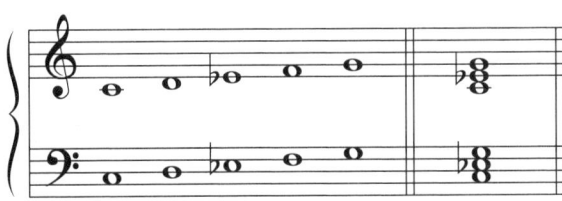

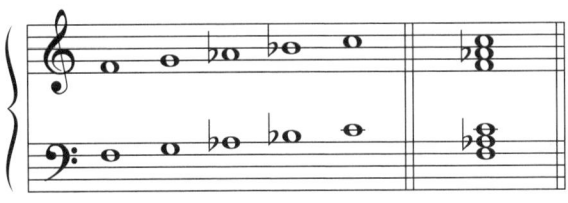

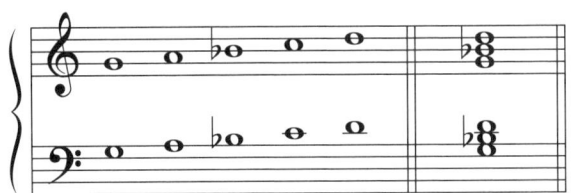

REVIEW: MAJOR AND MINOR FIVE FINGER PATTERNS (Pages 39-42)

Page 39

1. G Major, d minor, C Major, F Major, D Major, g minor

Page 40, No. 1, cont.

1. c minor, f minor

2.

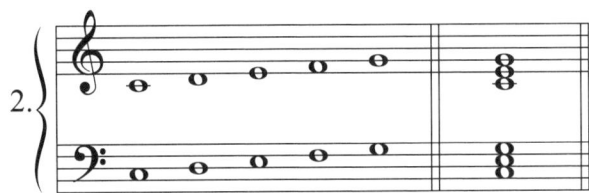

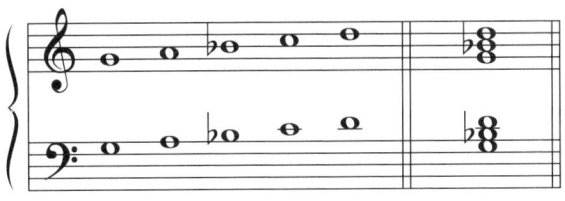

Preparatory Level, Pages 35-40

Page 41, No. 2, cont.

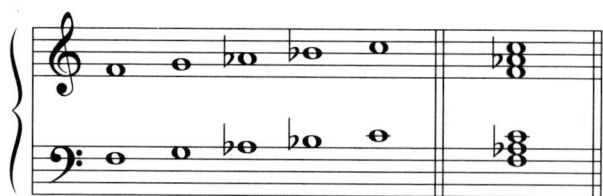

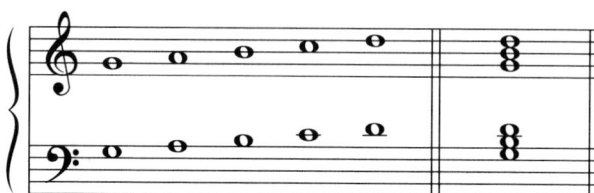

Page 42, No. 2, cont.

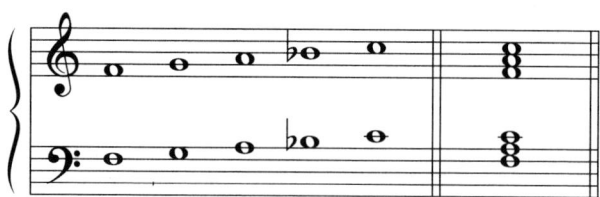

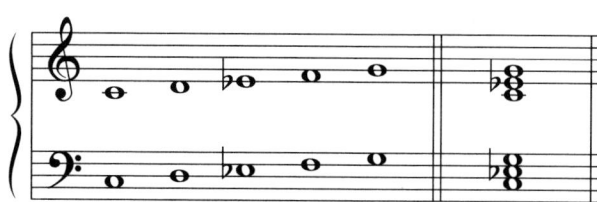

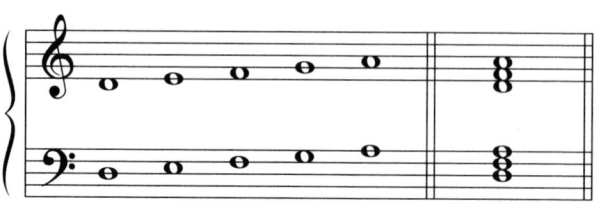

REVIEW: LESSONS 1-9 (Pages 43-44)

Page 43

1.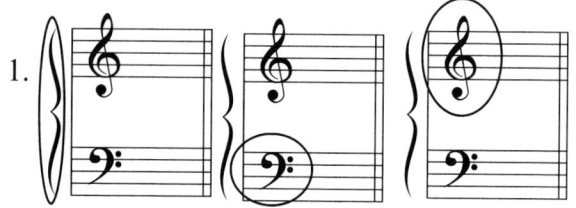

2. C, D, F, G, B♭, C, E♭
   F, C, A♭, B♭, E, A, E

3. Half, Half, Half, Whole
   Half, Whole, Half, Half

Page 44

4. 5th, 2nd, 3rd, 4th, 2nd, 4th
   2nd, 5th, 4th, 5th, 4th, 3rd

5.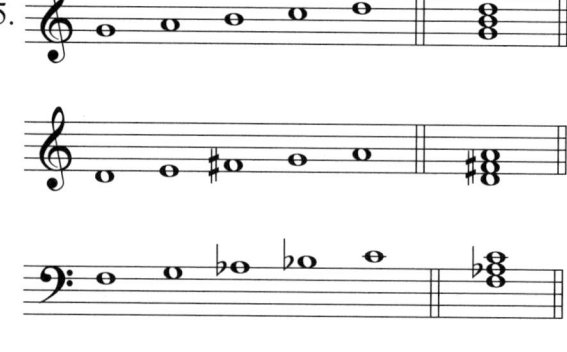

Preparatory Level, Pages 41-44

LESSON 10: C, F, AND G, MAJOR KEY SIGNATURES (Pages 45-48)

Page 46

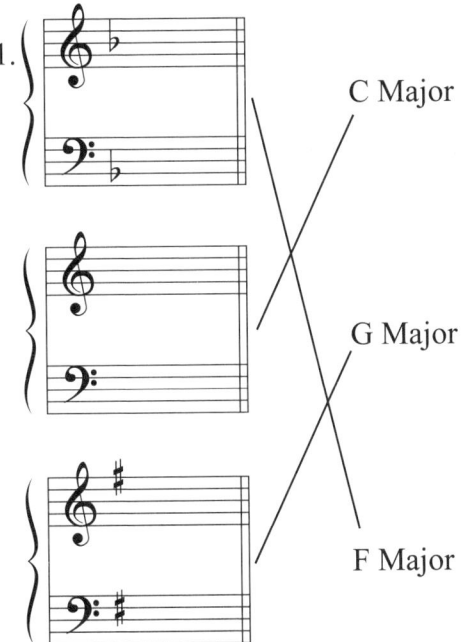

Page 47

2. F#
   G Major

   B♭
   F Major

   C Major

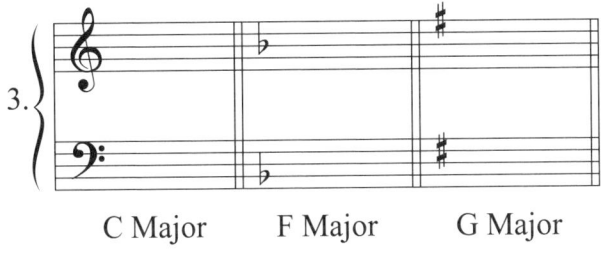

Page 48

4. a. G Major
   b. C Major
   c. F Major

LESSON 11: C, F, AND G, MAJOR SCALES (Pages 49-50)

Page 49

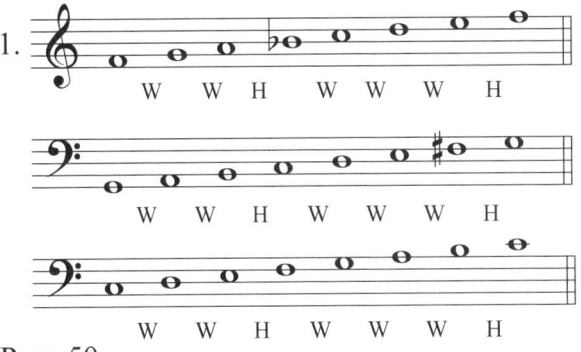

Page 50

1, cont.

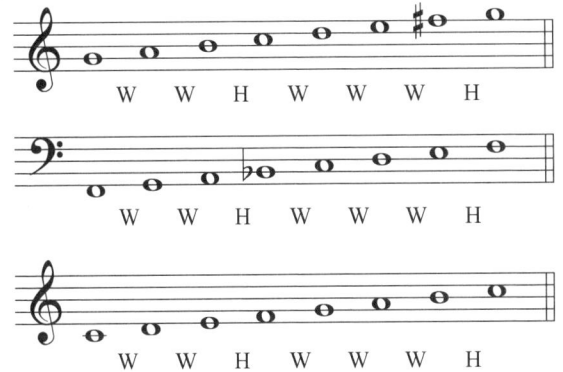

2. C Major

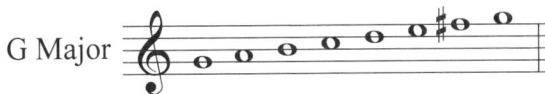

G Major

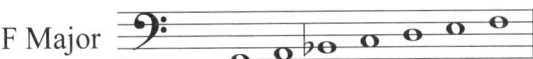

F Major

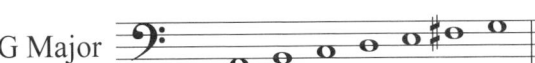

G Major

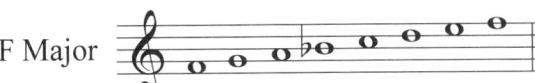

F Major

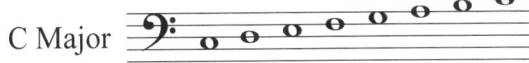

C Major

Preparatory Level, Pages 46-50

8

LESSON 12: TIME SIGNATURES (Pages 51-56)

Page 54

1. 2/4 : beats, one, one
   3/4 : three, one, one
   4/4 : measure, one, three, quarter, one

2. 1/2
   one
   two
   three

3.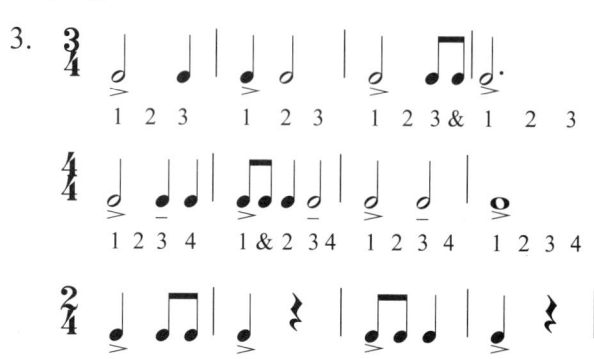

Page 55

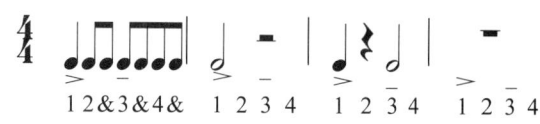

4. a.

   b.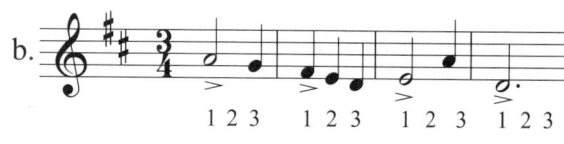

   c.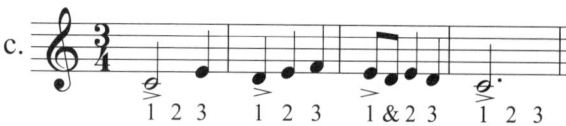

Page 55, No. 4, cont.

d.

e.

Page 56

5. quarter note; half note; half rest; eighth rest; whole note; eighth note; quarter rest; whole rest; dotted half note.

6. b, d, a, c

LESSON 13: SIGNS AND TERMS (Pages 57-58)

Page 58

1. d, c, a, b, h, e, i, f, k, g, j, l

REVIEW: LESSONS 10-13 (Pages 59-60)

Page 59

1. a.

   b.

   c.

2. a. Return to the original tempo.
   b. Staccato: detached
   c. Accent: play note louder than others
   d. Gradually slower

Preparatory Level, Pages 54-59

Page 60, No. 2, cont.

    e. Tie: hold second note
    f. Fermata: hold note longer than its value
    g. Forte: loud
    h. Repeat the music
    i. Piano: soft
    j. Slur: curved line indicating to play *legato*
    k. Return to the beginning and play to *fine*

3.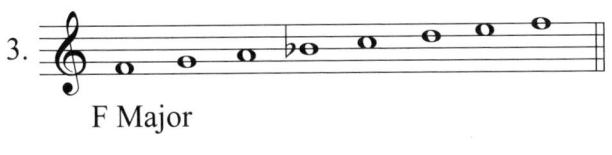
    F Major

    G Major

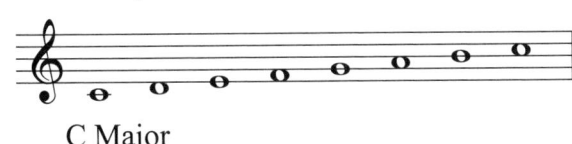
    C Major

REVIEW TEST (Pages 61-66)

1. a.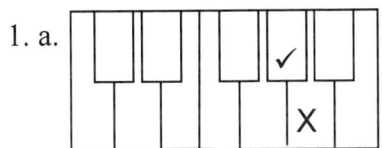
    b. Yes

2. a.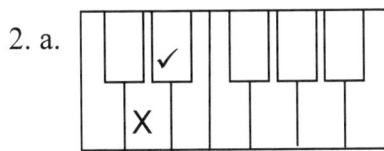
    b. No

3. a.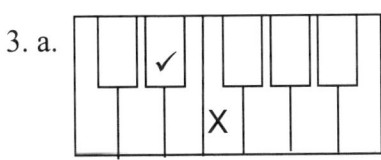
    b. No

Page 62

4. a. 3rd   b. 2nd   c. 5th   d. 3rd

5. a.

   b.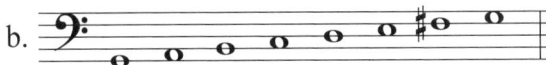

6.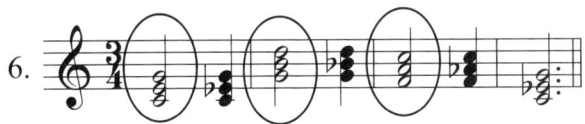

Page 63

7. 2, 1, 1/2, 3, 1

8. 3, 1, 4, 2, 5, 7, 6

Page 64

9. a. 4
   b. ♩.
   c. 6
   d. 3
   e. 8

Page 65

10. a. 4
    b. ♩.
    c. C Major
    d. 5th

Page 66

11. a. C
    b. D
    c. C
    d. 2nds
    e. 3
    f. Slowly
    g. Forte, loud
    h. Piano, soft

This page has purposely been left blank

LEVEL 1

LESSON 1: LETTER NAMES OF NOTES (Pages 1-2)

Page 2

1. D, F, A, C, G, D, G, B
   E, E, B, B, G, G, D, D, F

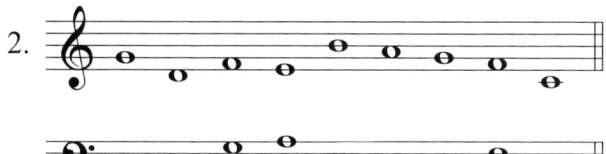

2.

3.

LESSON 2: SHARPS, FLATS, AND NATURALS (Pages 3-8)

Page 3

1.

Page 4

2. A♯, C♯, G♯, F♯, D♯, G♯, F♯, B♯
   F♯, E♯, G♯, C♯, F♯, A♯, B♯, E♯

Page 5

3.

Page 5, cont.

4. G♭, D♭, A♭, E♭, A♭, E♭, C♭, F♭
   E♭, E♭, B♭, G♭, A♭, D♭, F♭, C♭

Page 6

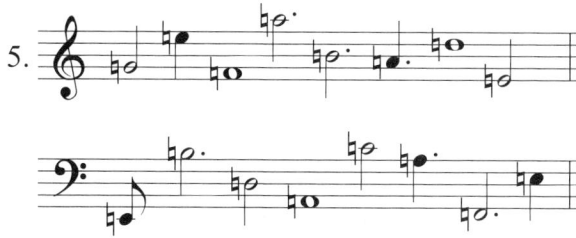

5.

Page 7

6. (Naturals are optional)
   E♮, G♮, B♮, F♮, D♮, A♮, E♮, A♮
   B♮, G♮, A♮, D♮, F♮, G♮, C♮, F♮

7. E♭, A♯, F♮, C♯, G♭, D♮, E♭, D♭
   B♭, F♯, C♯, E♮, G♭, A♭, D♯, F♯

Page 8

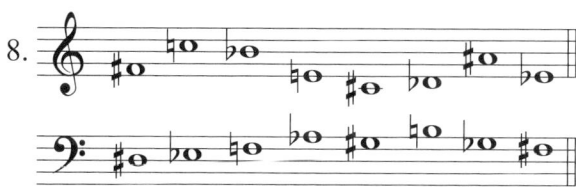

8.

9. Accidentals

LESSON 3: HALF STEPS AND WHOLE STEPS (Pages 9-10)

Page 9

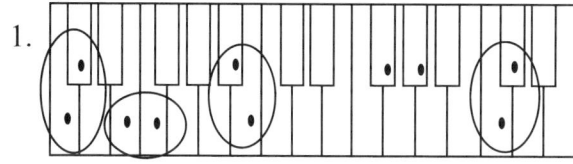

1.

Page 10

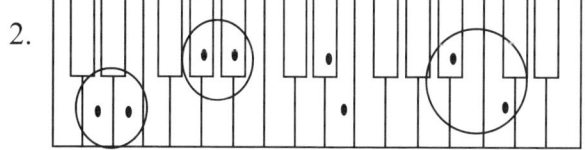

2.

Page 10, cont.

3. Whole   Whole
   Whole   Whole
   Half   Whole
   Whole   Half
   Half   Half
   Whole   Half

4. Whole, Half, Half, Whole, Whole, Whole
   Half, Whole, Whole, Half, Half, Whole

LESSON 4: INTERVALS (Pages 11-14)

Page 12

1. 4th, 5th, 3rd, 6th, 7th, 2nd, 4th, 6th
   4th, 8th (octave), 6th, 7th, 2nd, 4th, 5th, 3rd

2. 3rd, 8th (octave), 6th, 7th

Page 13

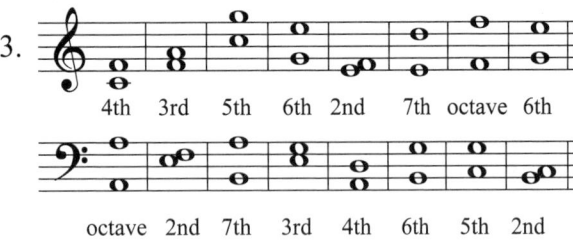

4. a. 3rd, 6th, 2nd, 3rd
   b. 5th, 3rd, 2nd, 4th

Page 14

Interval Game

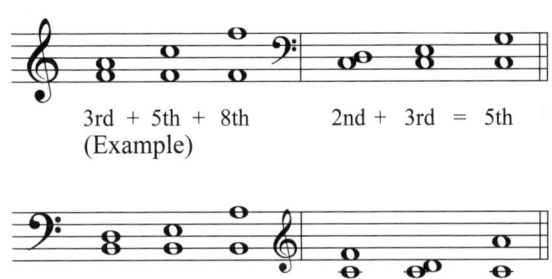

Page 14, Interval Game, cont.

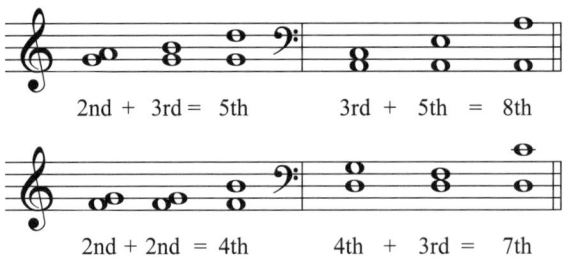

LESSON 5: MAJOR KEY SIGNATURES: C, G, D, AND F (Pages 15-18)

Page 16

1. G Major, C Major, F, Major, D Major

Page 17

3. a. C Major
   b. G Major
   c. F Major

Page 18, No. 3, cont.

d. C Major

LESSON 6: MAJOR SCALES: C, G, D, AND F (Pages 19-22)

Page 19

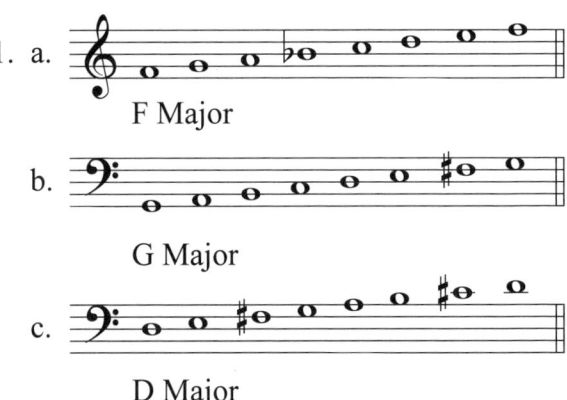

Level 1, Pages 10-19

Page 20, No. 1, cont.

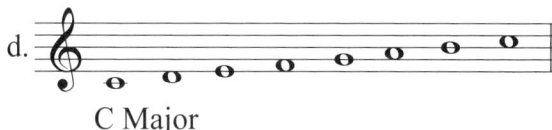
d. C Major

2. a.
C Major

b.
D Major

c.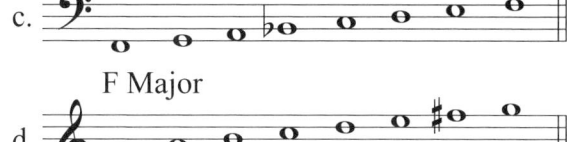
F Major

d.
G Major

Page 21: A Scale Game

a. D Major Scale
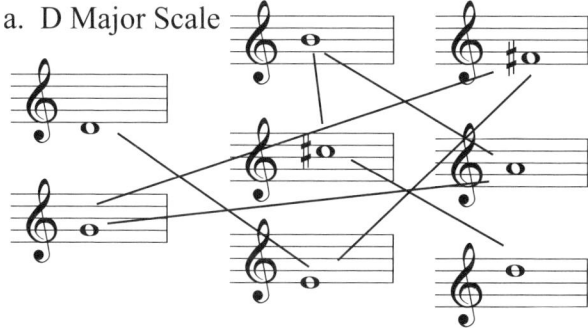

Page 22

b. F Major Scale
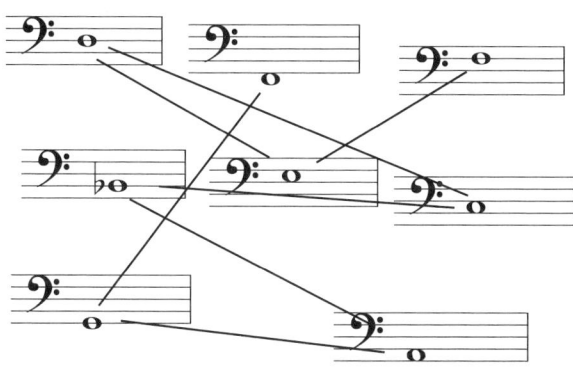

Page 22, cont.

c. G Major Scale
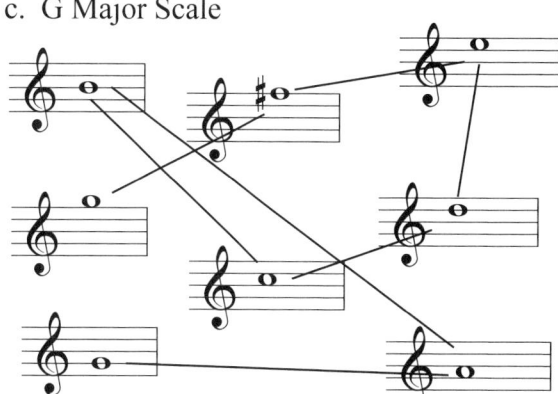

d. C Major Scale
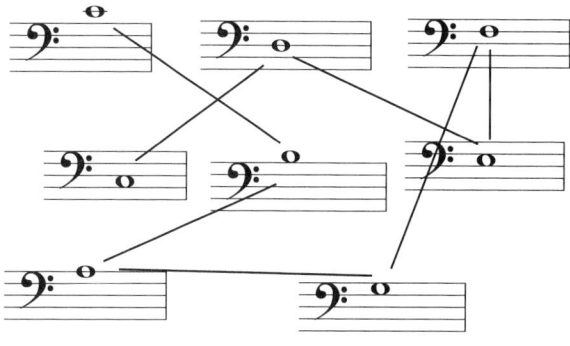

LESSON 7: C, F, AND G MAJOR AND MINOR FIVE FINGER PATTERNS AND TRIADS (Pages 23-30)

Page 25

1.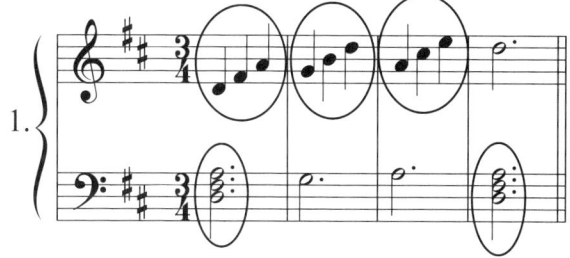

Level 1, Pages 20-25

Page 25, cont.

2. a.

b.

c.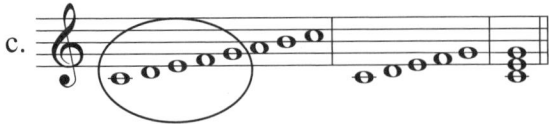

Page 26

3. F Major
   B♭

Page 27

4. a.

b.

c.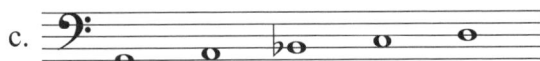

d.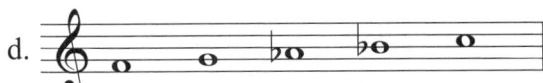

e.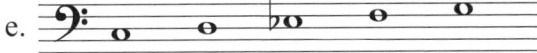

f.

Page 28

5. a. b.

c. d.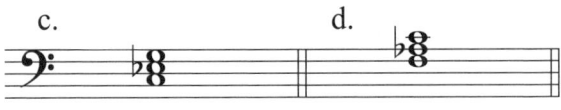

e. f.

Page 28

6. a. F Major
   b. C Major
   c. c minor

Page 29

   d. g minor
   e. G Major
   f. f minor
   g. F Major
   h. G Major
   i. c minor

Page 30

7.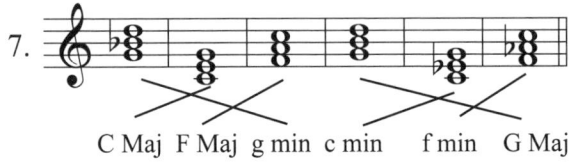

8. f minor, C Major, G Major, c minor, g minor, F Major

9.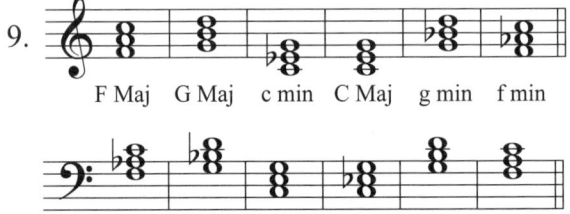

Level 1, Pages 25-30

LESSON 8: D, A, E, AND B♭ MAJOR AND MINOR FIVE FINGER PATTERNS AND TRIADS (Pages 31-36)

Page 31

1. E Major; F♯

2.

Page 32, No. 2, cont.

Page 33

3. a.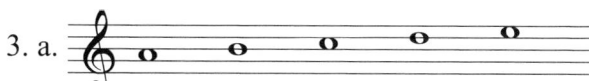

b.

c.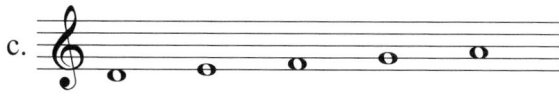

d.

e.

f.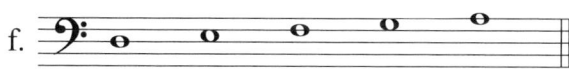

g.

Page 34

4.

5. a. D Major
   b. a minor
   c. e minor

Page 35

   d. A Major
   e. d minor
   f. E Major
   g. D Major
   h. E Major
   i. e minor
   j. B♭ Major
   k. b♭ minor

Page 36

6.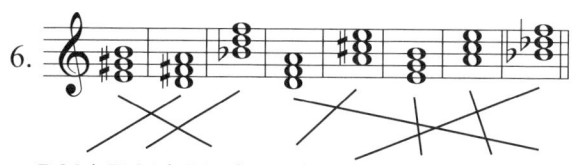

   D Maj B♭ Maj E Maj A Maj b♭ min e min a min d min

7. D Major, b♭ minor, A Major, a minor, B♭ Major, E Major, e minor, d minor

   b♭ minor, e minor, d minor, E Major, B♭ Major, a minor, A Major, D Major

8.

   EM am B♭M AM dm b♭m DM em

Level 1, Pages 31-36

REVIEW: MAJOR AND MINOR FIVE FINGER PATTERNS AND TRIADS
(Pages 37-38)

Page 37

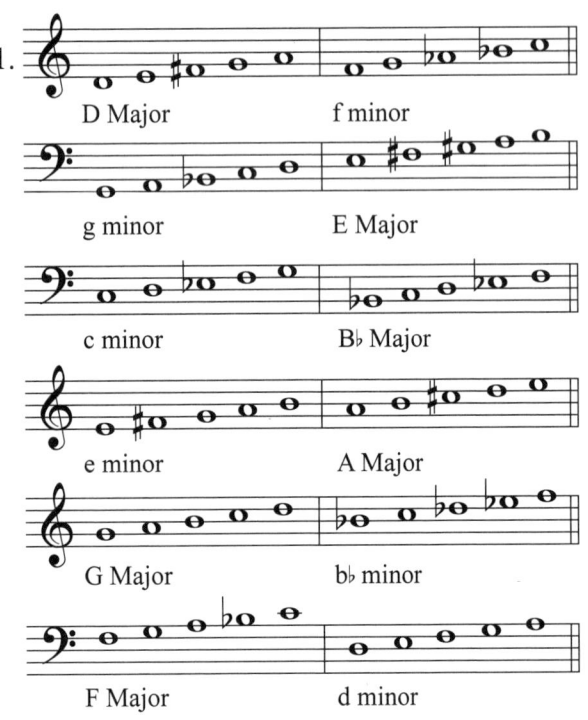

Page 38

2. g minor, D Major, F Major, c minor, A Major, e minor, B♭ Major

4. a. C Major
   b. G Major

LESSON 9: TRIADS OF THE SCALE
(Pages 39-40)

Page 39

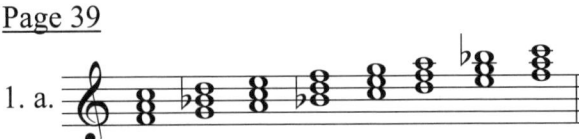

Page 40, No. 1, cont.

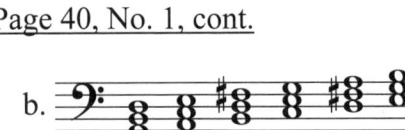

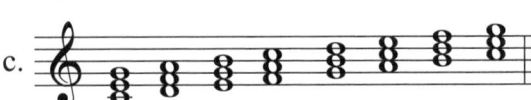

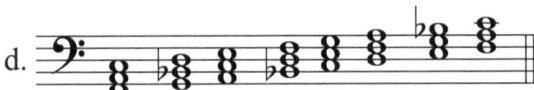

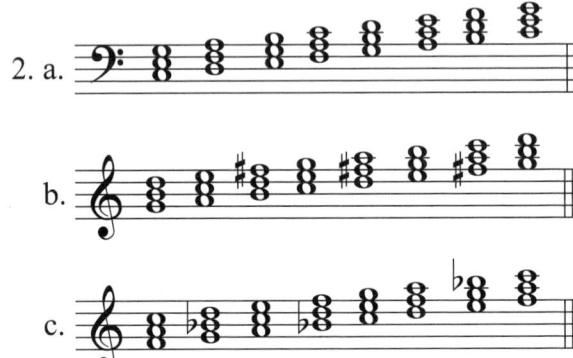

LESSON 10: PRIMARY TRIADS
(Pages 41-44)

Page 41

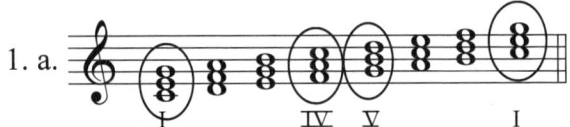

Page 42, No. 1, cont.

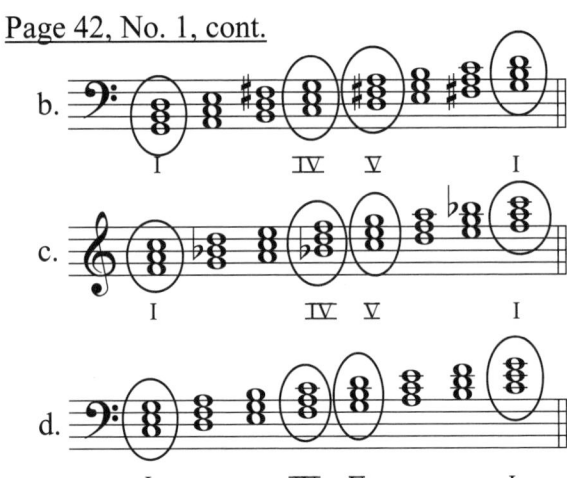

Page 42, No. 1, cont.

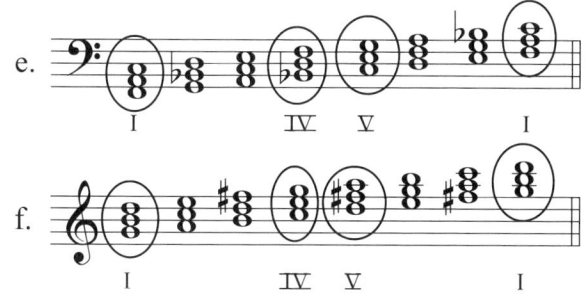

Page 43

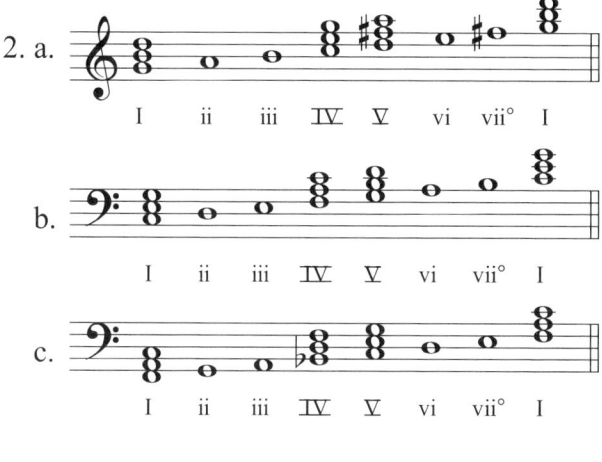

Page 44

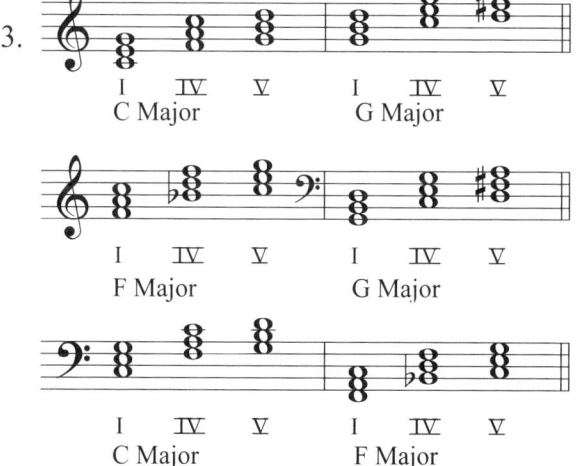

REVIEW: LESSONS 1-10 (Pages 47-52)

Page 47

1. A, E, A, F, D, D, G, A
   A, D, B, D, E, E, E, C

2. Whole, Half, Whole, Half, Half, Whole
   Half, Half, Half, Half, Whole, Whole

Page 48

3. 5th, 3rd, 4th, 8th (octave), 7th, 2nd
   4th, 4th, 3rd, 8th (octave), 6th, 5th

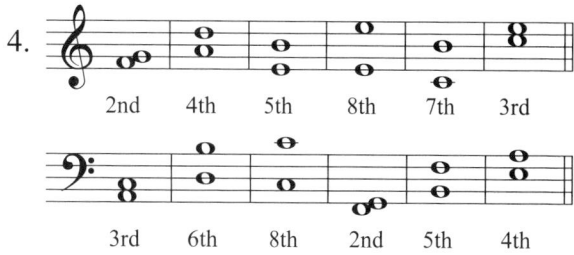

Page 49

5. D Major, C Major, F Major, G Major

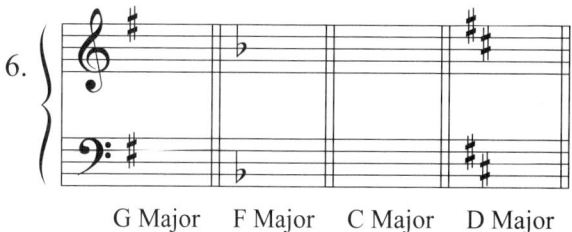

Page 50

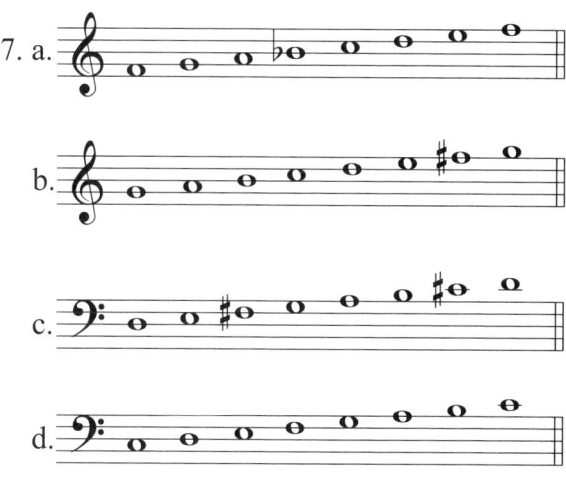

Page 50, No. 7, cont.

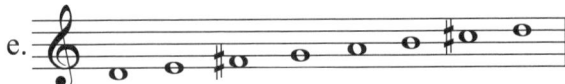

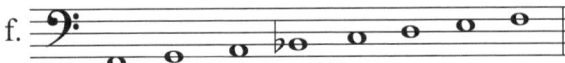

Page 51

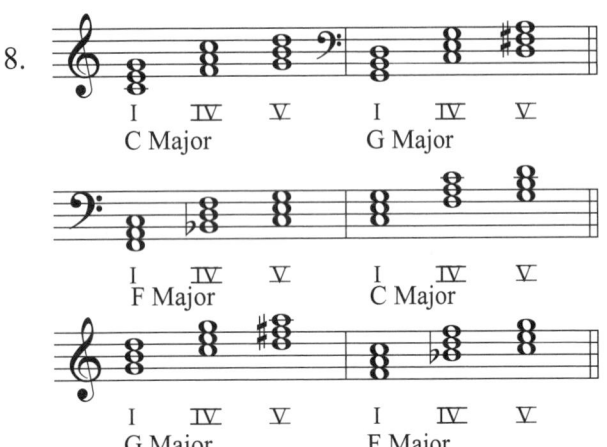

9. C Major, f minor, e minor, B♭ Major, D Major, A Major

   F Major, b♭ minor, c minor, G Major, E Major, a minor

Page 52

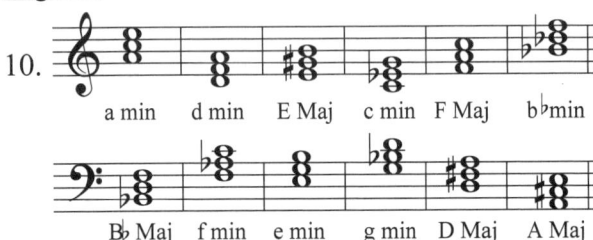

LESSON 11: TIME SIGNATURES (Pages 53-56)

Page 55

1. 2 = 2 beats per measure, first beat is strongest
   4 = Quarter note receives one beat

   3 = 3 beats per measure, first beat is strongest
   4 = Quarter note receives one beat

   4 = 4 beats per measure, first beat is strongest, third beat strong but not as strong as beat 1
   4 = Quarter note receives one beat

Page 55, cont.

Page 56

5. d, c, a, b

LESSON 12: SIGNS AND TERMS (Pages 57-62)

Page 60

1. c, d, a, h, g, e, f, b

Page 61

2. e, a, d, f, c, b

Page 62

3. b, d, a, c, g, e, f

LESSON 13: MOTIVE AND REPETITION (Pages 63-64)

Page 64

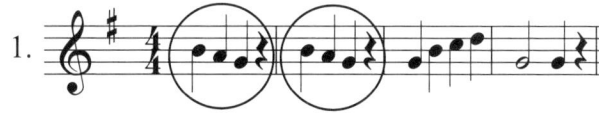
1.

2.

REVIEW: LESSONS 11-13 (Pages 65-70)

Page 65

1. 2 = two; first
   4 = Quarter note

   3 = measure, first
   4 = one beat

   4 = four; one and three
   4 = Quarter note

2. a.

Page 65, No. 2, cont.

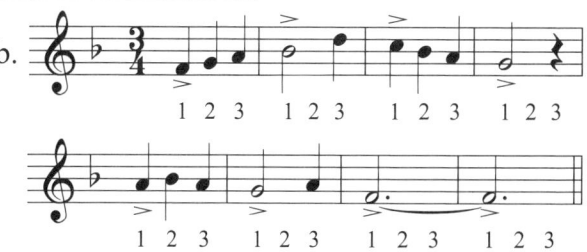
b.

Page 66

3. a. Accent: Play note louder than others
   b. Slur: curved line indicating to play *legato*
   c. Repeat sign: repeat the music
   d. Tenuto: Give note full value (stress the note)
   e. Play one octave higher than written
   f. Fermata: Hold the note longer

Page 67

   g. *Staccato:* detached
   h. Phrase: A musical sentence
   i. *Legato:* connect the notes
   j. First and second ending
   k. Use the damper pedal
   l. Symbols that indicate loud and soft
   m. Return to the beginning and play to *fine*
   n. Return to the original tempo

Page 68

   o. Gradually slower
   p. *forte:* loud
   q. *mezzo piano:* medium soft
   r. *pianissimo:* very soft
   s. *fortissimo:* very loud
   t. *mezzo forte:* medium loud
   u. *piano:* soft
   v. *crescendo:* gradually louder
   w. *decrescendo (diminuendo):* gradually softer

4.

Level 1, Pages 63-68

Page 69

5. 1. Moderately fast
    2. C Major
    3. *Staccato:* detached
    4. 6th
    5. Two

6.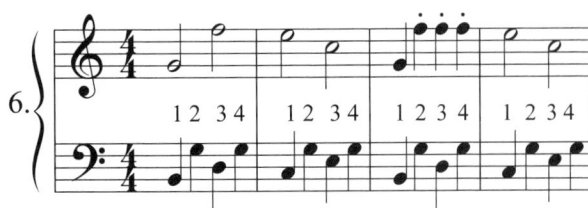

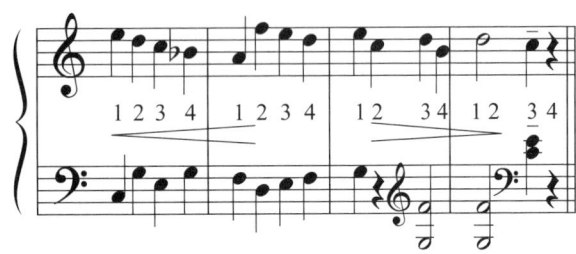

7. Gradually louder
8. Give note its full value (stress the note)

REVIEW TEST (Pages 71-77)

Page 71

1.

2. a.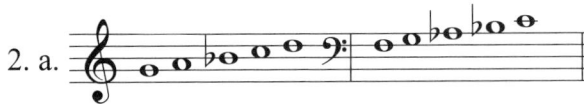

   b.

Page 72

3. C Major, F Major, D Major, G Major

Page 72, cont.

4. a.

   b.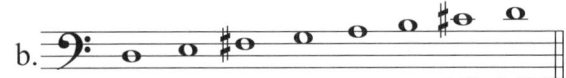

5. a.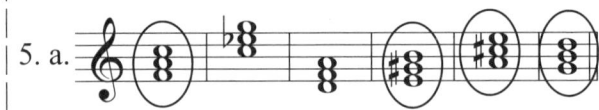

Page 73

   b. g minor, e minor, f minor

6. a & b.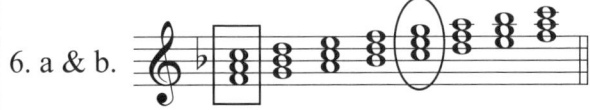

   c. Major

7.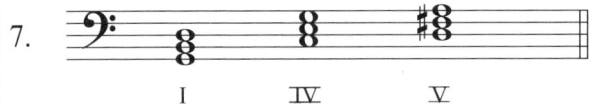
      I   IV   V

Page 74

8. a.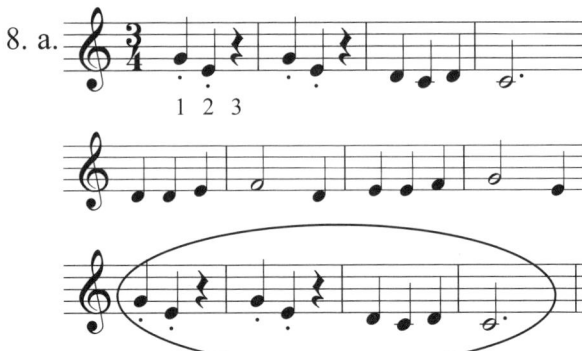

   b. 3

   c.

   d. C Major
   e. Medium loud (*mezzo forte*)
   f. Staccato

Page 75

9. a. G Major
    b. 1 and 4
    c. Yes
    d. 4
    e. Quarter note
    f. Loud
    g. Soft
    h. First and third in each measure

Page 76

10. a. F Major
    b. 2nd, 3rd, 3rd
    c. C Major

    d.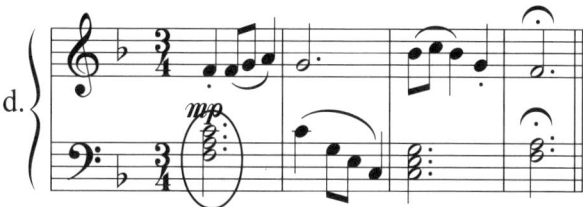

    e. 3
    f. Quarter note
    g. 6
    h. 3

Page 77

    i.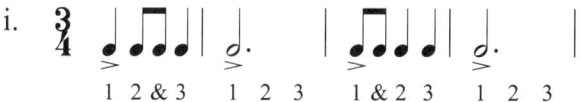

    j. Medium soft
    k. Legato

11. a. play loud *(forte)*
    b. return to the original tempo
    c. play *staccato*
    d. accent the note

Level 1, Pages 76-77

This page has purposely been left blank

LEVEL 2

LESSON 1: KEY SIGNATURES
(Pages 1-12)

Page 2

1. a. F♯, C♯
   b. F♯, C♯, G♯
   c. F♯,
   d. F♯, C♯, G♯, D♯

2.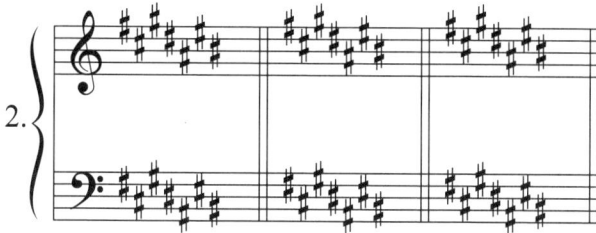

Page 3

3a. 1. F♯, C♯, G♯
    2. G♯
    3. A
    4. A

b. 1. F♯,
   2. F♯
   3. G
   4. G

Page 4

c. 1. F♯, C♯,
   2. C♯
   3. D
   4. D

d. 1. F♯, C♯, G♯ D♯
   2. D♯
   3. E
   4. E

Page 5

4. a. 1. G♯
      2. F♯, C♯, G♯

3.

b. 1. F♯
   2. F♯

3.

c. 1. C♯
   2. F♯, C♯

3.

Page 6

d. 1. D♯
   2 F♯, C♯, G♯, D♯

3.

5.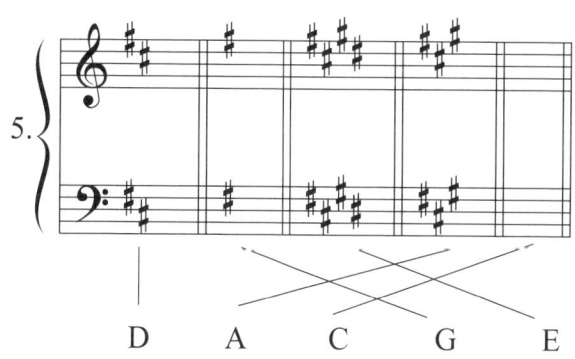

Level 2, Pages 1-6

Page 7

7. a. B♭, E♭
   b. B♭
   c. B♭, E♭, A♭

Page 8

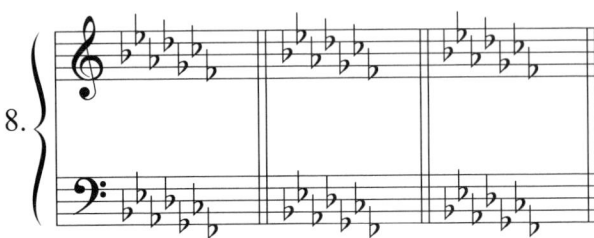

Page 9

9. a. 1. B♭
      3. F

   b. 1. B♭, E♭
      2. B♭
      3. B♭

   c. 1. B♭, E♭, A♭
      2. E♭
      3. E♭

Page 10

10. a. 2. B♭, E♭

    b. 2. B♭

c. 2. B♭, E♭, A♭

Page 11

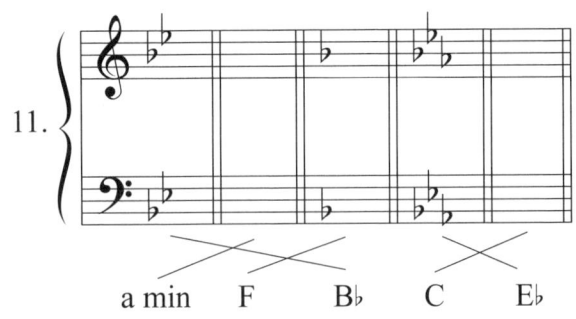

REVIEW: KEY SIGNATURES (Pages 13-16)

Page 13

1. F♯, C♯, G♯, D♯, A♯, E♯, B♯

2. B♭, E♭, A♭, D♭, G♭, C♭, F♭

3. F♯, C♯, G♯

4. B♭

5. c. A half step

6. No sharps or flats

7. G Major, E♭ Major, B♭ Major, C Major, F Major, E Major, A Major

Page 14

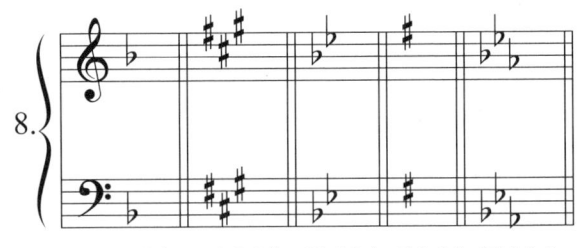

Page 14, No. 8, cont.

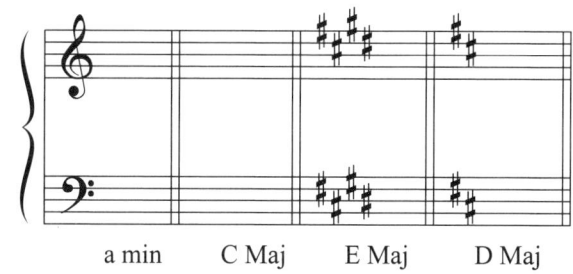

a min   C Maj   E Maj   D Maj

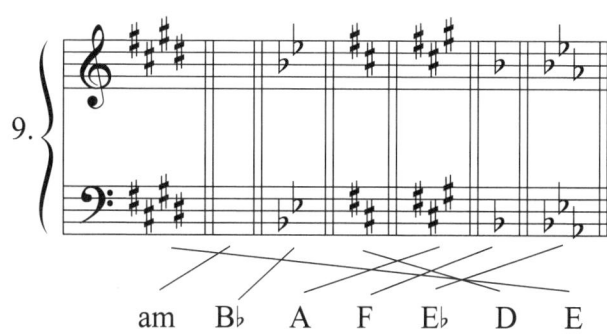

am   B♭   A   F   E♭   D   E

Page 15

10. a. D Major
    b. B♭ Major
    c. G Major
    d. F Major

LESSON 2: SCALES (Pages 17-20)

Page 17

1.
F Major

G Major

A Major

Page 18

D Major

Page 18, cont.

B♭ Major

E Major

Page 19

2.
C Major

B♭ Major

a natural minor

A Major

F Major

G Major

Page 20

E Major

a harm. minor

D Major

LESSON 3: INTERVALS (Pages 21-22)

Page 21

1. 4th, 8th, 5th, 3rd, 2nd, 6th, 2nd, 7th
   6th, 4th, 8th, 2nd, 7th, 5th, 3rd, 4th

Level 2, Pages 14-21

Page 22

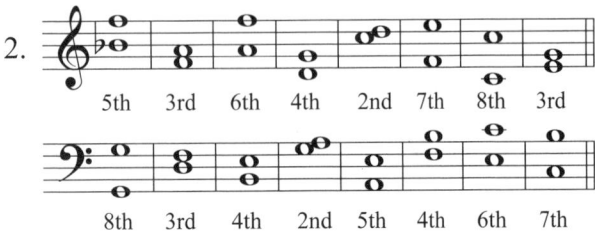

3. a. 3rd, 5th, 8th (octave), 4th
   b. 3rd, 7th, 5th, 2nd

LESSON 4: MAJOR AND MINOR TRIADS (Pages 23-28)

Page 23

1. E Major, B♭ Major, D Major, A Major, C Major, F Major

   G Major, B♭ Major, D Major, A Major, E Major, E♭ Major

Page 24

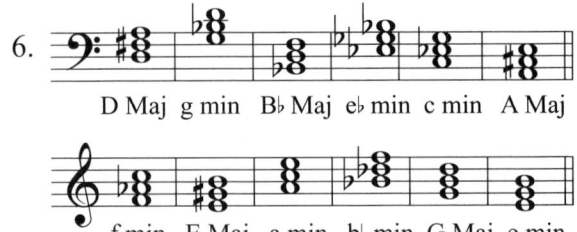

Page 25

3. g minor, e♭ minor, c minor, a minor, d minor, f minor

   e minor, b♭ minor, d minor, c minor, f minor, a minor

Page 26

5. f minor, E Major, a minor, d minor, B♭ Major, c minor

   b♭ minor, e♭ minor, g minor, A Major, D Major, e minor

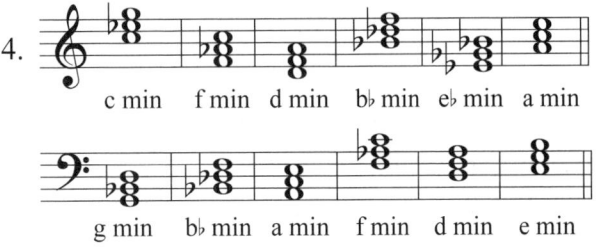

Page 27

7. a. G Major
   b. F Major
   c. D Major

Page 28

   d. B♭ Major
   e. d minor

LESSON 5: PRIMARY TRIADS (Pages 29-34)

Page 30

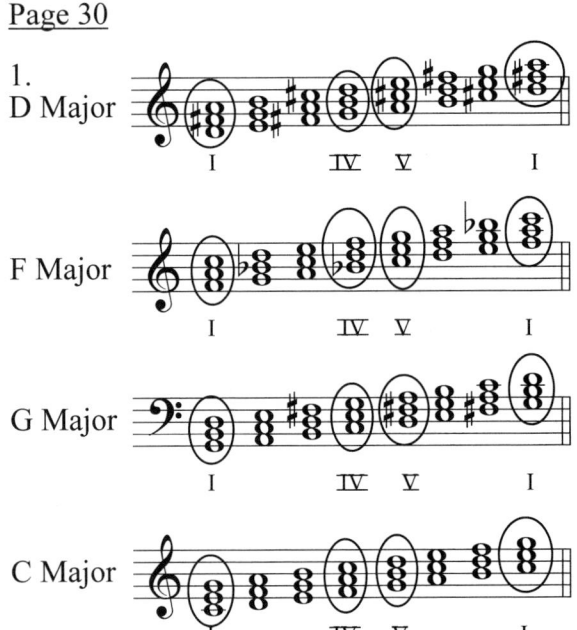

Page 30, cont.

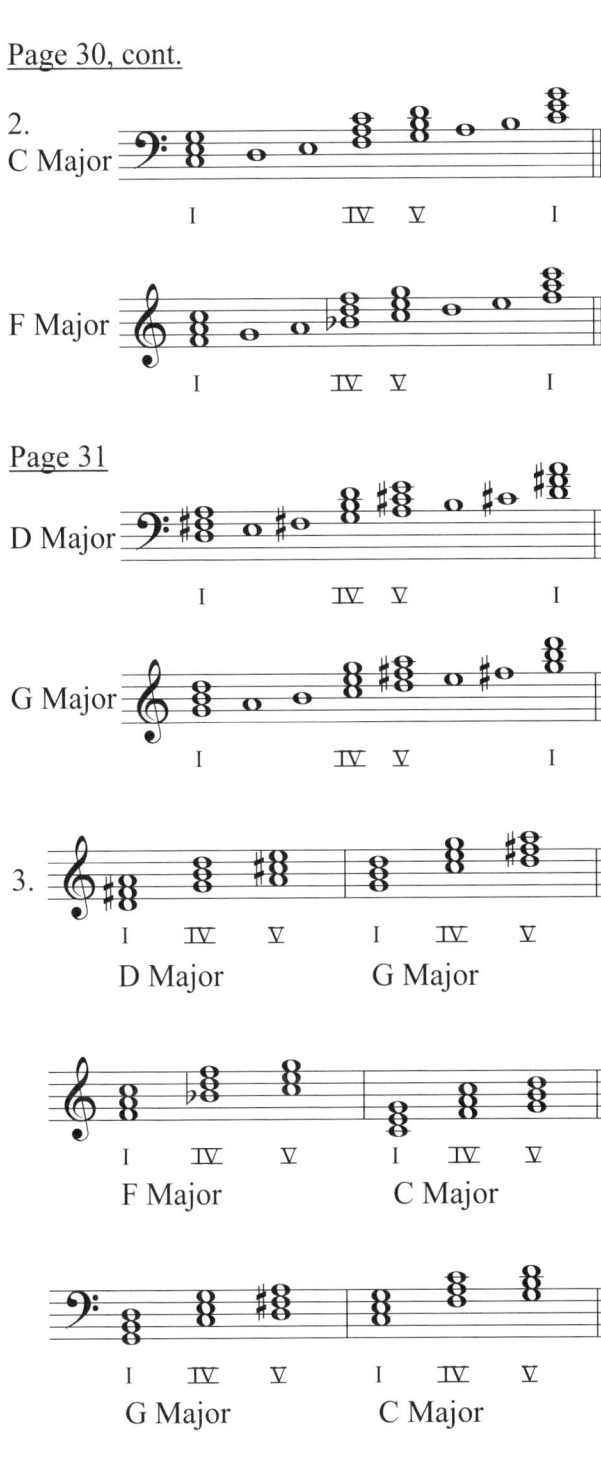

Page 32

4. V - Dominant
   I - Tonic
   IV - Subdominant

Page 33

5. a. Key of D Major: I
   b. Key of D Major: V
   c. Key of F Major: IV

Page 34

   d. Key of C Major: V
   e. Key of F Major: I
   f. Key of G Major: I

LESSON 6: AUTHENTIC, HALF, AND PLAGAL CADENCES (Pages 35-37)

Page 35

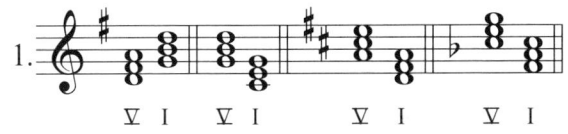
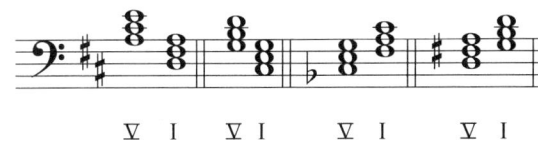

Page 36

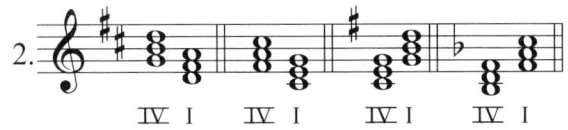
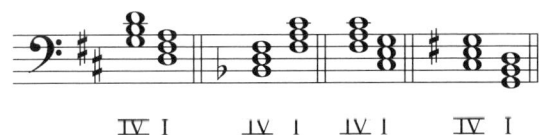

Page 37

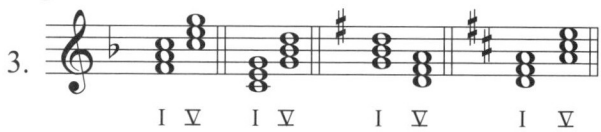
3.
I V   I V   I V   I V

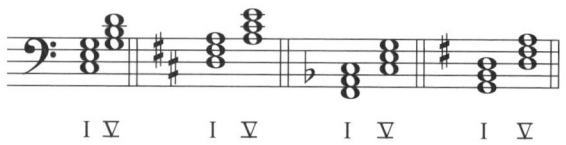
I V   I V   I V   I V

4. IV-I, Plagal; I-V, Half; I-V, Half;
   V-I, Authentic

   V-I, Authentic; I-V, Half; IV-I, Plagal;
   V-I, Authentic

REVIEW: LESSONS 1-6 (Pages 39-44)

Page 39

1. D Major, F Major, B♭ Major, G Major,
   E♭ Major, A Major, C Major

2.
EM FM B♭M AM DM am E♭M

Page 40

3.
D Major

A Major

E Major

B♭ Major

Page 40, No. 3, cont.

F Major

Page 41

a natural minor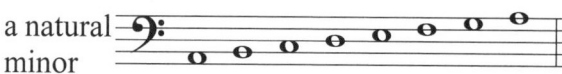

G Major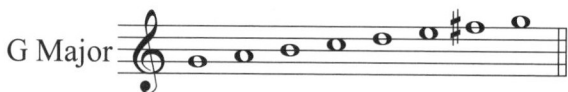

C Major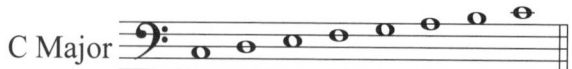

a harm. minor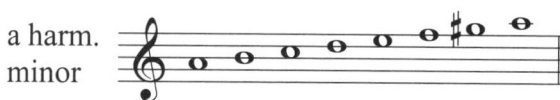

Page 42

4. e minor, B♭ Major, f minor, D Major,
   G Major, A Major

   b♭ minor, a minor, C Major, E Major,
   e♭ minor, F Major

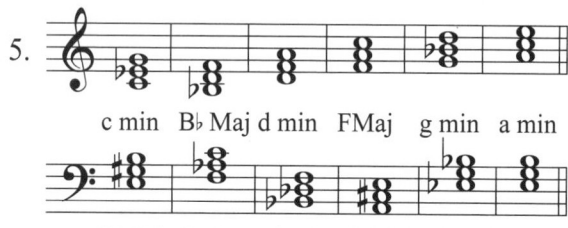
5.
c min B♭ Maj d min F Maj g min a min
E Maj f min b♭ min A Maj E♭ Maj e min

6. 4th, 5th, 3rd, 4th, 2nd, 6th
   6th, 3rd, 4th, 3rd, 4th, 6th

Page 43

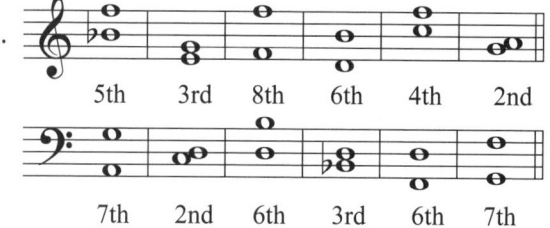
7.
5th 3rd 8th 6th 4th 2nd
7th 2nd 6th 3rd 6th 7th

Level 2, Pages 37-43

Page 43, cont.

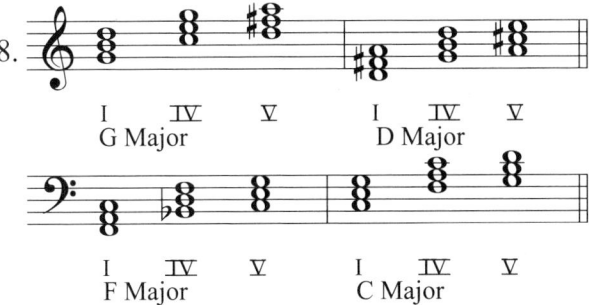

9. c
   b
   a

Page 44

10. V-I: Authentic
    I-V: Half
    V-I, Authentic
    IV-I, Plagal
    IV-I, Plagal
    I-V, Half

    I-V, Half
    IV-I, Plagal
    V-I, Authentic
    V-I, Authentic
    IV-I, Plagal
    I-V, Half

LESSON 7: TIME SIGNATURES (Pages 45-48)

Page 46

1. 2 = 2 beats per measure, first beat is strongest
    4 = Quarter note receives one beat

    3 = 3 beats per measure, first beat is strongest
    4 = Quarter note receives one beat

    4 – 4 beats per measure, first and third beats are strongest
    4 = Quarter note receives one beat

Page 46, cont.

2. a.
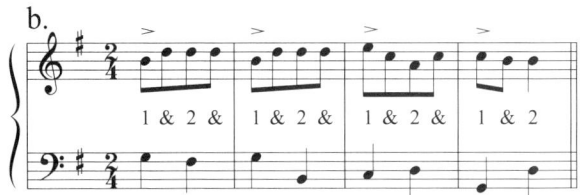

Page 47

b.

c.
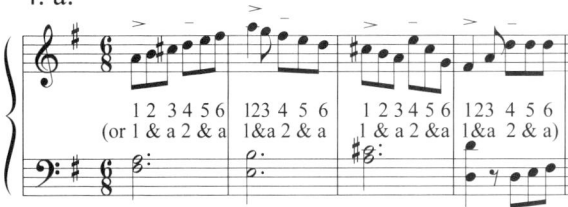

Page 48

3. 6   (or 2)
   one   (or three)

4. a.
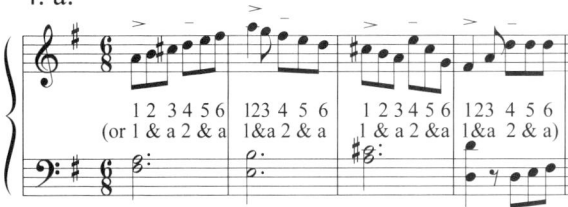

b.
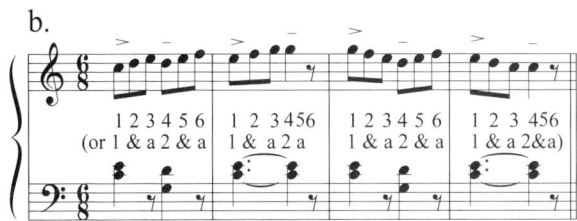

5.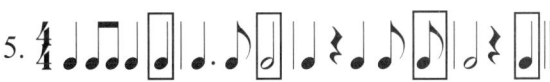

6. a. Quarter note   e. Whole rest
   b. Half note   f. Eighth rest
   c. Half rest   g. Whole note
   d. Eighth note   h. Half note

LESSON 8: SIGNS AND TERMS (Pages 49-54)

Page 51

1. c, d, a, h, g, e, f, b, k, i, j

Page 52

2. c, a or d, a or d, b, f, e

Page 53

3. d, c, b, a, g, e, f

Page 54

4. e, a, g, c, b, f, d, h

LESSON 9: MOTIF; REPETITION AND SEQUENCE (Pages 55-58)

Page 57

1. a. Repetition

b. Sequence

c. Repetition

Page 58

d. Sequence

e. Repetition

REVIEW: LESSONS 7-9 (Pages 59-62)

Page 59

1. 2, one
   Quarter note

   6, one and four   (or 2, one and two
   Eighth note   Dotted quarter)

   measure, one
   one beat

   4, one, three
   Quarter note

   $\frac{4}{4}$, common time

2. a.

b.

Page 60

1. Accent: play note louder than others
2. *tenuto:* hold note for full value (or stress the note)
3. Play one octave higher
4. Repeat the music
5. *fermata:* hold the note longer
6. *staccato:* detached
7: Slur: connect the notes; play *legato*

Page 61

8. *sforzando:* a sudden sharp accent
9. First and second endings
10. Connect the notes; play smoothly
11. A musical sentence
12. Symbols which indicate loud or soft
13. Return to beginning and play to *fine*
14. Return to original tempo
15. Gradually slower
16. *forte:* loud
17. *mezzo piano:* medium soft
18. *pianissimo:* very soft
19: *fortissimo:* very loud
20. *mezzo forte:* medium loud
21. *piano:* soft
22. *crescendo:* gradually louder
23. *decrescendo* or *diminuendo:* gradually softer
24. *fortississimo:* very very loud
25. *pianississimo:* very very soft

Page 62

26. The speed at which to play the music
27. Lively
28. Moderate walking tempo
29. Moderate or medium tempo
30. Fast or quick, cheerfully, merrily
31. *sforzando:* a sudden sharp accent
32. Use damper pedal
33. 4/4

Page 62, cont.

4. a. Repetition

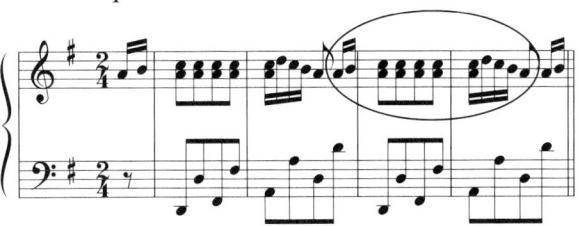

b. Sequence

REVIEW TEST (Pages 63-69)

Page 63

1. 4, 6, 5, 2, 3, 1

Page 64

2.
E Major
B♭ Major
D Major

3. Meas. 1: G Major   Meas. 4: F Major
   Meas. 2: d minor   Meas. 5: e minor
   Meas. 3: A Major   Meas. 6: c minor

Page 65

4. a.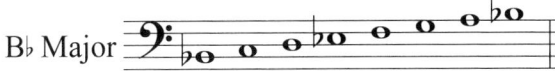

Level 2, Pages 60-65

Page 65, No. 4, cont.

b.

5.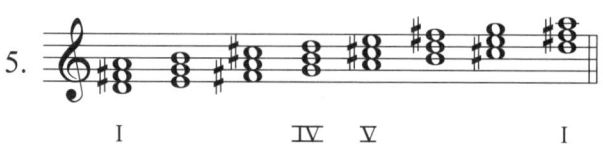

Page 66

6. a.    c: Authentic Cadence

   b. 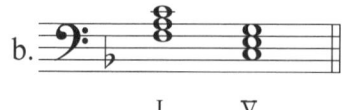   a: Plagal Cadence

   c.    b: Half Cadence

Page 67

7. a. A Major
   b. No
   c. Moderately fast
   d. *staccato:* detached
   e. Measure 1: 5th
      Measure 2: 4th
      Measure 4: 3rd
   f. *mezzo forte:* medium loud
   g. 2/4
   h. *legato* or slur: connect the notes

Page 68

8. a. D Major
   b. D Major
   c. fast, cheerfully
   d. 4/4
   e. Quarter
   f. *mezzo piano:* medium soft
   g. *crescendo:* gradually louder
   h. Measure 1: 2nd
      Measure 2-3: 2nd
      Measure 4: 5th
   i. First and third
   j.

Page 69

9. a. c minor
   b. 2
   c. Sequence
   d. *mezzo piano:* medium soft
   e. 2/4
   f.
   g. g minor

Level 2, Pages 65-69

LEVEL 3

LESSON 1: MAJOR KEY SIGNATURES (Pages 1-12)

Page 2

1. a. F#, C#
   b. F#, C#, G#
   c. F#
   d. F#, C#, G#, D#

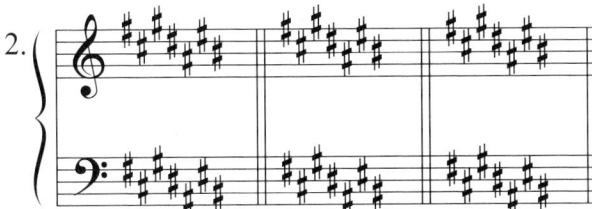

Page 3

3. a. 1. F#, C#, G#
      2. G#
      3. A
      4. A

   b. 1. F#
      2. F#
      3. G
      4. G

   c. 1. F#, C#
      2. C#
      3. D
      4. D

   d. 1. F#, C#, G#, D#
      2. D#
      3. E
      4. E

Page 4, No. 3, cont.

e. 1. F#, C#, G#, D#, A#
   2. A#
   3. B
   4. B

f. 1. F#, C#, G#, D#, A#, E#, B#
   2. B#
   3. C#
   4. C#

g. 1. F#, C#, G#, D#, A#, E#
   2. E#
   3. F#
   4. F#

Page 5

4. a. 1. G#
      2. F#, C#, G#   3.

   b. 1. F#
      2. F#   3.

   c. 1. D#
      2. F#, C#, G#, D#   3.

   d. 1. E#
      2. F#, C#, G#, D#, A#, E#,   3.

Page 6, No. 4, cont.

    e. 1. C#
       2. F#, C#   3.

    f. 1. B#
       2. F#, C#, G#, D#,   3.
          A#, E#, B#

    g. 1. A#
       2. F#, C#, G#, D#,   3.
          A#,
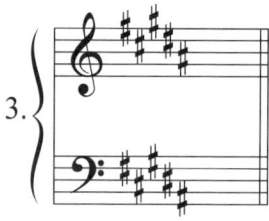

5.
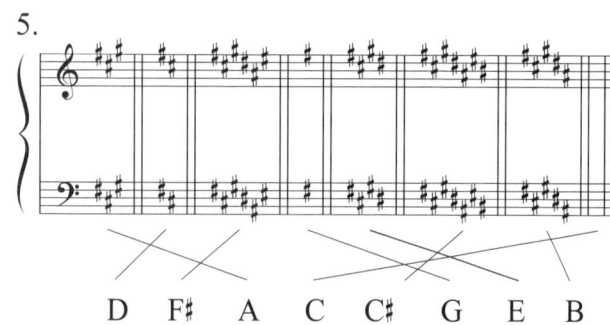

    D   F#   A   C   C#   G   E   B

Page 7

7. a. B♭, E♭
   b. B♭
   c. B♭, E♭, A♭

Page 8

8.
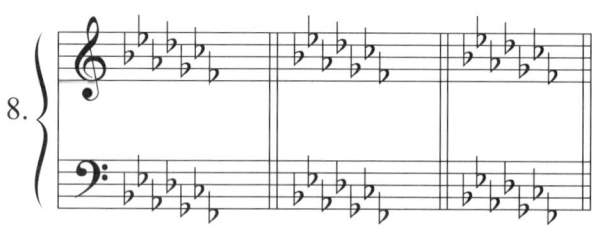

Page 9

9. a. 1. B♭
     3. F

   b. 1. B♭, E♭
     2. B♭
     3. B♭

   c. 1. B♭, E♭, A♭
     2. E♭
     3. E♭

   d. 1. B♭, E♭, A♭, D♭, G♭
     2. D♭
     3. D♭

Page 10, No. 9, cont.

   e. 1. B♭, E♭, A♭, D♭
     2. A♭
     3. A♭

   f. 1. B♭, E♭, A♭, D♭, G♭, C♭, F♭
     2. C♭
     3. C♭

   g. 1. B♭, E♭, A♭, D♭, G♭, C♭
     2. G♭
     3. G♭

Page 11

10. a. 2. B♭, E♭

    b. 2. B♭, E♭, A♭

Level 3, Pages 6-11

Page 11, No. 10, cont.

c. 2. B♭

d. 2. B♭, E♭, A♭, D♭, G♭, C♭,

e. 2. B♭, E♭, A♭, D♭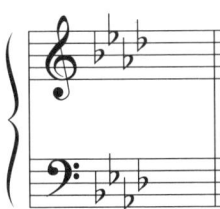

Page 12, No. 10, cont.

f. 2. B♭, E♭, A♭, D♭, G♭, C♭, F♭

g. 2. B♭, E♭, A♭, D♭, G♭

11.
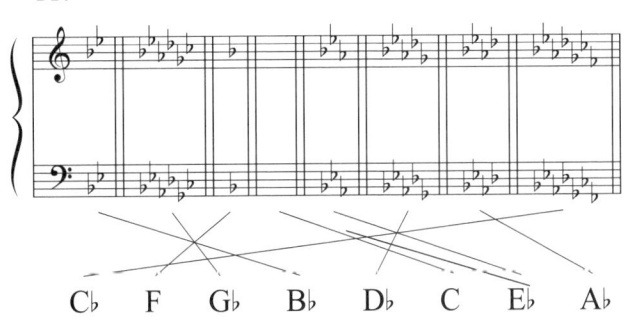

REVIEW: MAJOR KEY SIGNATURES
(Pages 13-14)

Page 13

1. F♯, C♯, G♯, D♯, A♯, E♯, B♯

2. B♭, E♭, A♭, D♭, G♭, C♭, F♭

3. F♯, C♯, G♯

4. B♭

5. A half step

6. A Major, G♭ Major, E♭ Major, F♯ Major, G Major, C♭ Major, F Major, B Major

   E Major, C Major, B♭ Major, A♭ Major, C♯ Major, D Major, D♭ Major

7.
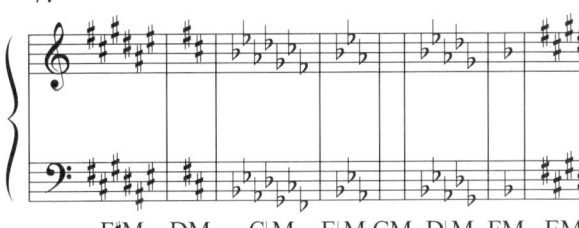

F♯M   DM   C♭M   E♭M   CM   D♭M   FM   EM

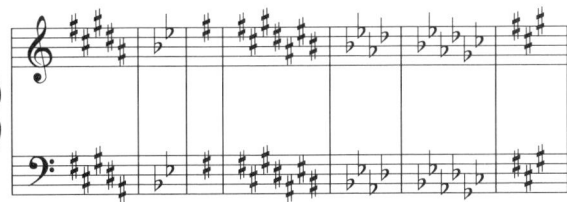

BM   B♭M   GM   C♯M   A♭M   G♭M   AM

8.
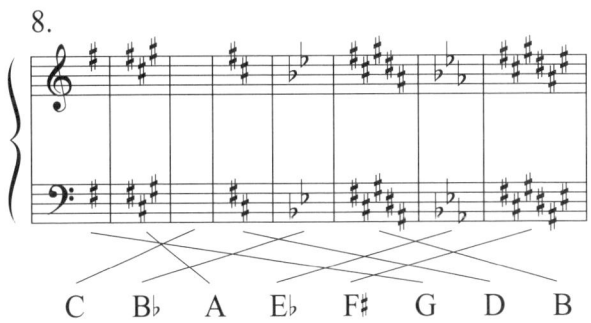

C   B♭   A   E♭   F♯   G   D   B

Page 14, No. 8, cont.

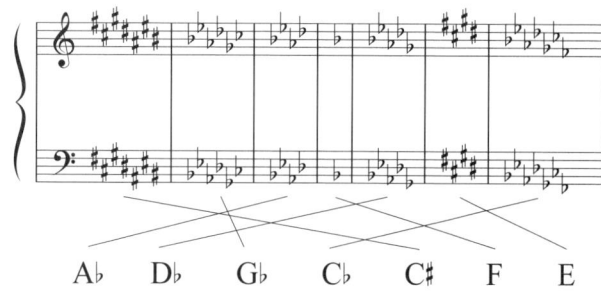

LESSON 2: MAJOR SCALES
(Pages 15-18)

Page 15

1.
F Major

G Major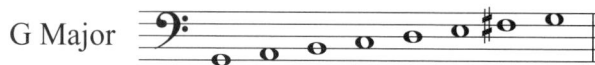

A Major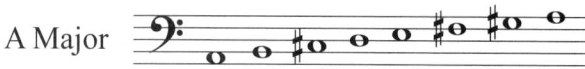

Page 16

B Major

D Major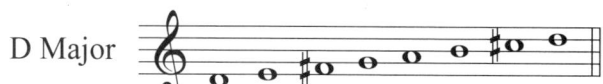

B♭ Major

E Major

E♭ Major

Page 17

2.
C Major

B♭ Major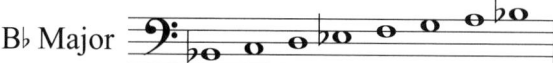

D Major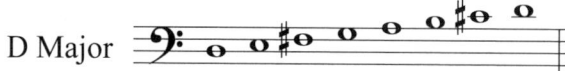

E♭ Major

F Major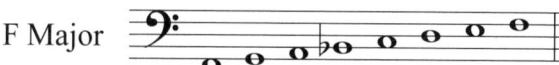

Page 18

G Major

E Major

A Major

B Major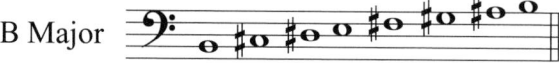

LESSON 3: MINOR KEY SIGNATURES AND SCALES (Pages 19-24)

Page 19

1. a. e minor
   b. a minor
   c. d minor

Page 20

2. a. F Major
   b. G Major
   c. C Major

3. a minor, e minor, d minor

4.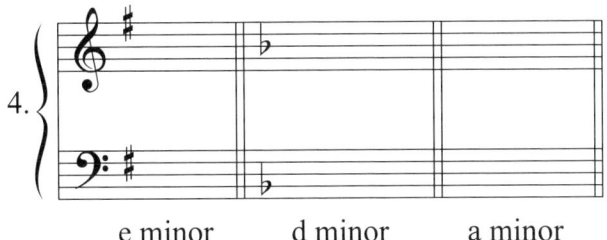
   e minor   d minor   a minor

Page 21

5.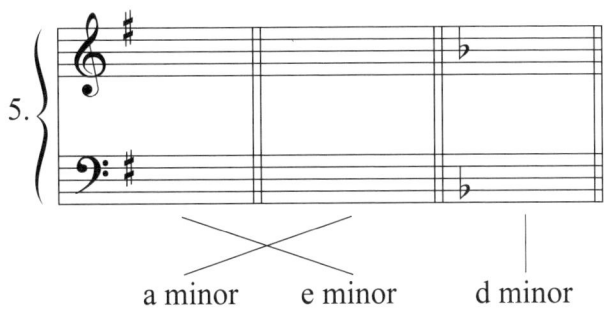
   a minor   e minor   d minor

7. a. D Major

Page 22, No. 7, cont.

   b. d minor
   c. a minor
   d. e minor
   e. F Major

Page 23

8. e natural minor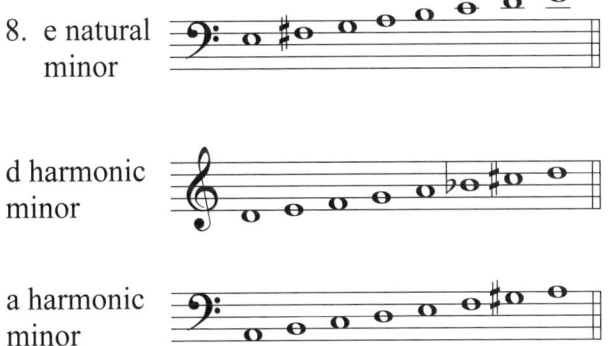
   d harmonic minor
   a harmonic minor

Page 24

e harmonic minor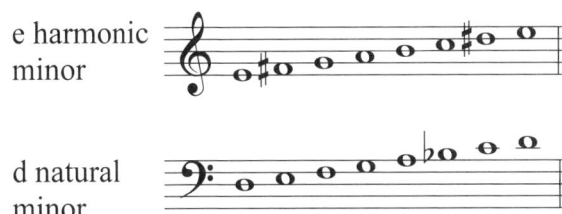
d natural minor

9. d natural minor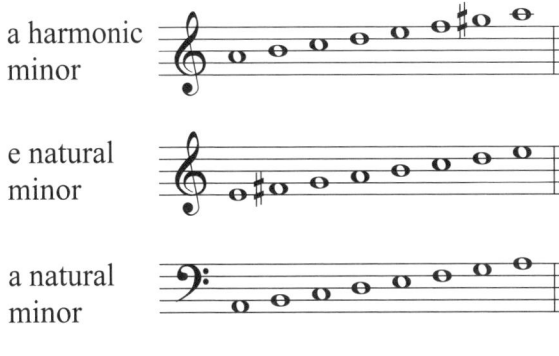
   a harmonic minor
   e natural minor
   a natural minor
   d harmonic minor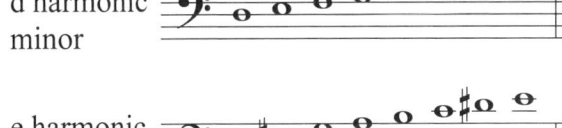
   e harmonic minor

LESSON 4: INTERVALS (Pages 25-26)

Page 25

1. P4, P5, M6, M3, P8, M7, M2, P4
   M3, M6, P4, M2, P8, P5, M7, M3

2.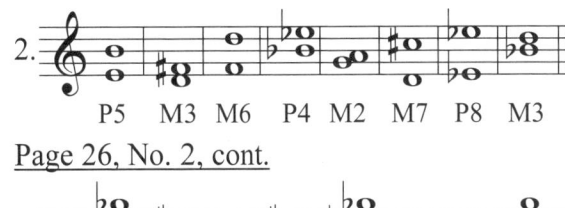
   P5 M3 M6 P4 M2 M7 P8 M3

Page 26, No. 2, cont.

P8 M3 P4 M2 P5 P4 M6 M7

Level 3, Pages 20-26

Page 26

2. a. P4, M3, M2, M3
    b. P4, M3, M2, M3
    c. P4, P4, M2, M3, M3, P8

LESSON 5: MAJOR AND MINOR TRIADS (Pages 27-30)

Page 27

1. E Major, B Major, G Major, G♭ Major, A♭ Major, B♭ Major, E Major, C♭ Major

   D Major, C♯ Major, E♭ Major, F Major, C Major, F♯ Major, A Major, D♭ Major

Page 28

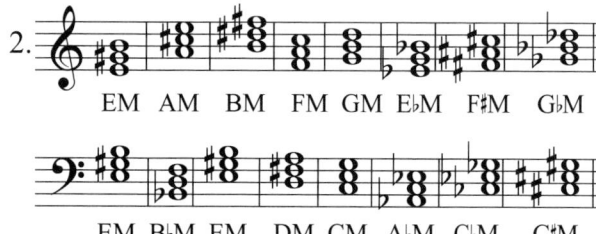

3. g minor, e minor, d♭ minor, f minor, f♯ minor, e♭ minor, c minor, d minor

   c♯ minor, g minor, g♭ minor, a minor, b♭ minor, a♭ minor, b minor, c♭ minor

Page 29

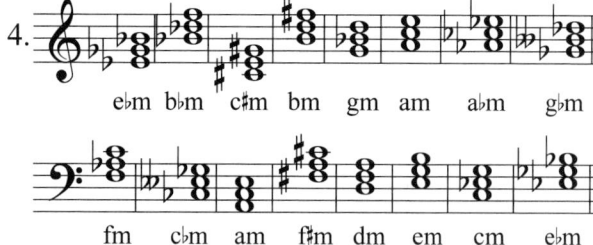

5. f minor, B♭ Major, c♭ minor, g minor, A♭ Major, G♭ Major, f♯ minor, C♯ Major

   C Major, f minor, e♭ minor, D Major, d♭ minor, E Major, a minor, B Major

Page 30

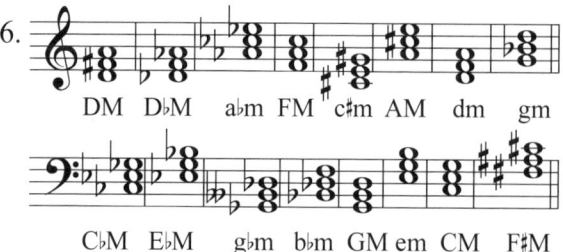

LESSON 6: TRIADS AND INVERSIONS Pages 31-38)

Page 31

1. A Major, C Major, d minor, f minor, e♭ minor, F Major

   g minor, E♭ Major, G Major, D Major, b♭ minor, F Major

Page 32

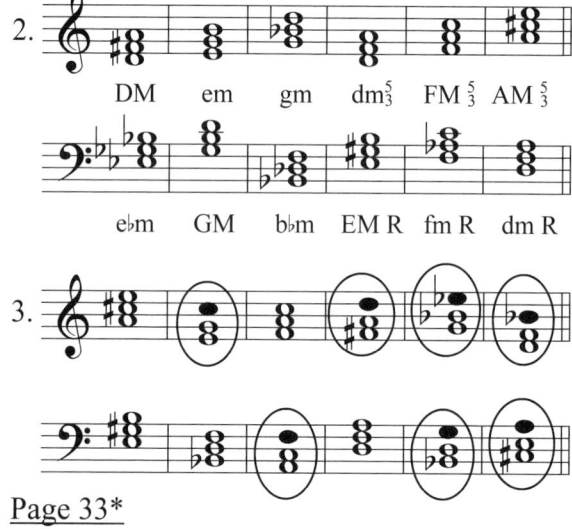

Page 33*

4. f minor ^{6}, C Major ^{6}, G Major ^{6}, c minor ^{6}, F Major ^{6}, g minor ^{6}, D Major ^{6}

   g minor ^{6}, C Major ^{6}, G Major ^{6}, c minor ^{6}, f minor ^{6}, F Major ^{6}, d minor ^{6}

*1st and $^6_3$ are also acceptable for inversions

Level 3, Pages 26-33

Page 33, cont.

5.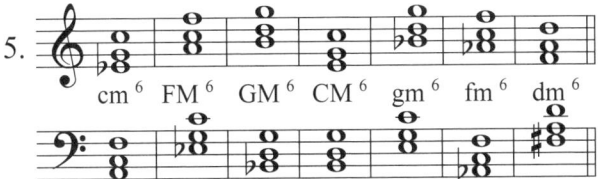
cm 6, FM 6, GM 6, CM 6, gm 6, fm 6, dm 6

FM 6/3, cm 1st, gm 6/3, GM 6/3, CM 6/3, fm 6/3, DM 1st

Page 34

6.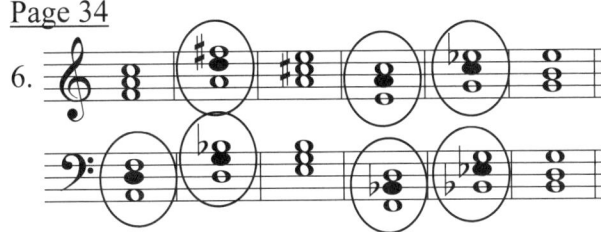

Page 35*

7. c minor 6/4, F Major 6/4, G Major 6/4, C Major 6/4, f minor 6/4, g minor 6/4, D Major 6/4

F Major 6/4, f minor 6/4, c minor 6/4, C Major 6/4, g minor 6/4, G Major 6/4, d minor 6/4

8.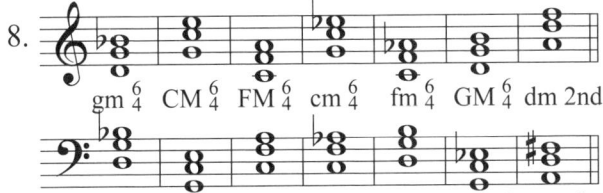
gm 6/4, CM 6/4, FM 6/4, cm 6/4, fm 6/4, GM 6/4, dm 2nd

gm 2nd, CM 6/4, FM 6/4, fm 6/4, GM 2nd, cm 6/4, DM 6/4

Page 36

9.

*2nd is also acceptable for inversions

Page 37

10. a. G Major

Page 38

   b. d minor 6/4
   c. a minor
   d. c minor 6, G Major
   e. F Major 6/4, F Major

LESSON 7: PRIMARY TRIADS
(Pages 39-44)

Page 40

1.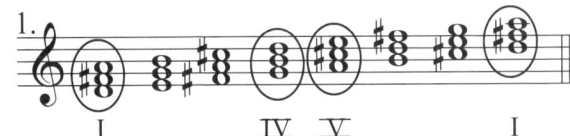
D Major — I, IV, V, I

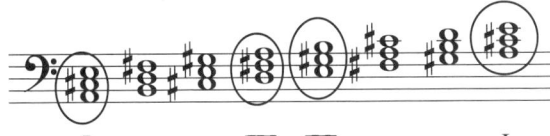
A Major — I, IV, V, I

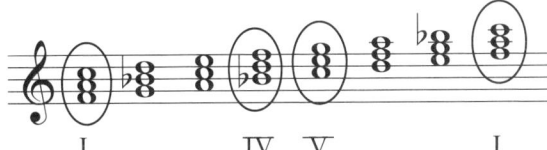
F Major — I, IV, V, I

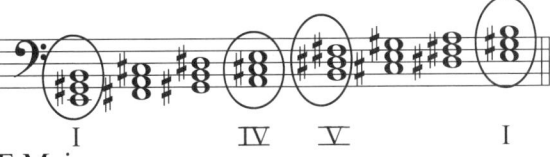
E Major — I, IV, V, I

Page 41

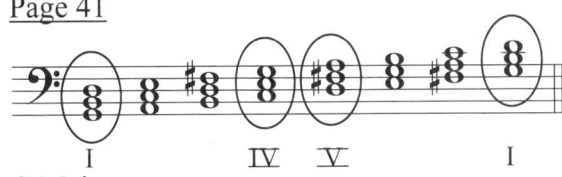
G Major — I, IV, V, I

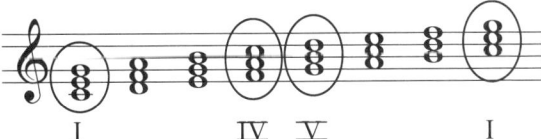
C Major — I, IV, V, I

Level 3, Pages 33-41

Page 41, cont.

2.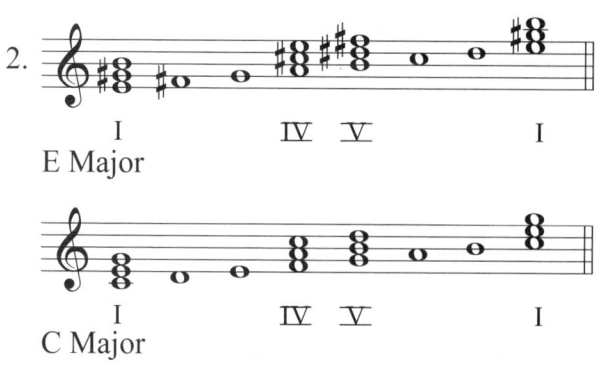

Page 42

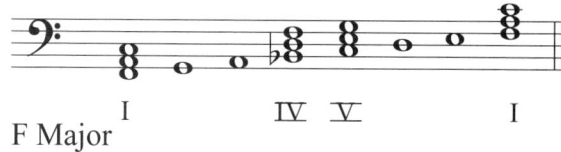
D Major

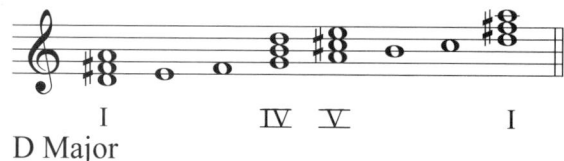
A Major

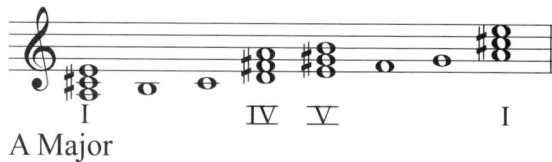
G Major

3.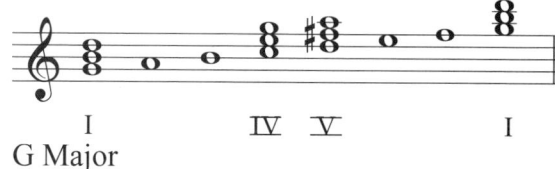

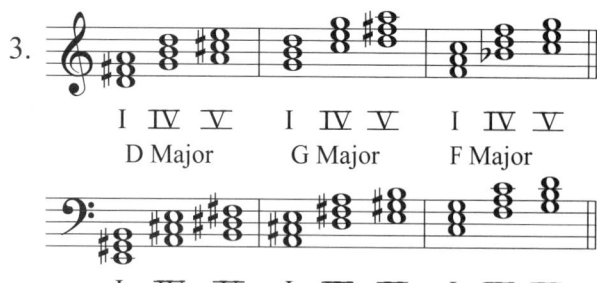

4. c
   a
   b

Page 43

5. a. Key of C Major: IV , V, I

Page 44, No. 5, cont.

   b. Key of D Major: V
   c. Key of D Major: I
   d. Key of F Major: I, V

LESSON 8: AUTHENTIC, HALF, AND PLAGAL CADENCES (Pages 45-48)

Page 45

1.

Page 46

2.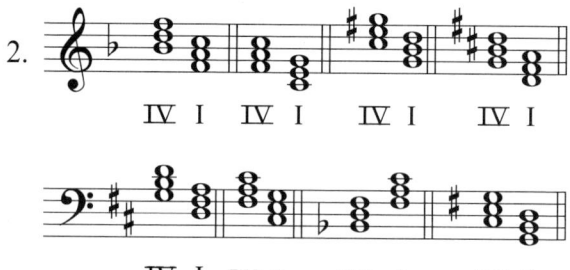

Page 47

3.

4. IV-I, Plagal; I-V, Half; V-I, Authentic;
   IV-I, Plagal

   I-V, Half; IV-I, Plagal; V-I, Authentic;
   V-I, Authentic

Page 48

5. a. Key of F Major; Authentic: V-I
   b. Key of C Major; Authentic: V-I
   c. Key of G Major; Half: I$^6_4$-V

REVIEW: LESSONS 1-8 (Pages 51-56)

Page 51

1. B Major, B♭ Major, A Major, G♭ Major, E Major, E♭ Major

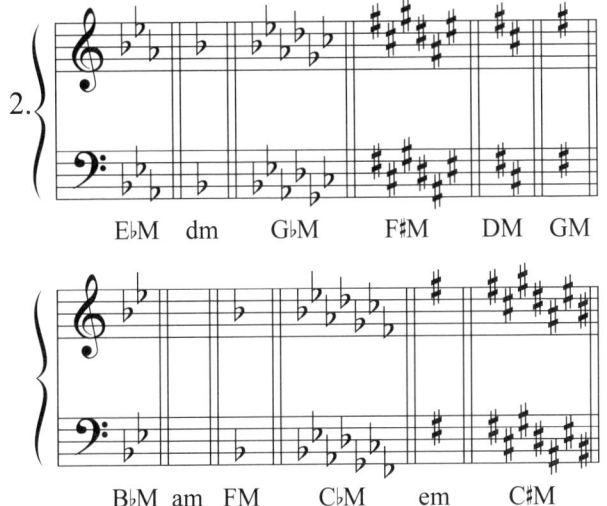

Page 52

3.
D Major

A Major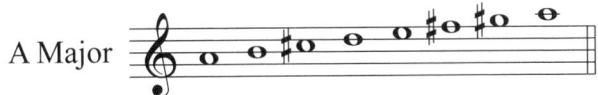

E Major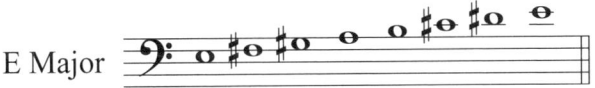

B♭ Major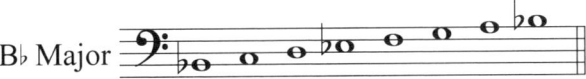

Page 52, No. 3, cont.

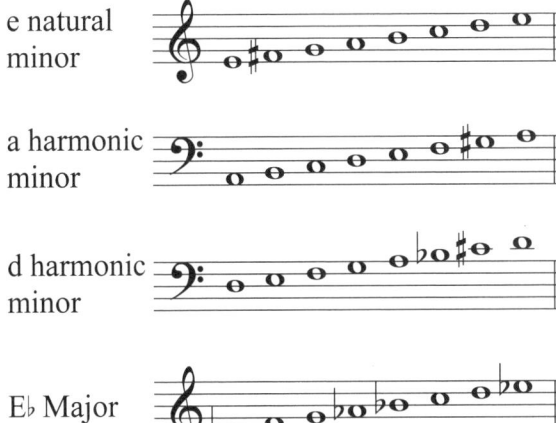

e natural minor

a harmonic minor

d harmonic minor

E♭ Major

4. e minor, c# minor, G Major, D♭ Major, F# Major, A Major

   E♭ Major, B♭ Major, D Major, b♭ minor, e♭ minor, c minor

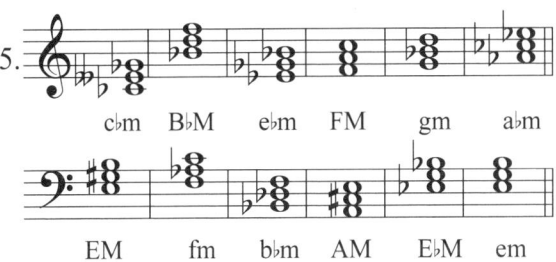

Page 54

6. G Major ^{6}, G Major $^6_4$, A Major, F Major ^{6}, g minor $^6_4$, c minor $^6_4$, D Major ^{6}

   d minor, B♭ Major, c minor ^{6}, F Major $^6_4$, f minor $^6_4$, C Major ^{6}, d minor $^6_4$

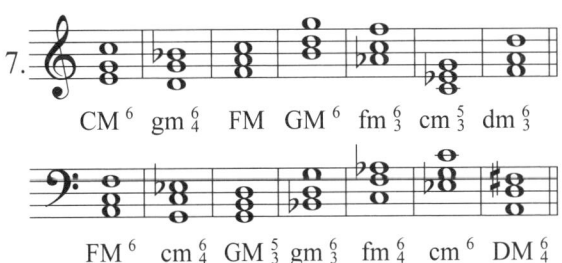

42

Page 55

8. P4, P5, M6, M3, M2, P8
   M7, P5, M3, M6, M2, M7

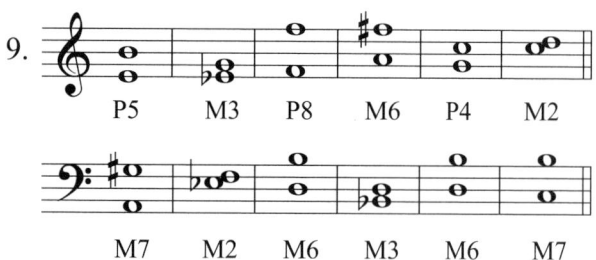

Page 56

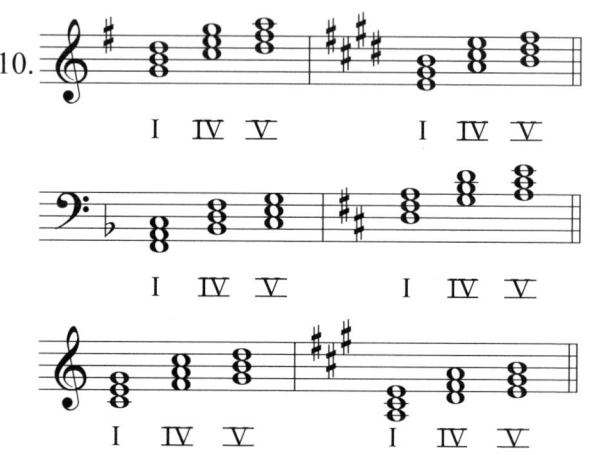

11. V-I, Authentic; IV-I, Plagal; IV-I, Plagal;
    I-V, Half

    V-I, Authentic; I-V, Half; V-I, Authentic;
    IV-I, Plagal

12. c
    a
    b

LESSON 9: TIME SIGNATURES (Pages 57-64)

Page 59

1. 2 = 2 beats per measure, first beat is strongest
   4 = Quarter note receives one beat

   3 = 3 beats per measure, first beat is strongest
   4 = Quarter note receives one beat

Page 59, No. 1, cont.

4 = 4 beats per measure, first and third
     beats are strongest
4 = Quarter note receives one beat

C = Common time or 4/4

¢ = Alla breve or 2/2

5 = 5 beats per measure
4 = Quarter note receives one beat

7 = 7 beats per measure
4 = Quarter note receives one beat

Page 60

2. a.

b.

c.

d.

Level 3, Pages 55-60

Page 61, No. 2, cont.

e.
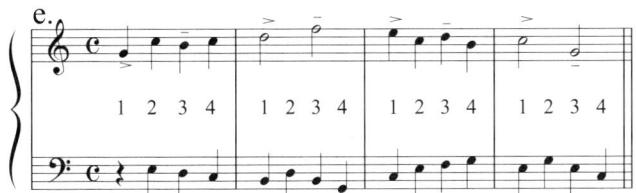

f.

Page 63

3. 6, one (or 2, three)
    measure, eighth note (or three measures,
                                    dotted quarter)
    12, eighth note (or 4, dotted quarter)
    measure, half note
    3, one beat
    12, half note

4. a.

b.

Page 64

c.

Page 64, No. 4, cont.

d.

e.

5. a. $\frac{6}{8}$ c. $\frac{2}{4}$
   b. $\frac{4}{4}$ d. $\frac{3}{4}$

LESSON 10: SIGNS AND TERMS (Pages 65-70)

Page 68

1. c, d, a, h, g, e, f, b, k, i, j

Page 69

2. d, c, f, e, b, a

3. c, d, b, a, g, e, f

Page 70

4. f, a, e, g, d, b, c

5. b, a, g, e, c, d, f, h

LESSON 11: MOTIF; REPETITION AND SEQUENCE (Pages 71-74)

Page 73

1. a. Sequence

Level 3, Pages 61-73

44

Page 73, No. 1, cont.

b. Sequence

c. Repetition

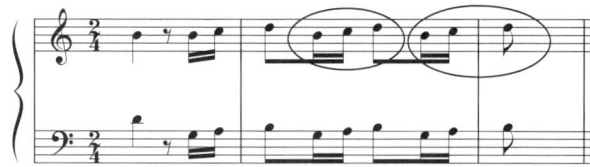

Page 74

d. Repetition

REVIEW: LESSONS 9-11 (Pages 75-78)

Page 75

1. 2, one
   quarter
   6, one and four (or 2, 1 and 2)
   eighth note (or dotted quarter)
   measure, one
   one beat
   4, one and three
   quarter note
   4/4, common time
   2/2, alla breve

2. a.

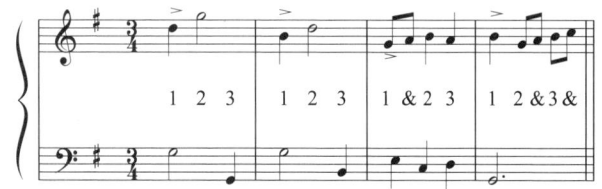

Level 3, Pages 73-77

Page 75, No. 2, cont.

b.

Page 76

3. 1. accent: play the note louder
   2. *tenuto:* hold for full value (stress the note)
   3. Play one octave higher
   4. Repeat the music
   5. *fermata:* hold the note longer
   6. *staccato:* detached
   7. Play smoothly, connect the notes
   8. *sforzando:* a sudden, sharp acccent

Page 77

9. First and second ending
10. Slur: play *legato,* connect the notes
11. Symbols that indicate loud and soft
12. Return to beginning and play to *fine*
13. Return to original tempo
14. Gradually slower
15. *forte:* loud
16. *mezzo piano:* medium soft
17. *pianissimo:* very soft
18. *fortissimo:* very loud
19. *mezzo forte:* medium loud
20. *piano:* soft
21. *crescendo:* gradually louder
22. *decrescendo:* gradually softer
23. *fortississimo:* very very loud
24. *pianississimo:* very very soft
25. The speed at which to play the music
26. Brisk, lively
27. Walking tempo
28. Moderate or medium tempo
29. Fast, quick, cheerfully, merrily
30. *sforzando:* a sudden sharp accent
31. Use damper pedal
32. 2/2
33. 4/4

Page 78, No. 3, cont.

34. Gradually faster
35. Slowly
36. With spirit
37. A musical sentence
38. Much or greatly
39. Use soft pedal
40. Little
41. Release soft pedal

4. a. Repetition

b. Sequence

REVIEW TEST (Pages 79-84)

1.

2.
a natural minor

E Major

B♭ Major

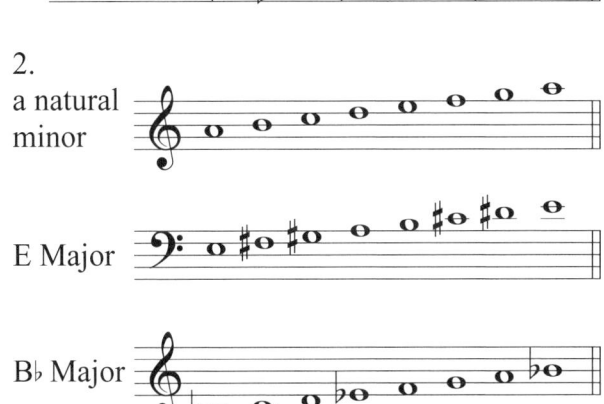

Page 80

3.
    I   IV   V

4. I, F Major
   IV, B♭ Major
   V, C Major

5.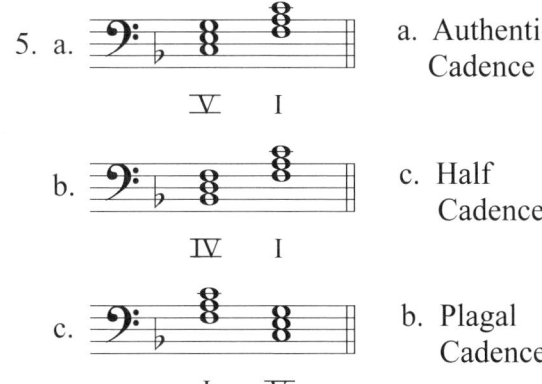

  a. Authentic Cadence
  c. Half Cadence
  b. Plagal Cadence

Page 81

6. a. Moderate tempo
   b. Medium soft
   c. C Major
   d. Alla Breve
   e. One (First in each measure)

   f.

   g. *crescendo:* gradually louder
   h. a. M3 b. P5 c. M3 d. M2 e. M6

Page 82

7. a. G Major
   b.

   c. *forte:* loud
   d. Walking tempo
   e. One (First in each measure)
   f. Authentic

Page 83

8. a. Fast, quick, cheerfully, merrily
    b. Repetition
    c. Common time or $\frac{4}{4}$
    d. C Major

Page 84

9. a. Moderate or medium tempo
    b. d minor
    c. Gradually slower
    d. Common time or $\frac{4}{4}$
    e. d minor
    f. P8

LEVEL 4

LESSON 1: MAJOR KEY SIGNATURES (Pages 1-12)

Page 2

1. a. F♯, C♯
   b. F♯, C♯, G♯
   c. F♯
   d. F♯, C♯, G♯, D♯, A♯, E♯

2.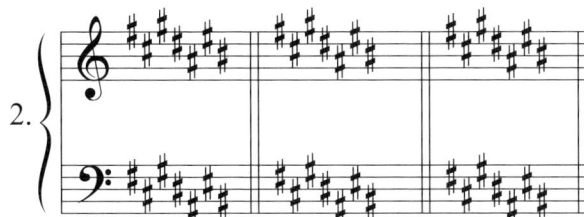

Page 3

3. a. 1. F♯, C♯, G♯
      2. G♯
      3. A
      4. A

   b. 1. F♯
      2. F♯
      3. G
      4. G

   c. 1. F♯, C♯, G♯, D♯, A♯
      2. A♯
      3. B
      4. B

   d. 1. F♯, C♯, G♯, D♯
      2. D♯
      3. E
      4. E

Page 4

   e. 1. F♯, C♯, G♯, D♯, A♯, E♯
      2. E♯
      3. F♯
      4. F♯

Page 4, No. 3, cont.

   f. 1. F♯, C♯, G♯, D♯, A♯, E♯, B♯
      2. B♯
      3. C♯
      4. C♯

   g. 1. F♯, C♯
      2. C♯
      3. D
      4. D

Page 5

   a. 1. A♯
      2. F♯, C♯, G♯, D♯, A♯
   3.

   b. 1. F♯
      2. F♯
   3.

   c. 1. C♯
      2. F♯, C♯
   3.

   d. 1. D♯
      2. F♯, C♯, G♯, D♯
   3.

Page 6, No. 4, cont.

e. 1. G♯
   2. F♯, C♯, G♯
   3.

f. 1. B♯
   2. F♯, C♯, G♯, D♯, A♯, E♯, B♯
   3.

g. 1. E♯
   2. F♯, C♯, G♯, D♯, A♯, E♯
   3.

5.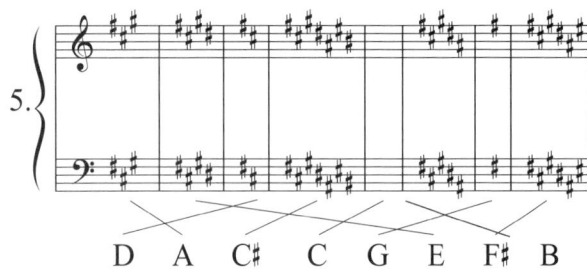
   D A C♯ C G E F♯ B

Page 7

7. a. B♭, E♭
   b. B♭, E♭, A♭, D♭
   c. B♭, E♭, A♭
   d. B♭

Page 8

8.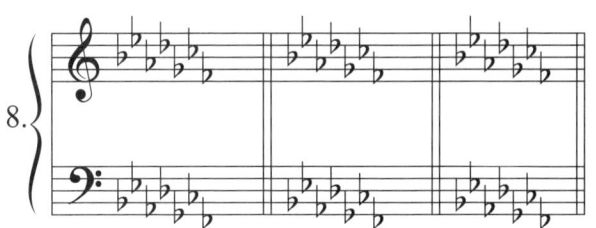

Page 9

9. a. 1. B♭
      3. F

   b. 1. B♭, E♭
      2. B♭
      3. B♭

   c. 1. B♭, E♭, A♭, D♭
      2. A♭
      3. A♭

   d. 1. B♭, E♭, A♭, D♭, G♭
      2. D♭
      3. D♭

Page 10, No. 9, cont.

e. 1. B♭, E♭, A♭, D♭, G♭, C♭, F♭
   2. C♭
   3. C♭

f. 1. B♭, E♭, A♭, D♭, G♭, C♭
   2. G♭
   3. G♭

g. 1. B♭, E♭, A♭
   2. E♭
   3. E♭

Page 11

10. a. B♭, E♭

    b. B♭, E♭, A♭

Level 4, Pages 6-11

Page 11, No. 10, cont.

LESSON 2: MAJOR SCALES
(Pages 13-16)

Page 13

c. B♭, E♭, A♭, D♭, G♭

1.
F Major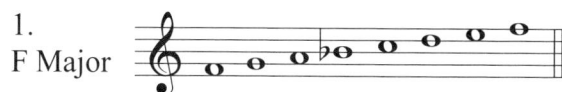

A Major

d. B♭, E♭, A♭, D♭, G♭, C♭

B♭ Major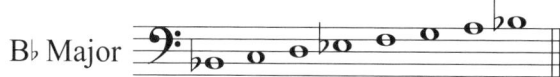

E Major

e. B♭, E♭, A♭, D♭, G♭, C♭, F♭

Page 14

F# Major

Page 12, No. 10, cont.

E♭ Major

f. B♭

2.
C Major

B♭ Major

g. B♭, E♭, A♭, D♭

D Major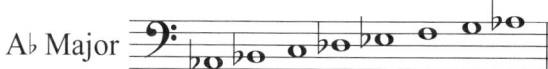

A♭ Major

Page 15

11.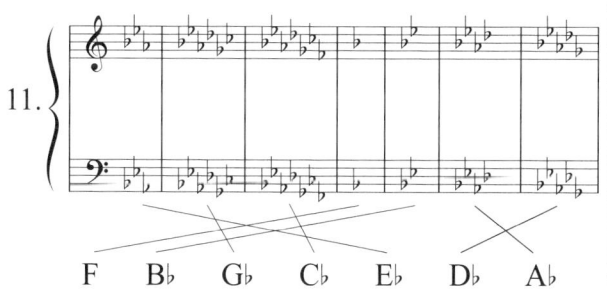

G Major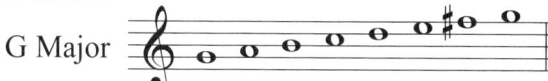

Level 4, Pages 11-15

Page 15, No. 2, cont.

C♭ Major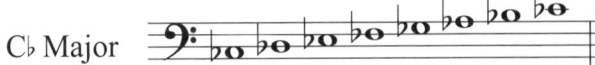

C♯ Major

F Major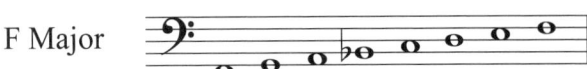

E♭ Major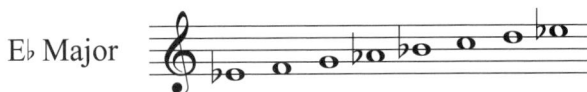

A Major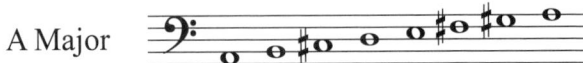

Page 16

B Major

D♭ Major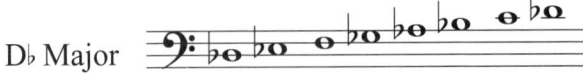

E Major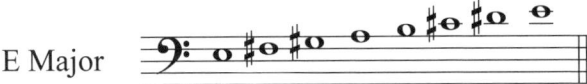

G♭ Major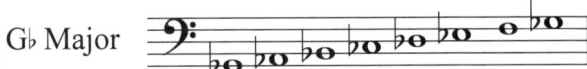

LESSON 3: MINOR KEY SIGNATURES AND SCALES (Pages 17-22)

Page 17

1. a. e minor
   b. c minor
   c. a minor
   d. d minor
   e. g minor
   f. b minor

Page 18

2. a. F Major
   b. G Major
   c. E♭ Major
   d. C Major
   e. B♭ Major
   f. D Major

3. g minor, d minor, b minor, a minor, c minor, e minor

4.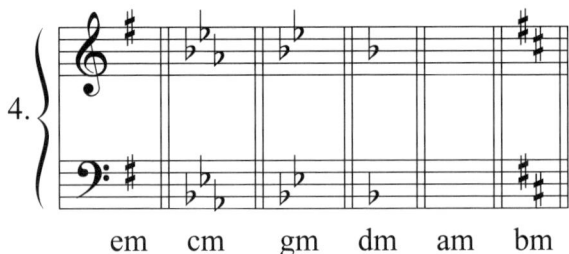
   em cm gm dm am bm

Page 19

5.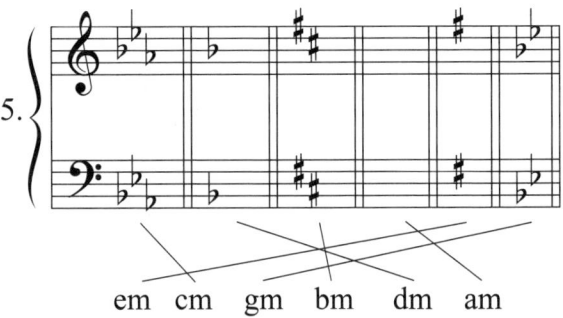
   em cm gm bm dm am

Page 20

7. g natural minor

Page 20, No. 7, cont.

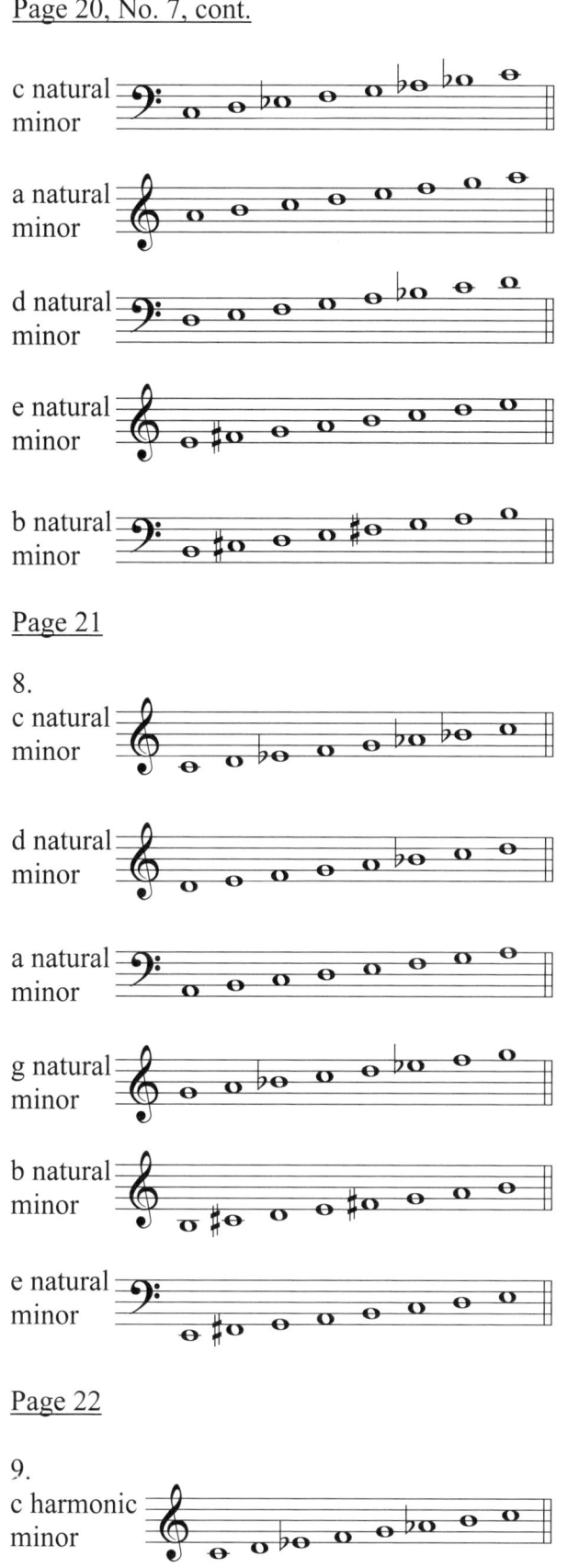

Page 21

8.

Page 22

9.

Page 22, No. 9, cont.

LESSON 4: INTERVALS (Pages 23-26)

Page 23

1. P4, P5, M6, M3, P8, P4, P5, M7
   M2, M6, M3, M7, P5, P4, M2, P8

2. P5 M3 M6 P4 M2 M7 P8 M3

Page 24, No. 2, cont.

P8 M3 P4 M2 P5 P4 M6 M7

3. m6, P4, P5, m2, M7, P8, M6, P5
   M2, P4, m7, M3, P8, m3, P4, M3

4. M2 m6 M3 P5 M7 m2 m7 P4

   M3 m3 M2 P4 P5 M6 P4 P8

Level 4, Pages 20-24

Page 25

5.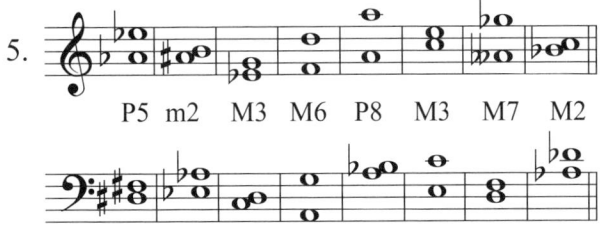
P5 m2 M3 M6 P8 M3 M7 M2

m3 P4 M2 m7 m2 m6 m3 P4

Page 26

6. a. P5, M3, P4, m3, m6, P5

   b. P4, P5, M2, m3, P5, m3

   c. P4, M3, P5, M3, M2, m3, P8

LESSON 5: MAJOR, MINOR, AND DIMINISHED TRIADS (Pages 27-30

Page 27

1.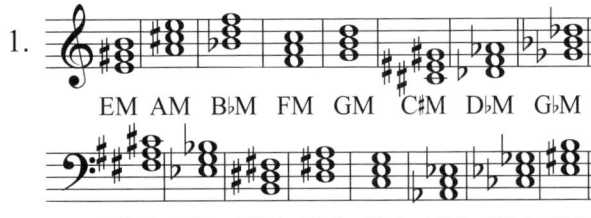
EM AM B♭M FM GM C♯M D♭M G♭M

F♯M E♭M BM DM CM A♭M C♭M EM

Page 28

2.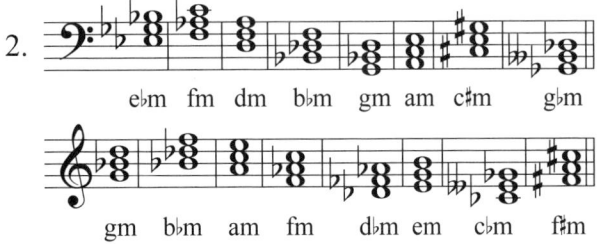
e♭m fm dm b♭m gm am c♯m g♭m

gm b♭m am fm d♭m em c♭m f♯m

Page 29

3.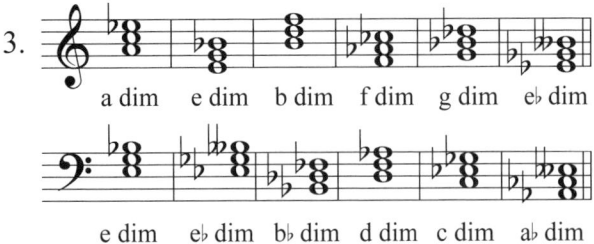
a dim e dim b dim f dim g dim e♭ dim

e dim e♭ dim b♭ dim d dim c dim a♭ dim

Page 29, cont.

4. f minor, E Major, c minor, A♭ Major,
   E♭ Major, b♭ minor, C♭ Major, f♯ minor

   D Major, g diminished, a diminished,
   C Major, B Major, f diminished,
   c♯ minor, G♭ Major

Page 30

5.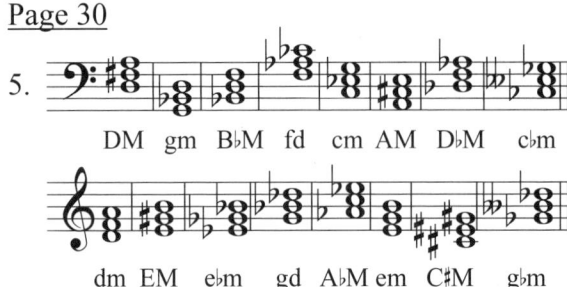
DM gm B♭M fd cm AM D♭M c♭m

dm EM e♭m gd A♭M em C♯M g♭m

LESSON 6: INVERSIONS OF TRIADS (Pages 31-34)

Page 32*

1. A Major $^6_4$, f minor ^{6}, D Major,
   a minor ^{6}, f minor $^6_4$, C Major

   F Major ^{6}, a minor ^{6}, C Major,
   G Major $^6_4$, A Major ^{6}, e minor

   c minor ^{6}, a minor $^6_4$, D Major ^{6},
   E Major $^6_4$, d minor, c minor ^{6}

Page 33

2.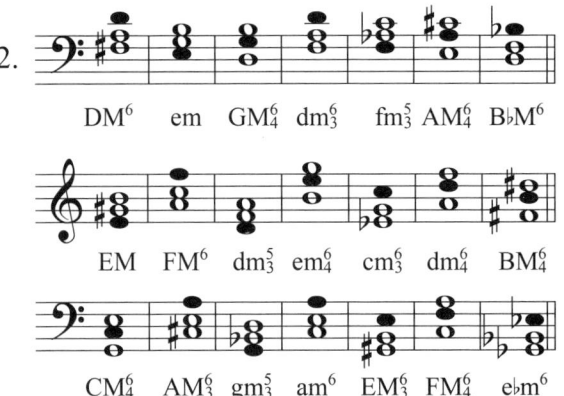
DM⁶ em GM$^6_4$ dm$^5_3$ fm$^5_3$ AM$^6_4$ B♭M⁶

EM FM⁶ dm$^5_3$ em$^6_4$ cm$^6_3$ dm$^6_4$ BM$^6_4$

CM$^6_4$ AM$^6_3$ gm$^5_3$ am⁶ EM$^6_3$ FM$^6_4$ e♭m⁶

* $^5_3$ is acceptable for root position
  $^6_3$ is acceptable for first inversion

Page 33, cont.

3. C Major   G Major
   f minor   E Major

Page 34, No. 3, cont.

e minor   d minor
a minor   F Major
g minor   c minor
D Major   A Major
b♭ minor   E♭ Major

LESSON 7: TRIADS AND INVERSIONS IN MUSIC LITERATURE (Pages 35-36)

Page 35

a. c minor $^6_4$, c minor ^{6}, G Major $^6_4$, c minor

Page 36

b. g minor, g minor ^{6}, D Major $^6_4$, F Major, F Major ^{6}, C Major $^6_4$

c. c minor, G Major ^{6}, a diminished

LESSON 8: PRIMARY AND SECONDARY TRIADS (Pages 37-40)

Page 38*

1. D Major — I ii iii IV V vi vii° I
   G Major — I ii iii IV V vi vii° I
   F Major — I ii iii IV V vi vii° I
   a harm. minor — i ii° III⁺ iv V VI vii° i

Page 39

2. C Major — I IV V   G Major — I IV V
   a minor — i iv V   F Major — I IV V
   E Major — I IV V   D Major — I IV V
   A Major — I IV V   C Major — I IV V

3. G Major — ii iii vi vii°   C Major — ii iii vi vii°
   F Major — ii iii vi vii°   G Major — ii iii vi vii°

Level 4, Pages 33-39

Page 40

4. f, g, a, e, d, c, b

5. Tonic, Supertonic, Mediant, Subdominant, Dominant, Submediant, Leading Tone

LESSON 9: ROMAN NUMERAL CHORD NAMES WITHIN A COMPOSITION (Pages 41-42)

Page 42

1. a. Key of a minor: i, iv$_4^6$

   b. Key of F Major: I^6, $\underline{IV}$, $\underline{V}$, ii, ii^6

   c. Key of C Major: I, $\underline{V}^6$

   d. Key of F Major: I$_4^6$, iii^6, $\underline{IV}_4^6$, $\underline{V}$, ii$_4^6$

LESSON 10: THE DOMINANT SEVENTH CHORD (Pages 43-44)

Page 43

1.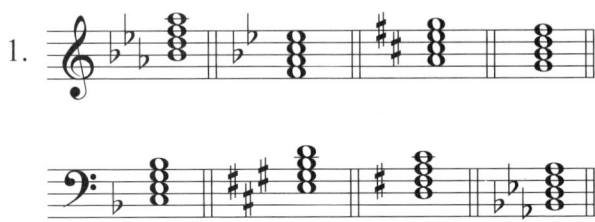

Page 44

2.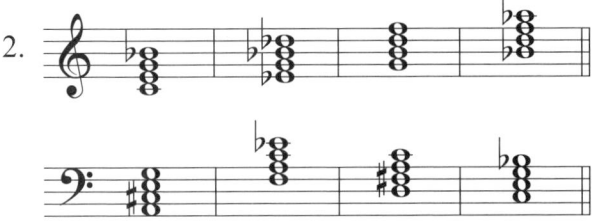

Page 44, cont.

3. a. B♭ Major   b. F Major

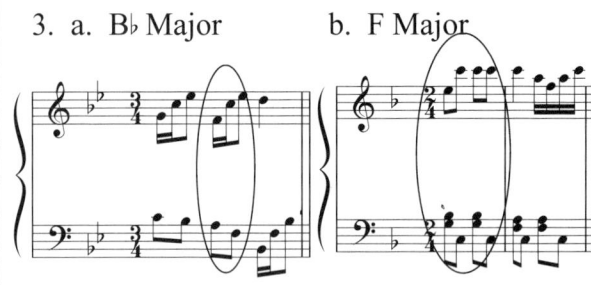

c. C Major   d. C Major

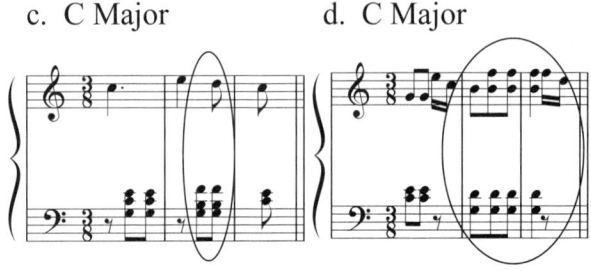

LESSON 11: AUTHENTIC, HALF, AND PLAGAL CADENCES (Pages 45-48)

Page 45

1a.
1b.

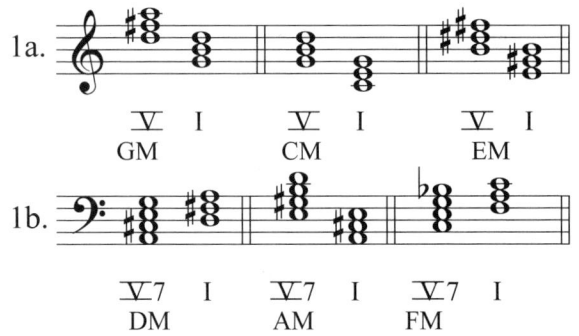

Page 46

2.

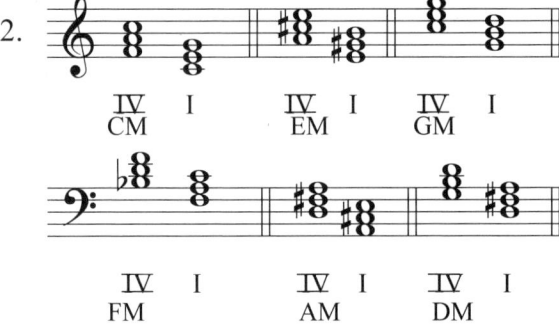

Page 46, cont.

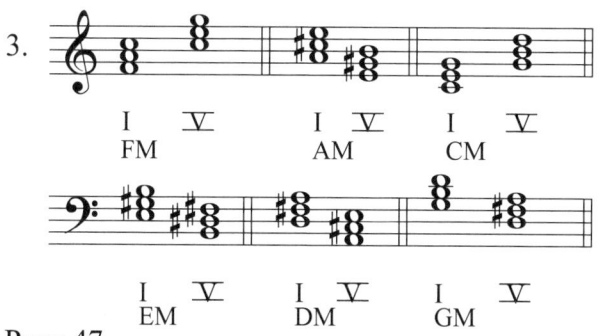

Page 47

4. IV-I, Plagal; IV-I, Plagal, V⁷-I, Authentic;
   IV$_4^6$-I, Plagal

   V-I, Authentic; I-V^6, Half;
   V^6-I, Authentic; IV-I, Plagal

5. a. Key of F Major: I$_4^6$-V, Half

Page 48

   b. Key of F Major: V^6-I, Authentic

   c. Key of F Major: V-I, Authentic

   d. Key of C Major: I-V^6, Half

REVIEW: LESSONS 1-11 (Pages 51-62)

Page 51

1. a. B Major, A♭ Major, D Major, B♭ Major,
      E♭ Major, E Major, D♭ Major, F♯ Major

   b. g minor, e minor, d minor, a minor,
      c minor, b minor

Page 52

Page 52, No. 2, cont.

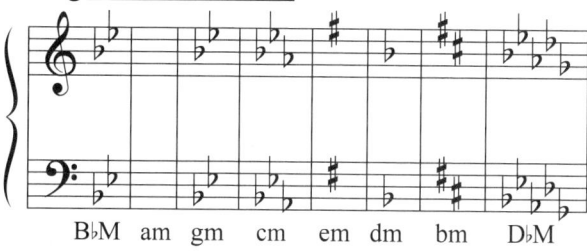

3.
D Major

B♭ Major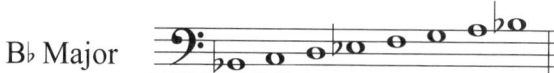

Page 53

c natural minor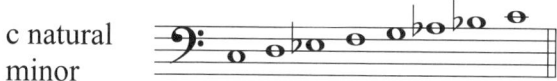

g harmonic minor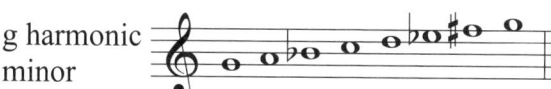

b harmonic minor

G♭ Major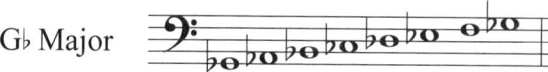

4. E Major ^{6}, d diminished, D Dominant ^{7},
   A Major $_4^6$, F♯ Major, f minor $_4^6$

   f minor ^{6}, a minor $_4^6$, C♭ Major,
   B♭ Dominant ^{7}, a diminished, e minor $_4^6$

Page 54

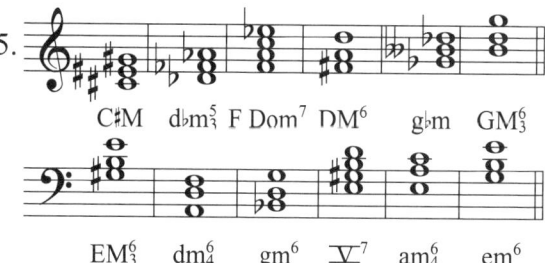

Level 4, Pages 46-54

Page 54, cont.

6. P4, m2, P4, P5, M3, P4
   m3, P5, m6, M6, M7, P5

Page 55

7.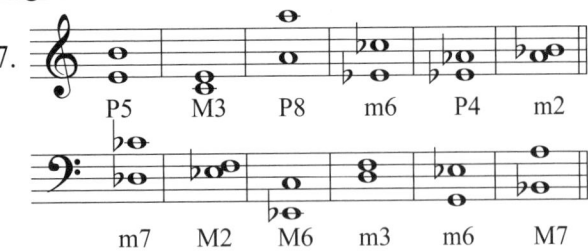
   P5 M3 P8 m6 P4 m2
   m7 M2 M6 m3 m6 M7

8. h, c, a, d, b, g, e, f

Page 57

9. a. F Major
   b. F Major
   c. Triad a: F Major, I
      Triad b: F Major, I⁶
      Triad c: C Major: V $\frac{6}{4}$
      Triad d: F Major: I
      Triad e: C Major: V⁶
   d. 1: m2   2: M2   3: M2   4: P5
      5: M3   6: m6   7: P8
   e. Half
      Authentic

Page 59

10. a. e minor
    b. Harmonic
    c. Triad a: e minor, $\frac{5}{3}$ (root)
       Triad b: a minor, $\frac{6}{4}$ (second)
       Triad c: e minor, $\frac{5}{3}$ (root)
       Triad d: B Major, $\frac{5}{3}$ (root)
    d. No
    e. 1: M2   2: m2   3: m3   4: M6
       5: P8   6: P4   7: m3
    f. Half
    g. Authentic

Page 60

11. a. g minor
    b. Harmonic

Page 60, No. 11, cont.

c. B♭ Major
d. Relative

Page 61

e. Triad a: g minor $\frac{6}{3}$ (first)
   Triad b: g minor $\frac{6}{4}$ (second)
   Triad c: D Major $\frac{5}{3}$ (root)
   Triad d: g minor $\frac{5}{3}$ (root)
f. 1: m2   2: M3   3: P4   4: P5
   5: M3   6: m3   7: P4
g. Half
h. Authentic

LESSON 12: TIME SIGNATURES
(Pages 63-70)

Page 65

2 = 2 beats per measure, beat 1 strongest
4 = Quarter note receives one beat

3 = 3 beats per measure, beat 1 strongest
4 = Quarter note receives one beat

4 = 4 beats per measure, beats 1 & 3 strong
4 = Quarter note receives one beat

𝄴 = $\frac{4}{4}$ or common time

𝄵 = $\frac{2}{2}$ or alla breve

5 = 5 beats per measure
4 = Quarter note receives one beat

7 = 7 beats per measure
4 = Quarter note receives one beat

Page 66

2. a.

Level 4, Pages 54-66

Page 66, No. 2, cont.

b.

c.

d.

Page 67

e.

Page 68

3. 6, one (or 2, 1/3)
   measure, eighth note (or 3 measures,
      dotted quarter
   12, eighth note (or 4, dotted quarter)
   measure, half note
   3, one beat
   12, half note (or 4, dotted whole)

Page 69

4. a.

b.

c.

Page 70

d.

Level 4, Pages 66-70

Page 70, cont.

5. 6/8 3/4 6/8 3/4

LESSON 13: SIGNS AND TERMS
(Pages 71-76)

Page 74

1. e, d, a, c, g, b, f, i, k, h, j

2. f, g, e, a, c, d, b

Page 75

3. d, c, b, a, g, e, f

4. h, a, f, g, b, d, e or i, e or i, c

Page 76

5. b, e, d, f, a, c, l, i, k, h, j, g

6. e, f, b, c, d, a, h, g

LESSON 14: TRANSPOSITION
(Pages 77-80)

Page 79

a. Original key: C Major
   Transposed to: D Major

b. Original key: G Major
   Transposed to: F Major

Page 80

2.
Melody 1
Melody 2

Level 4, Pages 70-84

LESSON 15: MOTIF; REPETITION, SEQUENCE, IMITATION
(Pages 81-84)

Page 82

1. a. Sequence

b. Sequence

c. Imitation

d. Repetition

Page 84

e. Repetition

Page 84, No. 1, cont.

f. Imitation

LESSON 16: THE FOUR PERIODS OF MUSIC HISTORY (Pages 85-86)

1. Baroque, 1600-1750, Bach, Handel, Scarlatti
   Classical, 1750-1830, Mozart, Haydn, Clementi
   Romantic, 1830-1900, Tchaikovsky, Chopin, Schumann
   20th & 21st Centuries or Contemporary, 1900-present, Kabalevsky, Bartók

REVIEW: LESSONS 12-16 (Pages 87-90)

Page 87

1. 2, one
   Quarter note

   6, one and four (or 2, one and 2)
   Eighth note (or dotted quarter note)

   measure, one
   one beat

   measure (or 3 measures)
   one beat (or 1/3 beat)

   4, one and three
   Quarter note

   12 (or 4)
   Eighth note (or dotted quarter)

Page 87, cont.

2. a.

b.

Page 88

3. 1. Slightly faster than Andante
   2. In a singing style
   3. Very fast
   4. Expressively
   5. Lightly
   6. Slightly slower than Allegro
   7. Suffix meaning little
   8. Suddenly
   9. Suffix meaning little
   10. Trill
   11. Major and minor keys with the same letter name
   12. The manner in which notes are executed; includes *staccato* and *legato*

4. a. Sequence

Level 4, Pages 84-88

Page 89

b. Repetition

c. Sequence

7. Baroque: 1600-1750
   Classical: 1750-1830
   Romantic: 1830-1900
   20th/21st Centuries (Contemp.) 1900-present

Page 90

8.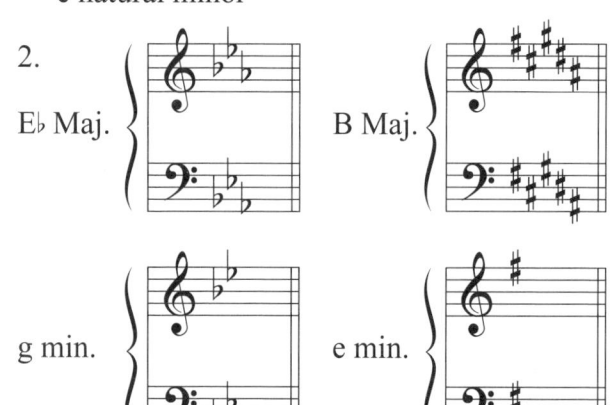

11. a. 3/4   b. 4/4 (C) or 2/2 (¢)

REVIEW TEST (Pages 91-98)

1. F Major
   A♭ Major
   c harmonic minor
   e natural minor

2. E♭ Maj. B Maj.
   g min.   e min.

Page 92

3. a.
   i   iv   V

   b.
   ii   iii   vi   vii°

   c.
   I ii iii IV V vi vi° I

Page 93

4. a. A Major
   b. Tonic
   c.
   d. 2/4
   e. Repetition
   f. Medium or moderate tempo

Page 94

5. a. a minor
   b. harmonic
   c. Yes
   d. a. P4   b. M2   c. M6   d. m2
      e. M3   f. m3
   e. 2 1/2
   f. Left hand
   g. First in each measure

Page 95

6. a. G Major
   b. *piano:* soft
      crescendo: gradually louder
      decrescendo (diminuendo): gradually softer
      mezzo forte: medium loud

Page 95, No. 6, cont.

c. Triad a: G Major, I
   Triad b: D Major, V
   Triad c: C Major, IV⁶
   Triad d: G Major, I⁶
d. Half

e.

Page 96

7. g, e, h, a, f, b, c, i, d

Page 97

8. a. E♭ Major
   b. g minor
   c. a. P4   b. M3   c. M2   d. P5
      e. m6   f. M3
   d. Beat 4, measure 3: B♭ Major ⁵₃ (root)
      Beat 1, measure 4: E♭ Major ⁵₃ (root)
   e. Authentic
   f.

Page 98

9. a. F Major
   b. Triad 1: F Major ⁵₃ (root)
      Triad 2: B♭ Major ⁶₄ (second)
   c. a. M3   b. P5   c. M3   d. M6   e. M2
   d. Imitation
   e. 4/4
   f. First and third in each measure

Level 4, Pages 95-98

This page has purposely been left blank

LEVEL 5

LESSON 1: MAJOR AND MINOR KEY SIGNATURES (Pages 1-10)

Page 2

1. a. F♯, C♯
   b. F♯, C♯, G♯
   c. F♯
   d. F♯, C♯, G♯, D♯, A♯, E♯

2.

Page 3

3. D Major, C♯ Major, B Major, A Major, E Major, C Major

4.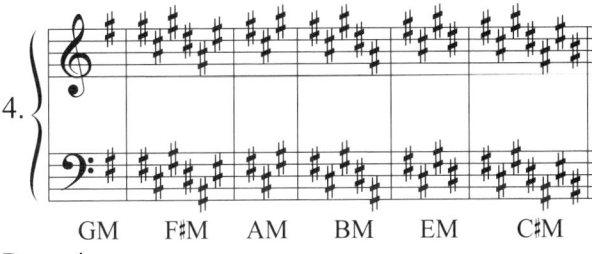

   GM F♯M AM BM EM C♯M

Page 4

5. a. B♭, E♭
   b. B♭, E♭, A♭, D♭
   c. B♭, E♭, A♭
   d. B♭, E♭, A♭, D♭, G♭

6.

Page 5

7. C♭ Major, B♭ Major, A♭ Major, D♭ Major, F Major, E♭ Major, G♭ Major

Page 6

8.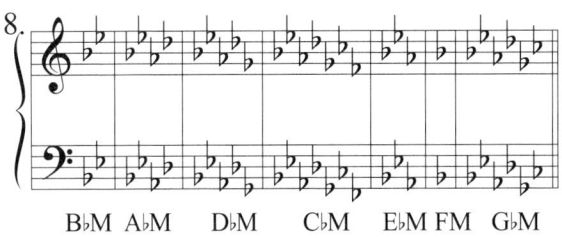

   B♭M A♭M D♭M C♭M E♭M FM G♭M

Page 8

10. a. e minor
    b. c minor
    c. a minor
    d. d minor
    e. g minor
    f. b minor
    g. f minor

11. a. F Major
    b. G Major
    c. A♭ Major
    d. E♭ Major
    e. C Major
    f. B♭ Major
    g. D Major

Page 9

12. d minor, b minor, c minor, g minor, f minor, e minor, a minor

13.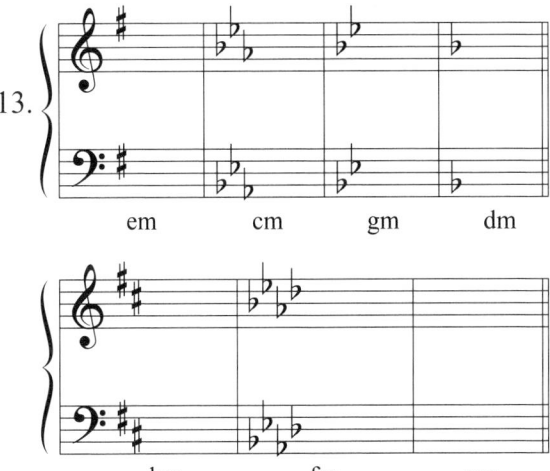

    em cm gm dm

    bm fm am

Level 5, Pages 1-9

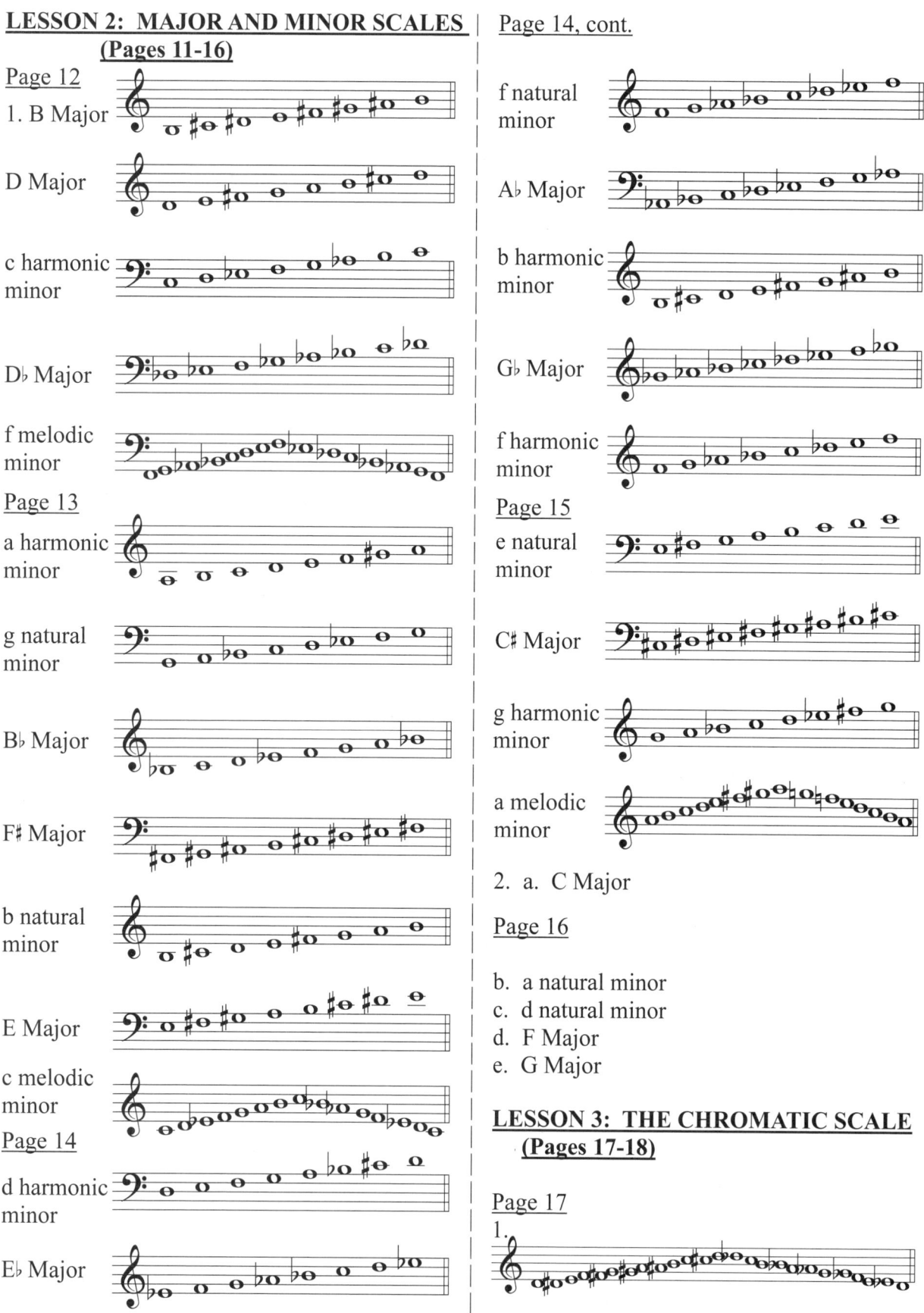

Page 17, No. 1, cont.

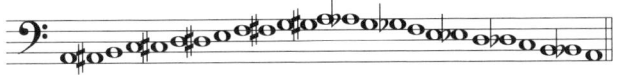

Page 18

LESSON 4: INTERVALS (Pages 19-22)

Page 20

1. P4, M3, P8, M2, P4, M6, M7, P5
   M6, M3, P8, P5, P4, M7, M2, M7

2.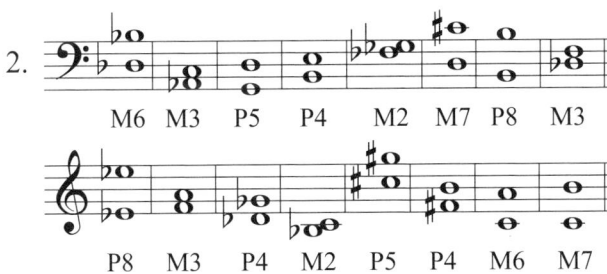

Page 21

3. m6, M2, m3, m6, P4, m7, m2, M2
   m7, M7, M3, P5, m6, M7, m3, M6

4.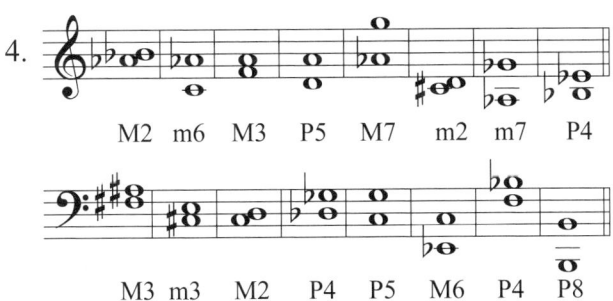

Page 22

5. a. m3, m3, M2, m6, P4, P8, P8
   b. m3, m3, M2, P4, M3, m3
   c. P5, M6, P4, m2, M3, M3, m2, P5

LESSON 5: MAJOR, MINOR, AND DIMINISHED TRIADS (Pages 23-26)

Page 23

1.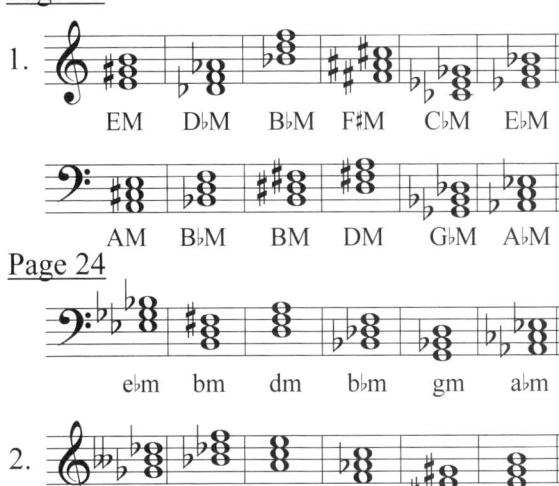

Page 24

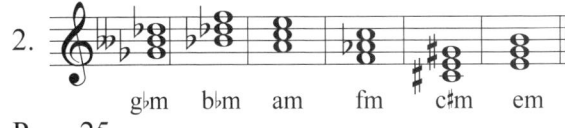

2.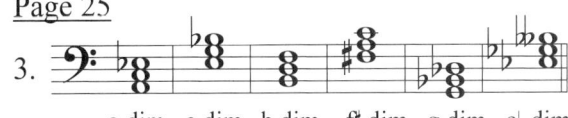

Page 25

3.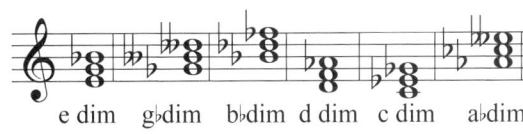

4. f minor, B Major, D Major, g minor,
   a diminished, c# minor

   c♭ minor, A♭ Major, e diminished,
   b♭ minor, f# minor, D♭ Major

Page 26

5.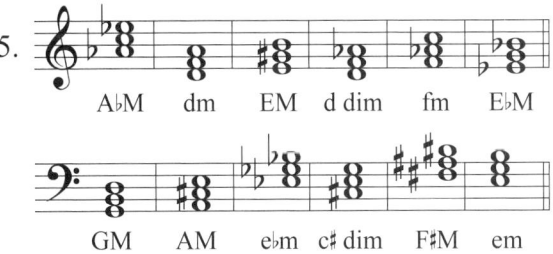

LESSON 6: INVERSIONS OF TRIADS (Pages 27-32)

Page 28*

1. A Major $^6_4$, d minor ^{6}, E Major, b♭ minor ^{6}, C Major ^{6}, c minor ^{6}

   g diminished, c minor $^6_4$, G♭ Major ^{6}, F♯ Major $^6_4$, f minor ^{6}, d minor

   a minor, A♭ Major $^6_4$, E♭ Major $^6_4$, B Major $^6_4$, e♭ diminished, c diminished

Page 29

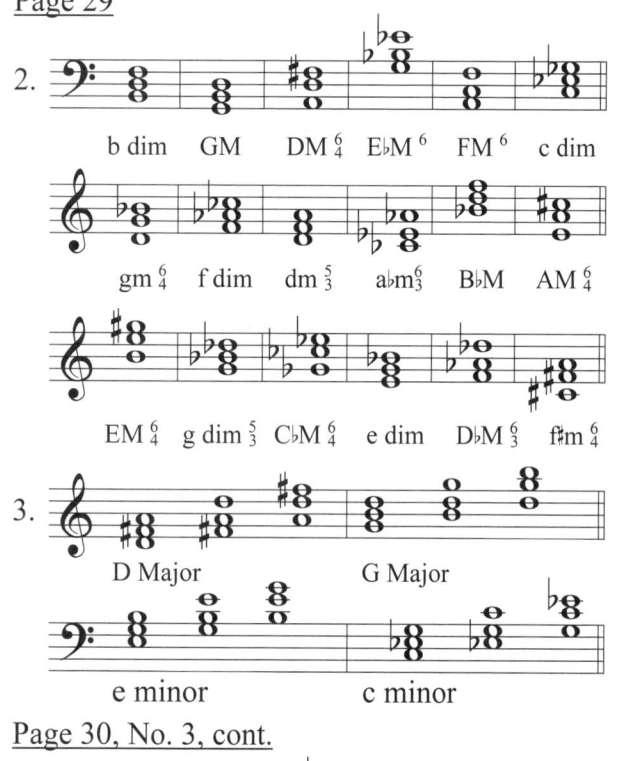

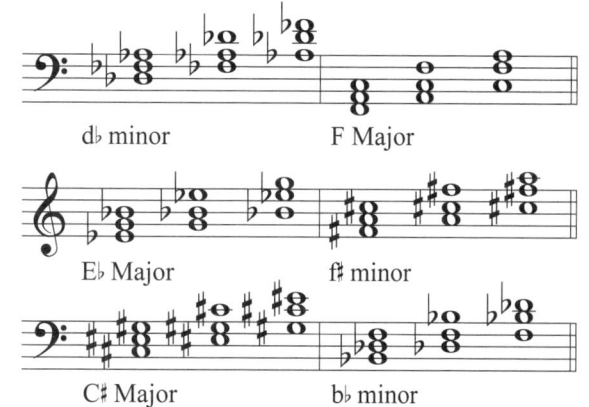

Page 30, No. 3, cont.

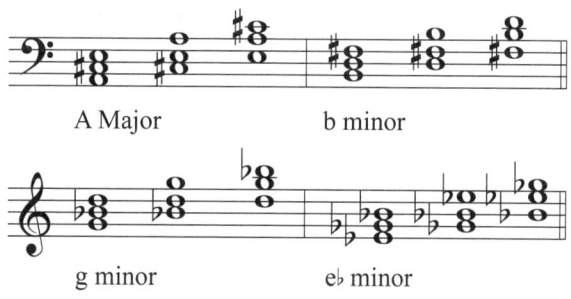

Page 31

4. a. G Major, a minor, d minor ^{6}, C Major $^6_4$, C Major

Page 32

   b. e minor, D Major, G Major, C Major ^{6}, G Major $^6_4$, D Major, G Major

   c. A Major, B Major $^6_4$, A Major

LESSON 7: PRIMARY AND SECONDARY TRIADS (Pages 33-40)

Page 34*

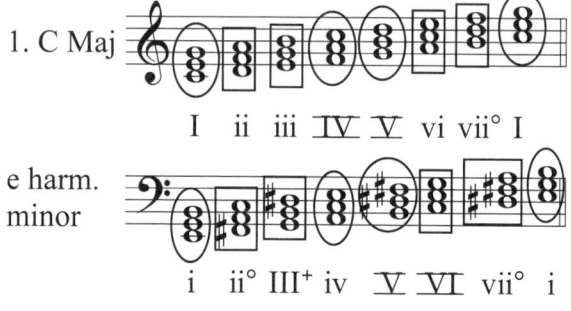

Page 35

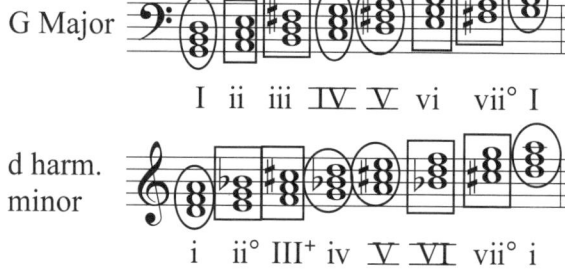

*$^5_3$ for root position and $^6_3$ for first inversion are acceptable

Level 5, Pages 28-35

Page 35, cont.

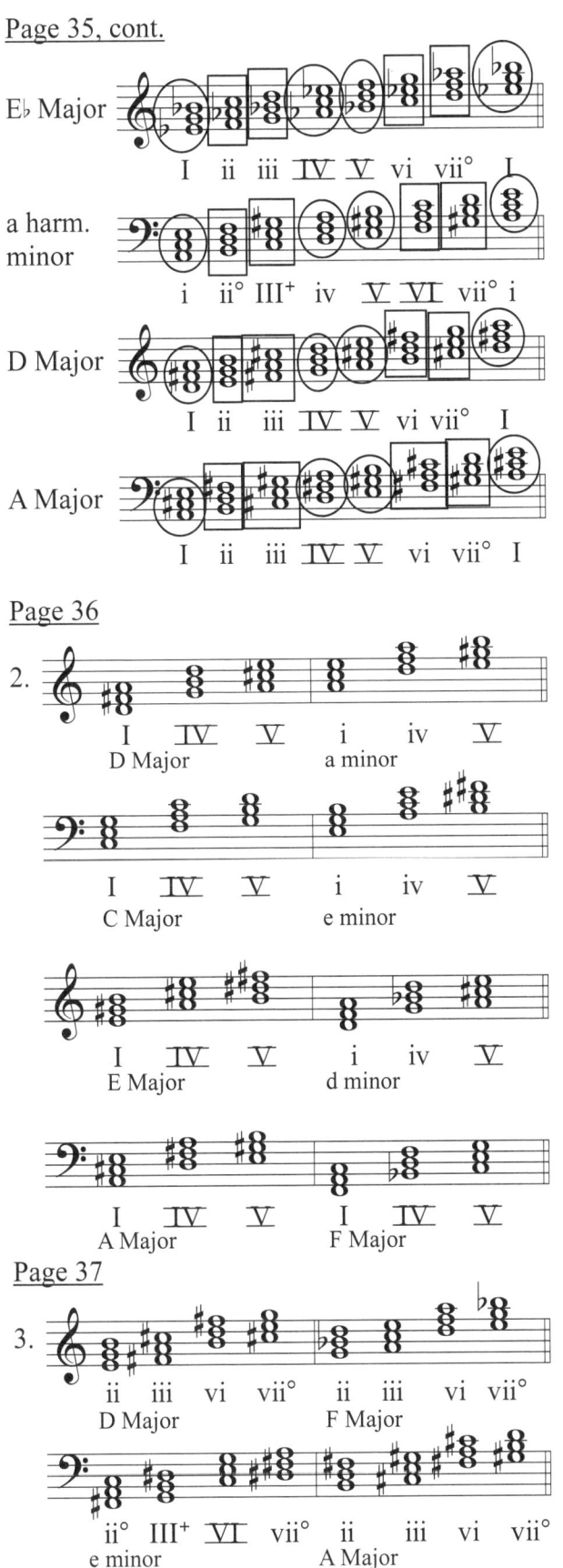

Page 36

Page 37

Page 37, No. 3, cont.

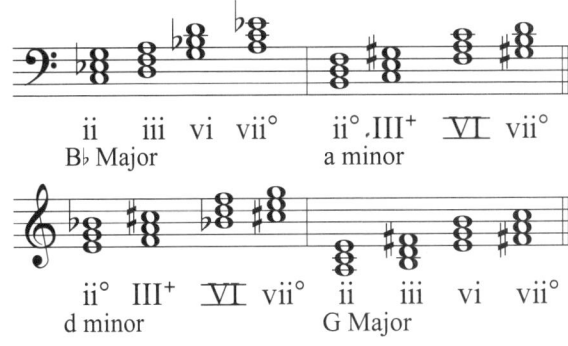

Page 38

4. f, g, a, e, d, c, b

5. tonic, supertonic, mediant, subdominant, dominant, submediant, leading tone

Page 40

6. a. Key of G Major: I I^6 IV I V

b. Key of C Major: I I^6 V ii^6 i iii

c. Key of G Major: I I$^6_4$ IV$^6_4$ IV^6 ii I

LESSON 8: THE DOMINANT SEVENTH CHORD (Pages 41-44)

Page 42

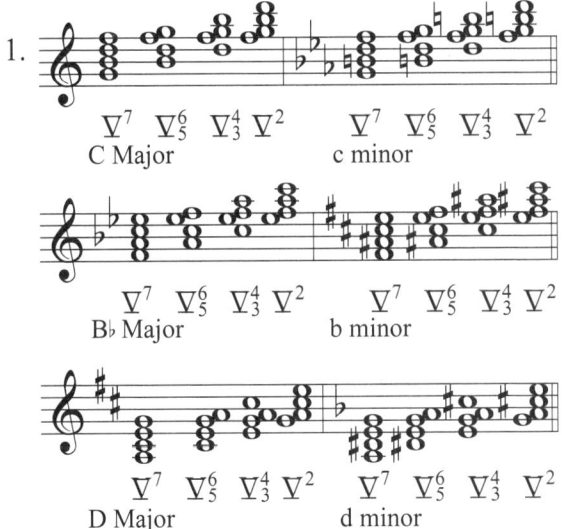

* $^4_2$ is acceptable for third inversion

Level 5, Pages 35-42

Page 42, cont.

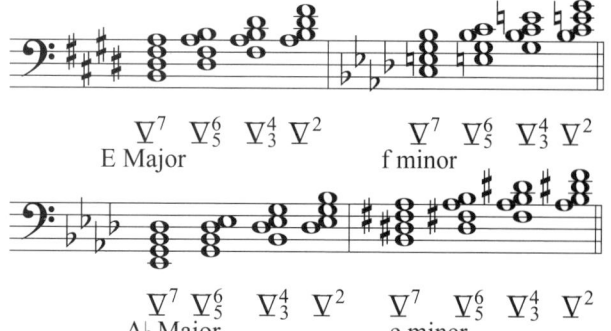

Page 43

2. a. V^6_5
   b. V
   c. V^7
   d. V
   e. V^6_4
   f. V^7

Page 44, No. 2, cont.

   g. V^7
   h. V^7

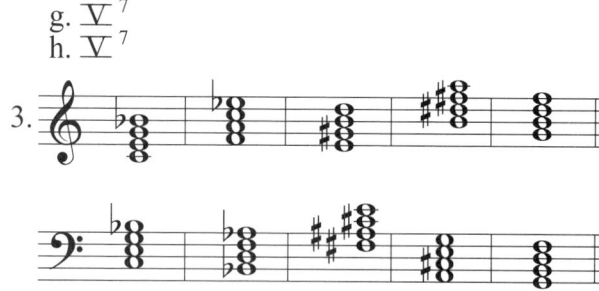

LESSON 9: AUTHENTIC, HALF, AND PLAGAL CADENCES (Pages 45-52)

Page 45

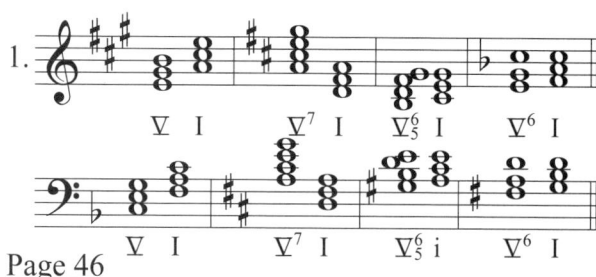

Page 46

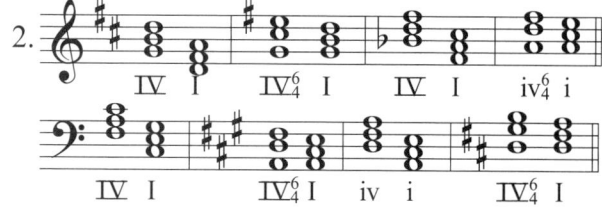

Page 47

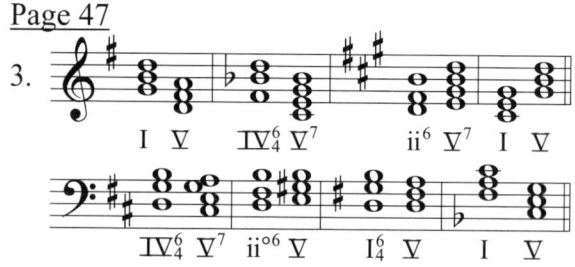

4. IV^6_4 - I, Plagal
   V^7 - I, Authentic
   I - V^6_5, Half
   iv - i, Plagal

   I - V^6, Half
   V - I, Authentic
   IV^6_4 - I, Plagal
   V - i, Authentic

Page 48

5. a. Key of F Major: V^6_4 - I, Authentic
   b. Key of C Major: V - I, Authentic

Page 49

   c. Key of F Major: IV^6_4 - I, Plagal
   d. Key of G Major: I^6_4 - V, Half
   e. Key of g minor: iv^6_4 - I, Plagal

Page 50, No. 5, cont.

   f. Key of C Major: I - V, Half
   g. Key of G Major: ii^6 - V, Half

REVIEW: LESSONS 1-9 (Pages 53-60)

Page 53

1. G♭ Major, A♭ Major, E Major, F♯ Major, G Major, D♭ Major, C♯ Major

2. g minor, a minor, b minor, c minor, f minor, e minor, d minor

Level 5, Pages 42-53

Page 53, cont.

3.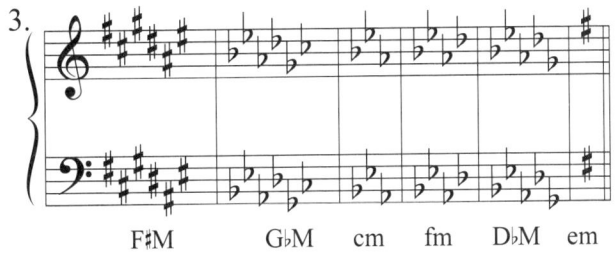

F#M   G♭M   cm   fm   D♭M   em

Page 54, No. 3, cont.

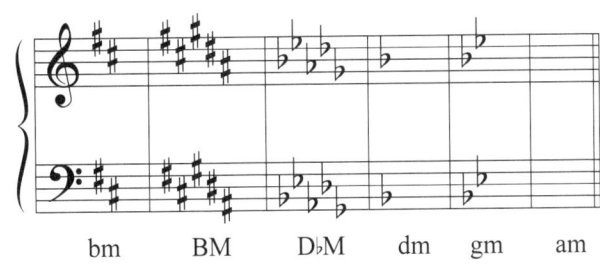

bm   BM   D♭M   dm   gm   am

4.
D Major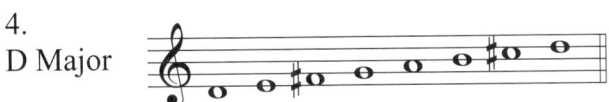

b natural minor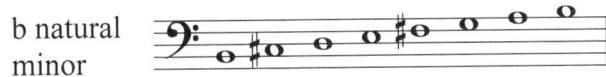

e harmonic minor

B Major

Page 55

f melodic minor

c natural minor

A♭ Major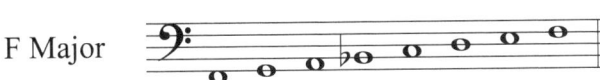

F Major

Page 55, cont.

5. E Major ^{6}, c minor ^{6}, f minor, g minor ^{6}, B♭ Major $^6_4$, d diminished

   a minor $^6_4$, E♭ Major, g minor $^6_4$, C Major ^{6}, a♭ minor, B Major ^{6}

Page 56

6.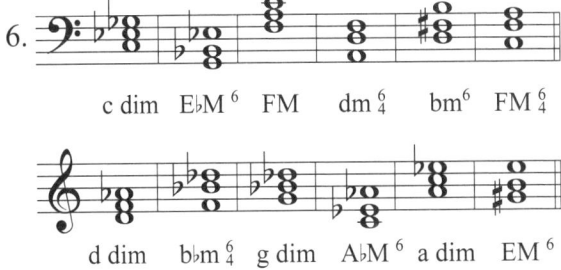

c dim   E♭M ^{6} FM   dm $^6_4$ bm^6 FM $^6_4$

d dim   b♭m $^6_4$ g dim   A♭M ^{6} a dim   EM ^{6}

7. P4, M3, M2, P8, M2, M7, P5, m6
   P5, P4, m3, P4, m6, m7, P8, M2

8.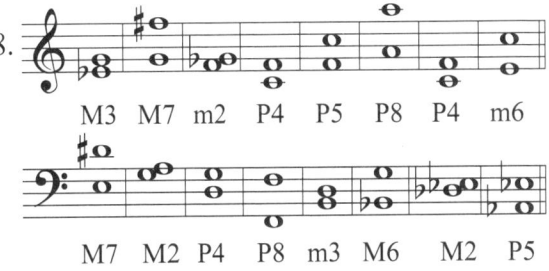

M3   M7   m2   P4   P5   P8   P4   m6

M7   M2   P4   P8   m3   M6   M2   P5

Page 57

9. a. f minor
   b. Harmonic
   c. Triad a: C Major $^6_3$ (first)
      Triad b: f minor $^5_3$ (root)
      Triad c: f minor $^6_4$ (second)
      Triad d: f minor $^5_3$ (root)
      Triad e: b♭ minor $^6_4$ (second)
      Triad f: b♭ minor $^5_3$ (root)
   d. 1. P4   2. m2   3. m3   4. M6
      5. P8   6. m6   7. P5
   e. Authentic

Page 58

10. a. C Major
    b. G Major
    c. Triad a: C Major, I
       Triad b: d minor, ii^6
       Triad c: C Major, I
       Triad d: G Major, V
       Triad e: C Major, I
    d. 1. m2   2. M2   3. m6   4. P5
       5. P8   6. M6   7. M2

Page 59

    e. Authentic
    f.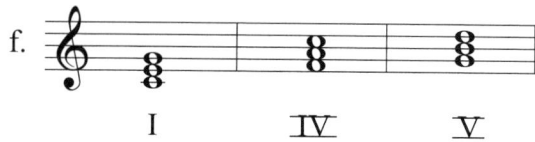
       I   IV   V

11. a. Tonic
    b. Supertonic
    c. Mediant
    d. Subdominant
    e. Dominant
    f. Submediant
    g. Leading Tone

Page 60

12. a. F Major
    b. Triad a: F Major, I
       Triad b: B♭ Major, IV$^6_4$
       Triad c: C Major, V^6
       Triad d: C Major, V
       Triad e: g minor, ii
       Triad f: F Major, I
    c. 1. M3   2. m3   3. M3   4. M3
       5. m2   6. m6   7. P4
    d. Authentic
    e.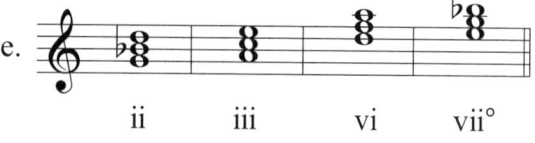
       ii   iii   vi   vii°

LESSON 10: TIME SIGNATURES
(Pages 61-68)

Page 65

1. 2 beats per measure
   Quarter note receives one beat

   3 beats per measure
   Quarter note receives one beat

   3 beats per measure (or 1 beat)
   Eighth note receives one beat (or dotted quarter)

   Common Time or $\frac{4}{4}$

   Alla Breve or $\frac{2}{2}$

   2 beats per measure
   Half note receives one beat

   7 beats per measure
   Quarter note receives one beat

   6 beats per measure (or 2 beats)
   Eighth note receives one beat (or dotted quarter)

2. a. 2 Equal beats per measure

Page 66

   b. 2 equal beats per measure
   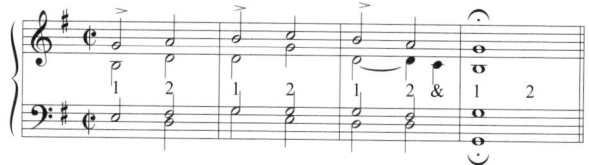

   c. 6 equal beats per measure (or 2)

Page 66, No. 2, cont.

  d. 4 equal beats per measure

  e. 3 equal beats per measure

Page 67

  f. 3 equal beats per measure

  g. 4 equal beats per measure

  h. 6 equal beats per measure (or 2)

Page 68

3. a. 6/8   b. 3/4   c. 3/4   d. 6/8

4. a. ♪ ♪ ♪. ♪
    b. 𝅗𝅥 𝅗𝅥 ♩ ♩

5. a. 𝄽 ᜎ 𝄽 𝄽
    b. 𝄽 ᜎ ᜎ 𝄽

LESSON 11: SIGNS AND TERMS
(Pages 69-76)

Page 73

1. c, g, a, j, i, d, f, b, k, e, h

2. d, f, c, e, a, b

Page 74

3. c, a, b, d, g, e, f

4. i, a, f, g, b, d, e or j, e or j, c, h

Page 75

5. e, g, f, k, b, m, d, n, j, c, a, o, i, l, h

Page 76

6. d, f, a, h, k, g, c, i, e, b, l, j

LESSON 12: MOTIF; REPETITION, SEQUENCE, IMITATION
(Pages 77-80)

Page 78

1. a. Repetition

Page 79

  b. Imitation

Level 5, Pages 66-79

Page 79

c. Repetition

d. Sequence

Page 80

e. Sequence

f. Sequence

LESSON 13: TRANSPOSITION (Pages 81-84)

Page 83

1. a. Original key: C Major
      Transposed to: D Major

   b. Original key: D Major
      Transposed to: G Major

Page 84

LESSON 14: THE FOUR PERIODS OF MUSIC HISTORY, THE THE BAROQUE PERIOD (Pages 85-88)

Page 87

1. Harpsichord, clavichord, organ
2. Ornamentation; cadenzas; figured bass
3. Trills, mordents
4. Polyphonic
5. Keyboard instruments could not produce *cresc.* and *dim.*
6. J.S. Bach, Germany
   G.F. Handel, Germany
   Domenico Scarlatti, Italy
   Henry Purcell, England

LESSON 15: THE CLASSICAL PERIOD (Pages 89-90)

Page 90

1. Sonata form
2. Homophonic
3. Alberti Bass
4. To set off a new theme or section
5. Obvious melody, clear harmony
6. Franz Josef Haydn, Austria
   Wolfgang Amadeus Mozart, Austria
   Muzio Clementi, Italy
   Ludwig van Beethoven, Germany

Level 5, Pages 79-90

LESSON 16: THE ROMANTIC PERIOD (Page 91-92)

Page 92

1. Descriptive titles
2. More complicated, chromaticism
3. Lyric melodies
4. Syncopation, dotted rhythms, cross rhythms, triplets
5. Franz Schubert, Austria
   Robert Schumann, Germany
   Peter Tchaikovsky, Russia
   Edvard Grieg, Norway

LESSON 17: THE 20th & 21st CENTURIES (CONTEMPORARY) (Pages 93-96)

Page 95

1. a. Bitonality
   b. Quartal harmony
   c. Atonality
   d. Polytonality

Page 96

2. They are avoided
3. Irregular and changing meters
4. Polyphonic texture
5. Classical forms (Sonatas, etc.)
6. Béla Bartók, Hungary
   Dmitri Kabalevsky, Russia
   Alexander Tcherepnin, Russia
   Serge Prokofiev, Russia

REVIEW: LESSONS 10-17 (Pages 97-100)

Page 97

1. a. 6 equal beats per measure (or 2)

Page 97, cont.

b. 4 then 3 equal beats per measure

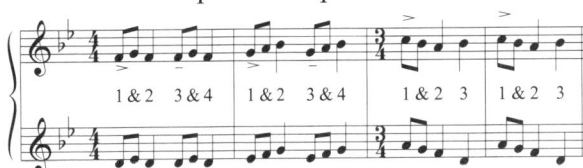

Page 98

2. a. Very slowly, large
   b. Animated, with spirit
   c. With brilliance
   d. Lively
   e. With
   f. Tranquilly, peacefully
   g. Two names for the same pitch
   h. With motion
   i. A persistently repeated pattern
   j. Mordent
   k. Turn
   l. Appoggiatura

Page 99

3. a. Repetition
   b. Sequence
   c. Imitation

Page 100

4. Baroque: 1600-1750
   Classical: 1750-1830
   Romantic: 1830-1900
   20th & 21st Centuries (Contemporary): 1900-present

5. F, F, T, T, T, F, T, F, T

6.

REVIEW TEST (Pages 101-106)

Page 101

1. E♭ Major, c minor
   G Major, e minor
   B♭ Major, g minor
   C Major, a minor

2.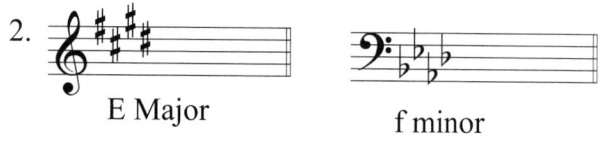
   E Major   f minor

   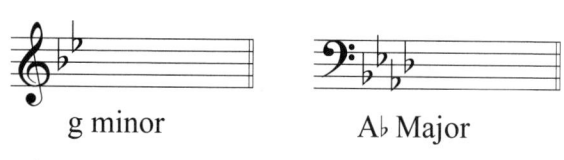
   g minor   A♭ Major

3.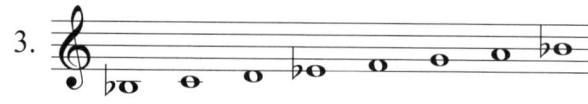

Page 102

4a.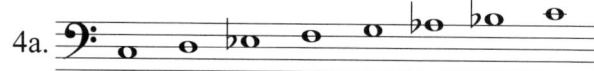

4b.

5. Ex. 1: B♭ Major   Ex. 2: a diminished
   Ex. 3: g minor   Ex. 4: e minor
   Ex. 5: D♭ Major   Ex. 6: f diminished

6. a. Animated; with spirit
   b. Tranquilly, peacefully
   c. Two different names for the same pitch
   d. Lively
   e. With brilliance
   f. With motion
   g. Very slowly; large
   h. Lightly

Page 103

7. a. a minor
   b. No
   c. Natural
   d. a. i, Tonic   b. VI, Submediant

Page 103, No. 7, cont.

e.

f. 4
g. First and third in each measure
h. 20th & 21st Centuries (Contemporary)
i. Repetition

Page 104

8. a. A Major
   b. No
   c. Trill
   d. 1. M2   2. P4   3. P4   4. M3
      5. m2   6. P8
   e. Romantic
   f. Schubert, Tchaikovsky, Grieg, for example

9. d, c, a, b

Page 105

10. a. C Major
    b. G Major
    c. V
    d. Triad 1: G Major, V^6
       Triad 2: C Major, I^6
       Triad 3: G Major, V
    e. Authentic
    f. First in each measure
    g. Classical

Page 106

11. a. B Major
    b. D Major
    c. $\frac{6}{8}$, first and fourth in each measure
    d. First in each measure
    e. Fermata, hold the note longer than its value
    f. Little by little gradually faster
    g. Tenuto; hold for full value (stress the note)

LEVEL 6

LESSON 1: MAJOR AND MINOR KEY SIGNATURES (Pages 1-10)

Page 4

1. A Major, B♭ Major, G Major, F♯ Major, C♭ Major

   A♭ Major, E Major, D Major, C Major, D♭ Major

   C♯ Major, G♭ Major, B Major, E♭ Major, F Major

Page 5, No. 2, cont.

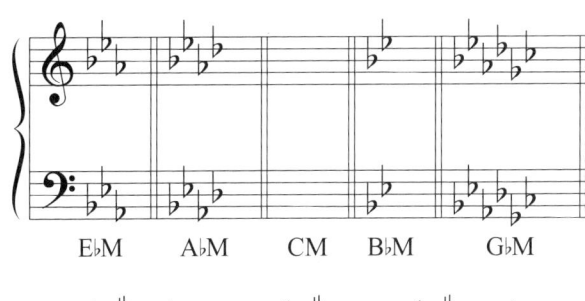

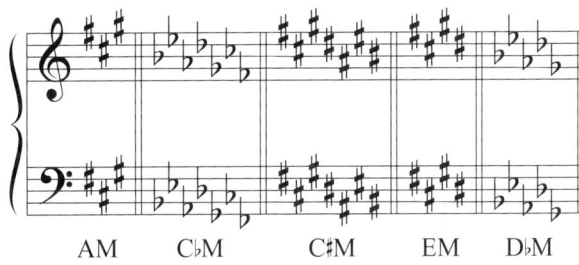

Page 6

3. a. e minor
   b. c minor
   c. a minor
   d. d minor
   e. g minor
   f. b minor
   g. f minor
   h. f♯ minor
   i. b♭ minor

4. a. F Major
   b. G Major
   c. A♭ Major
   d. E♭ Major
   e. C Major
   f. A Major
   g. B♭ Major
   h. D Major
   i. D♭ Major

Page 7

5. f♯ minor, g minor, e minor, f minor, b minor

   a minor, b♭ minor, c minor, d minor

Page 8
7. a. c minor
   b. a minor
   c. B♭ Major

Page 9
   d. d minor
   e. D Major
   f. E♭ Major

LESSON 2: MAJOR AND MINOR SCALES (Pages 11-16)

Page 12

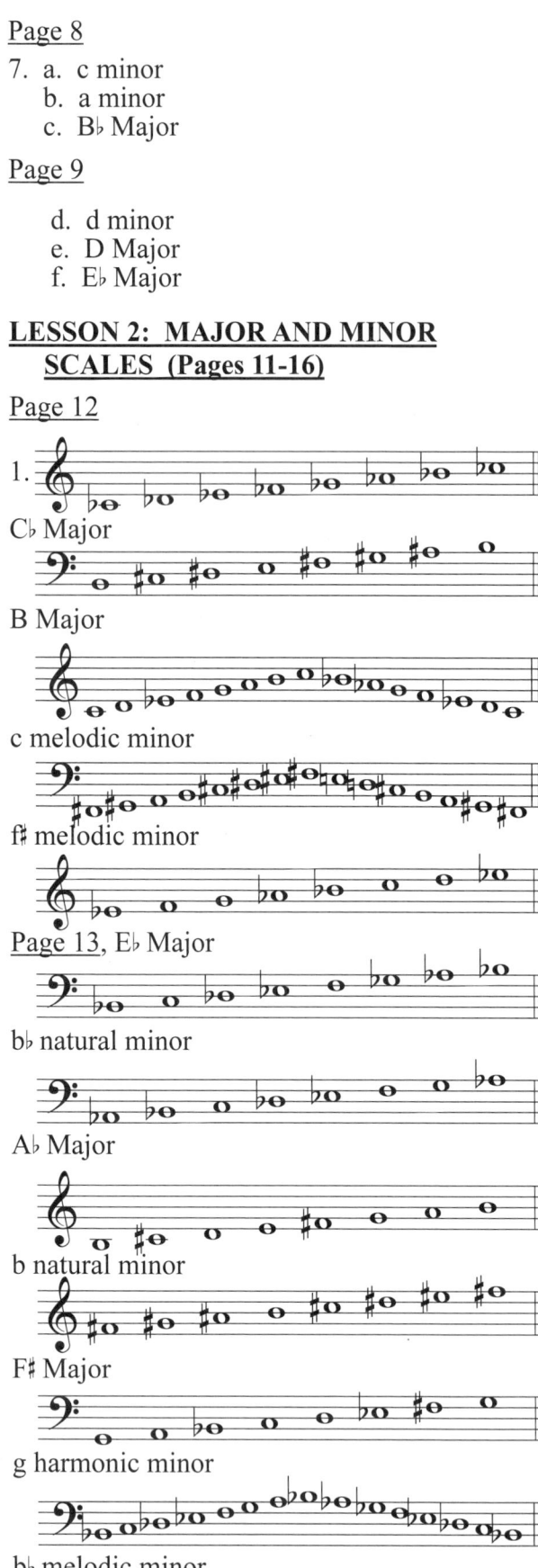

Page 14

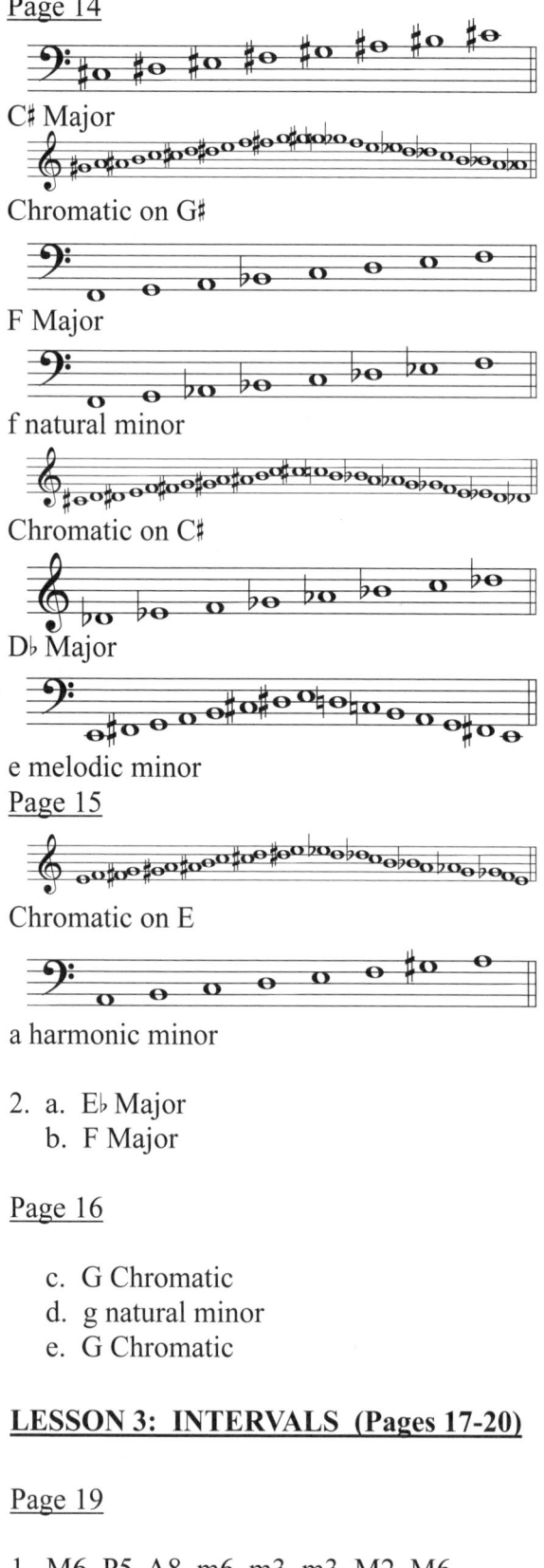

2. a. E♭ Major
   b. F Major

Page 16
   c. G Chromatic
   d. g natural minor
   e. G Chromatic

LESSON 3: INTERVALS (Pages 17-20)

Page 19

1. M6, P5, A8, m6, m3, m3, M2, M6
   d4, A7, A2, A4, d6, A5, m7, P4

Page 19, cont.

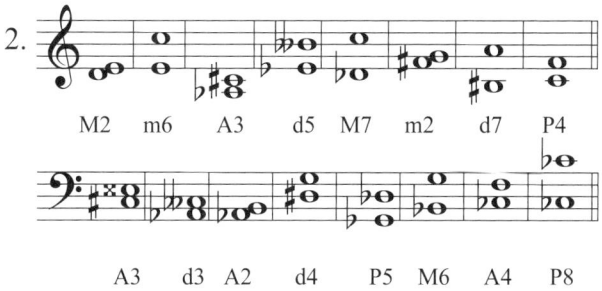

Page 20

3. a. M2, M3, P4, P5, m3, P4
   b. M2, P5, M3, P4, M3, P4
   c. P4, m6, P4, P5, P8, m3

LESSON 4: MAJOR, MINOR, AUGMENTED, AND DIMINISHED TRIADS AND INVERSIONS (Pages 21-28)

Page 22

Page 23

2. f minor, d♭ minor, A♭ Major, E♭ Major, e minor, b♭ minor

   D Augmented, g♭ minor, c minor, G Major, a diminished, B Augmented

Page 25

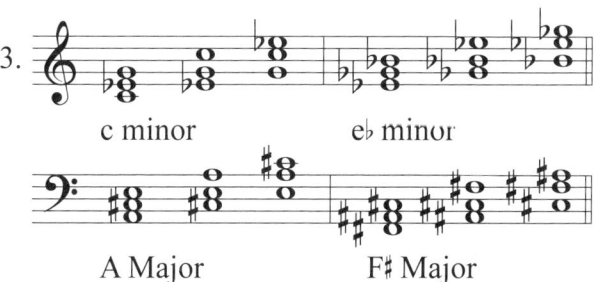

Page 25, No. 3, cont.

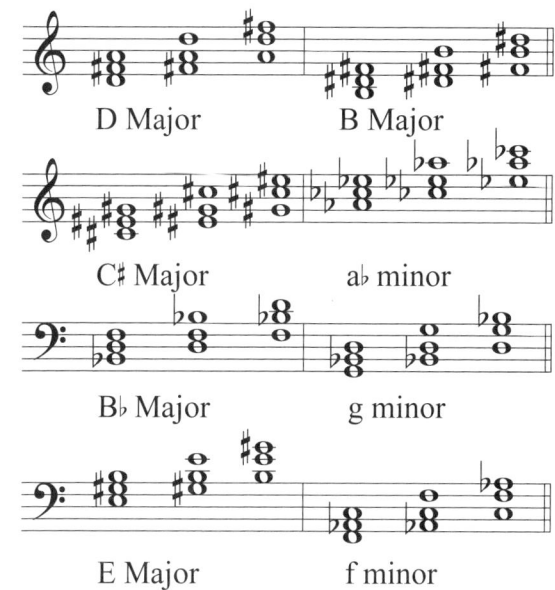

Page 26*

4. A Major $^6_4$, d minor, d minor $^6_4$, a minor ^{6}, C♯ Major $^6_4$, b♭ minor ^{6}

   E Major $^6_4$, B Augmented, E♭ Major ^{6}, A♭ Major $^6_4$, G Major $^6_4$, B♭ Major ^{6}

   F Major, G♭ Major $^6_4$, c minor, F♯ Major, C Augmented, C♭ Major

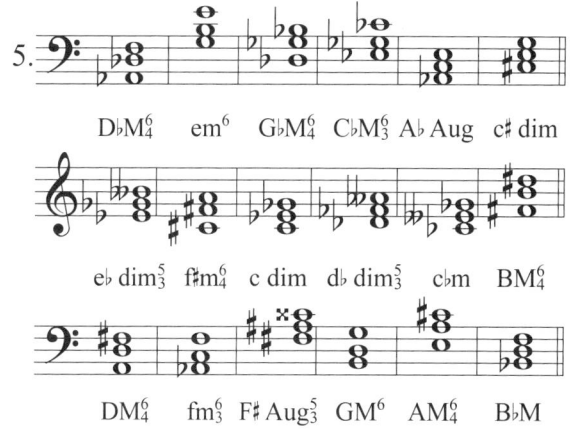

Page 27

6. a. B♭ Major ^{6}, e diminished, g minor $^6_4$, E♭ Major, F Major

*Also accept $^5_3$ for root position and $^6_3$ for 1st inversion

Level 6, Pages 19-27

Page 28, No. 6, cont.

b. e minor, C Major, e minor $^6_4$, b minor ^{6}, D Major, G Major $^6_4$

c. e minor $^6_4$, B Major, e minor, G Major $^6_4$, D Major

LESSON 5: PRIMARY AND SECONDARY TRIADS (Pages 29-36)

Page 30*

1.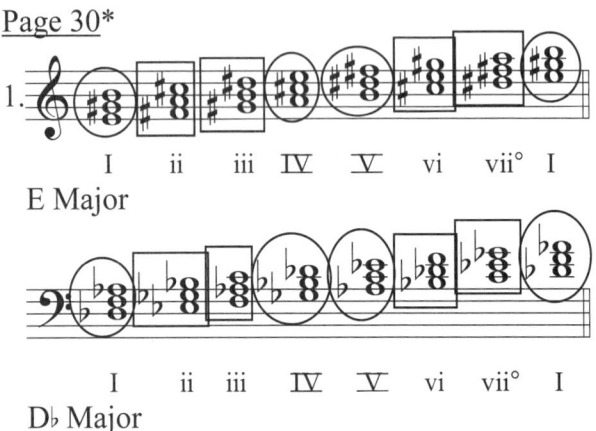
E Major / D♭ Major

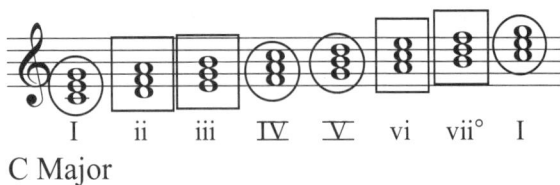
C Major

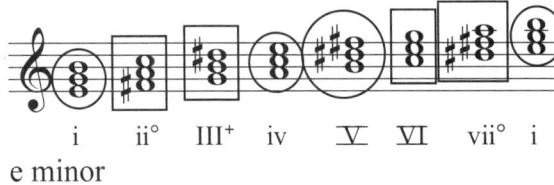
e minor

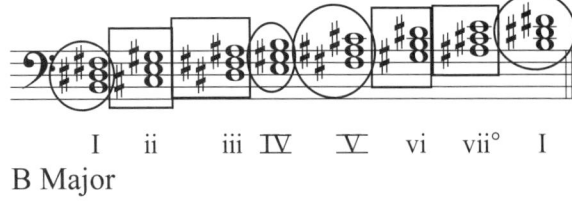
B Major

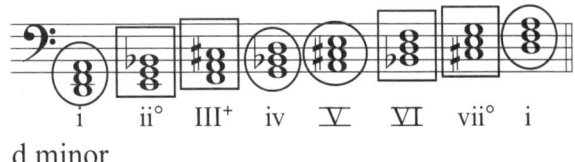
d minor

Page 31

2.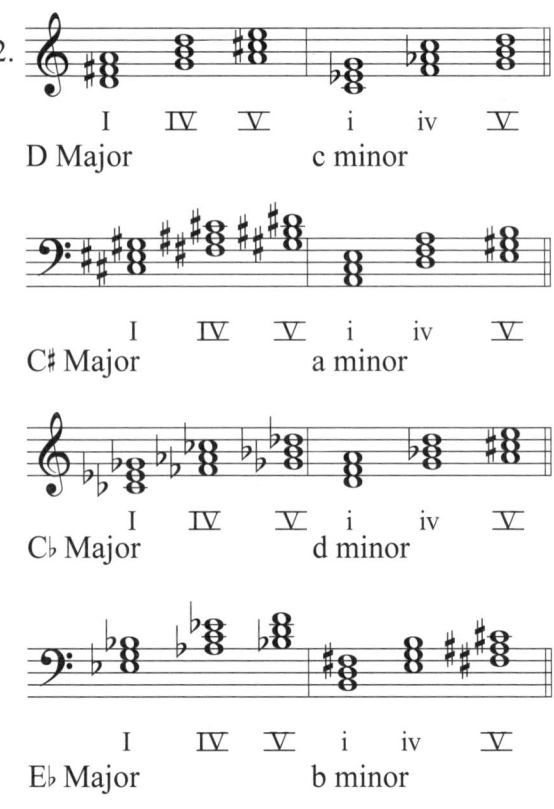
D Major / c minor
C♯ Major / a minor
C♭ Major / d minor
E♭ Major / b minor

Page 32

3.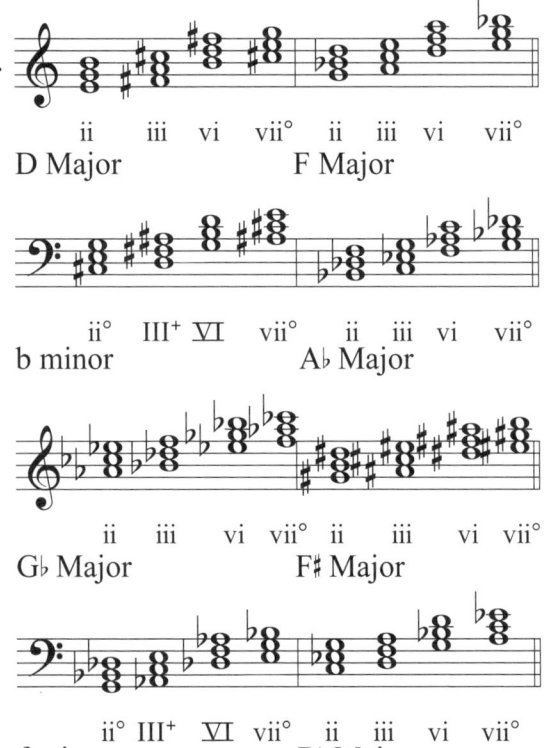
D Major / F Major
b minor / A♭ Major
G♭ Major / F♯ Major
f minor / B♭ Major

Page 33

4. f, g, a, e, d, c, b

5. Tonic, Supertonic, Mediant, Subdominant, Dominant, Submediant, Leading Tone

Page 35

6. a. Key of d minor: V^6, iv^6, VI, iv, iv^6, V

   b. Key of E♭ Major: I^6, IV, V, vi, vii°, I

   c. Key of G Major: ii^6, I^6, I, V

Page 36, No. 6, cont.

   d. Key of D Major: IV, I$^6_4$, vi

   e. Key of B♭ Major: I^6, vi$^6_4$, V

LESSON 6: THE DOMINANT SEVENTH CHORD (Pages 37-40)

Page 38

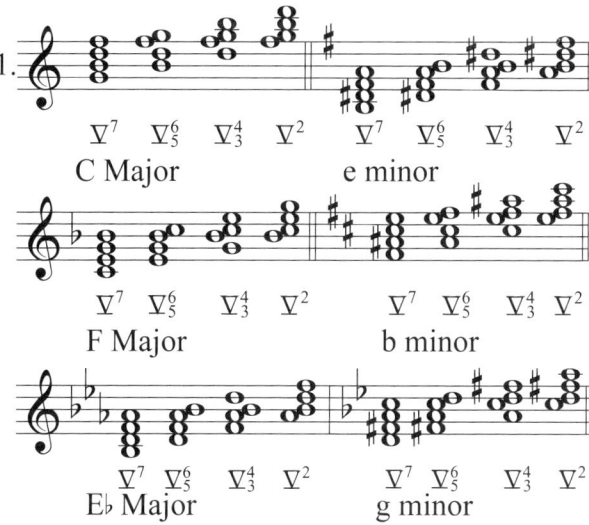

*$^4_2$ is acceptable for third inversion

Page 38, No. 2, cont.

Page 39

3. a. V
   b. V
   c. V^7
   d. V
   e. V^7
   f. V
   g. V$^6_4$
   h. V$^4_3$

Page 40, No. 3, cont.

   i. V^6
   j. V^7
   k. V
   l. V
   m. V$^6_5$
   n. V^6
   o. V$^4_3$
   p. V$^6_5$

LESSON 7: AUTHENTIC, HALF, PLAGAL, AND DECEPTIVE CADENCES (Pages 41-48)

Page 41

1.

Page 42

Page 43

5. IV_4^6 - I, Plagal
   iv-i, Plagal
   I - V, Half
   V -i, Authentic

   V -vi, Deceptive
   V -VI, Deceptive
   V_5^6 -I, Authentic
   I - V_5^6, Half

Page 44

Page 45

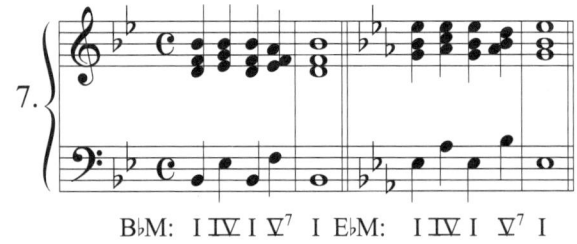

Page 45

8. a. Key of D Major: V^7- vi
      Deceptive Cadence
   b. Key of a minor: iv_4^6 - i
      Plagal Cadence

Page 46

   c. Key of E♭ Major: V - vi
      Deceptive Cadence
   d. Key of e minor: iv-i
      Plagal Cadence
   e. Key of G Major: V - I
      Authentic Cadence

Page 47

   f. Key of E♭ Major: V^7 - I
      Authentic Cadence
   g. Key of G Major: I_4^6 - V
      Half Cadence
   h. Key of C Major: I - V
      Half Cadence

Page 48

   i. Key of F Major: V^7- I
      Authentic Cadence
   j. Key of d minor: iv^6- V
      Half Cadence

REVIEW: LESSONS 1-7 (Pages 51-58)

Page 51

1. F# Major, A♭ Major, E Major, E♭ Major, A Major, F Major, D Major

2. a minor, b minor, g minor, c minor, f# minor, f minor, e minor

3.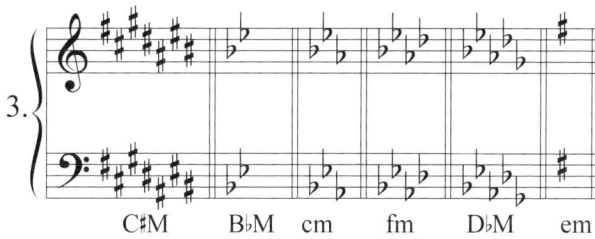
   C#M   B♭M   cm   fm   D♭M   em

Page 52, No. 3, cont.

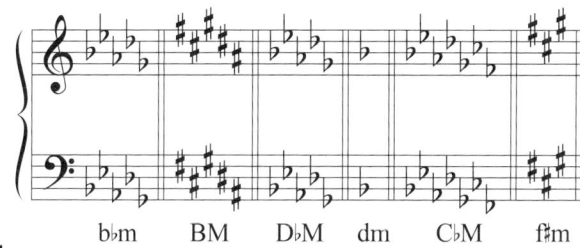
b♭m   BM   D♭M   dm   C♭M   f#m

4.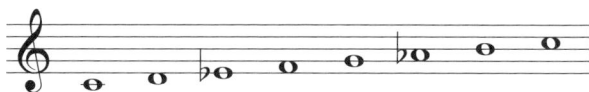
Chromatic on E

c harmonic minor

f# harmonic minor

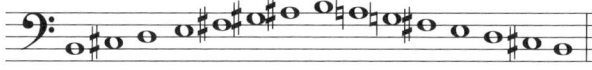
G♭ Major

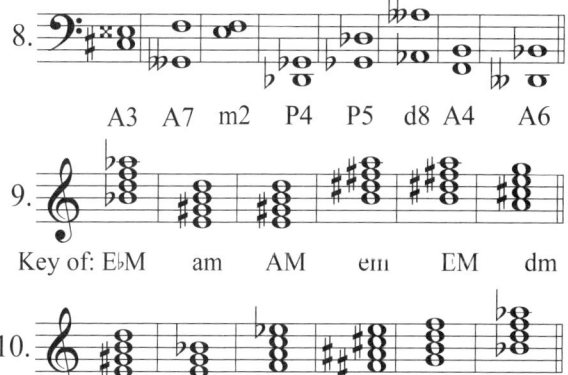
b melodic minor

Page 53, No. 4, cont.

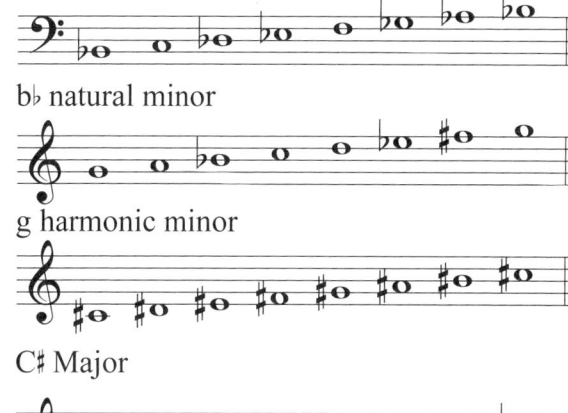
b♭ natural minor

g harmonic minor

C# Major

D♭ Major

d melodic minor

5. E Major ^{6}, d minor, B Major $^6_4$, f# diminished, c minor $^6_4$, A Major ^{6}

   c# minor $^6_4$, e♭ minor ^{6}, A♭ Major, f minor $^6_4$, G Augmented, B♭ Major

Page 54

6.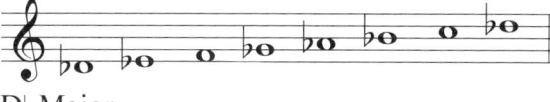
E Aug   b♭m$^5_3$ F#M$^6_4$ fm$^6_4$ C♭M$^6_3$ g dim

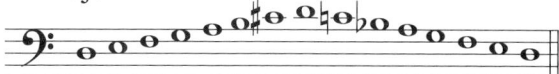
d dim$^5_3$ e dim   B♭ Aug$^5_3$ am$^6_3$ A Aug   FM^6

7. P4, d8, M7, A3, d6, M6, m2, A5

8.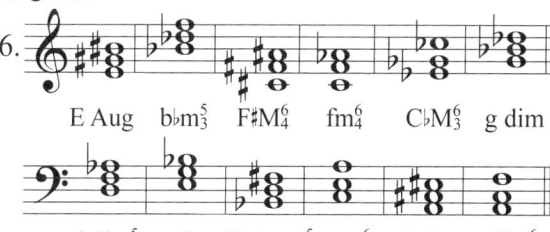
A3   A7   m2   P4   P5   d8   A4   A6

9.
Key of: E♭M   am   AM   em   EM   dm

10.

Page 55

11. D Major, A Major, F Major, C Major,
    B♭ Major, E♭ Major

12. Tonic, Supertonic, Mediant, Subdominant,
    Dominant, Submediant, Leading Tone

13.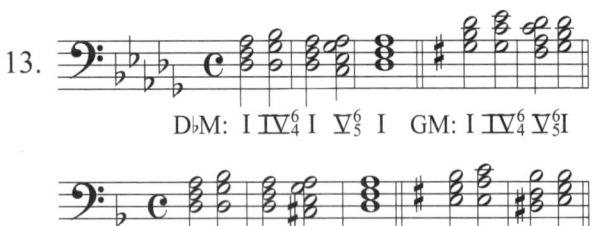

Page 56

14. a. g minor
    b. Harmonic
    c. Triad a: g minor, i⁶
       Triad b: D Dominant 7, V$^4_3$
       Triad c: D Major, V⁶
       Triad d: g minor, i
       Triad e: D Major, V
    d. 1. M3   2. M3   3. P4   4. M2
       5. M2   6. m3   7. P8
    e. Half

Page 57

15. a. B♭ Major
    b. Triad a: B♭ Major, I$^6_4$
       Triad b: F Dominant 7, V⁷
       Triad c: F Dominant 7, V⁷
       Triad d: B♭ Major, I
    c. 1. m7   2. M6   3. M2   4. P4
    d. Measure 6: V⁷
       Measure 7: I
       Type of cadence: Authentic

Page 58

16. a. C Major
    b. Triad a: F Major, IV$^6_4$
       Triad b: C Major, I
       Triad c: C Major, I
       Triad d: G Major, V
    c. 1. m6   2. M6   3. m2   4. P5
       5. m2   6. m2   7. M3
    d. Half
    e.
       ii   iii   vi   vii8

LESSON 8: TIME SIGNATURES
  (Pages 59-66)

Page 62

1. 2 beats per measure
   Quarter note receives one beat

   3 beats per measure
   Quarter note receives one beat

   3 beats per measure
   Eighth note receives one beat

   $\frac{4}{4}$ or Common Time

   $\frac{2}{2}$ or Alla Breve

   2 beats per measure
   Half note receives one beat

   7 beats per measure
   Quarter note receives one beat

   6 beats per measure (or 2)
   Eighth note receives one beat
     (or dotted quarter)

Page 63

2.

3.

Page 64

4. $\frac{3}{4}$

Page 65

5. a.

b.

Page 65

c.

d.
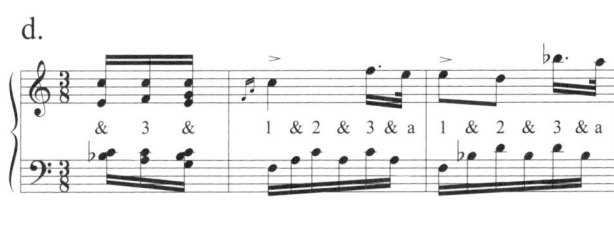

Page 66, No. 2, cont.

e.
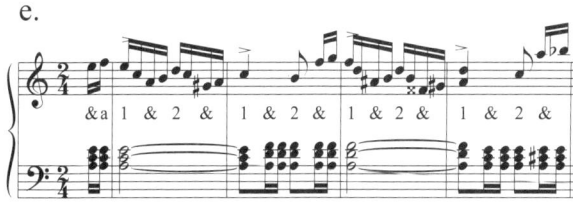

f.

g.

h.

LESSON 9: SIGNS AND TERMS (Pages 67-74)

Page 71

1. c, e, j, a, k, i, f, d, h, g, b

2. e, b, d, a, f, c, g

Page 72

3. c, d, b, a, g, e, f

4. i, a, f, g, b, d, e or j, e or j, c, h

Page 73

5. d, e, a, f, b, c

6. d, f, a, h, b, g, c, i, e, j

Level 6, Pages 65-73

Page 74

7. e, g, f, k, b, a, d, n, j, c, m, o, i, l, h, r, q, s, p, t

LESSON 10: MOTIVE; REPETITION, IMITATION, SEQUENCE (Pages 75-80)

Page 77

a. Sequence

b. Sequence

c. Repetition

Page 78

d. Sequence

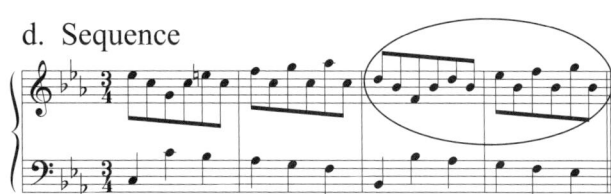

e. Imitation

Page 78, No, 1, cont.

f. Repetition

g. Imitation

LESSON 11: TRANSPOSITION (Pages 79-80)

Page 80

LESSON 12: MODULATION (Pages 81-82)

Page 81

1. a. Modulates to: G Major

Page 82

   b. Modulates to: G Major

   c. Modulates to: E♭ Major

Level 6, Pages 74-82

LESSON 13: THE FOUR PERIODS OF MUSIC HISTORY; THE BAROQUE PERIOD (Pages 83-86)

Page 84

1. Harpsichord, Clavichord, Organ
2. Figured Bass, Ornamentation, Cadenzas
3. Trills, mordents, other ornaments
4. Polyphonic
5. Keyboard instruments could not produce *crescendos* and *diminuendos*

Page 85

1. Germany
2. Baroque
3. Harpsichord, Clavichord, Organ

Page 86

4. Musical director and organist at St. Thomas' School in Leipzig, Germany
5. No
6. Two-part Inventions, Three-part Sinfonias, Preludes and Fugues, Toccatas, French and English Suites, Partitas
7. Scarlatti, Handel (other names are possible)

LESSON 14: THE CLASSICAL PERIOD (Pages 87-92)

Page 88

1. Sonata form
2. Homophonic
3. Alberti Bass
4. To set off new sections
5. Obvious melodies, clear harmonic structure

Page 89

1. Classical
2. Court musician for Archbishop of Salzburg, and professional composer. First professional composer.
3. Child prodigy, traveled and performed, wrote music at an early age.
4. Salzburg, Austria
5. Clementi, Kuhlau (other names are possible)

Page 91

1. Vienna
2. Director of Music to Prince Esterhazy at Eisenstadt
3. Sonata form and four-movement format for symphony
4. Cut off fellow student's pigtail, Farewell Symphony leaves two performers on stage, Surprise Symphony has loud chord in slow movement
5. Classical

Page 92

1. Developed Sonata form further
2. Yes
3. Composer and teacher
4. Classical transitioning to Romantic

LESSON 15: THE ROMANTIC PERIOD (Pages 93-96)

Page 93

1. Descriptive titles that reflect emotion, people, places, things
2. Became more complicated, more chromaticism

Page 94

3. Lyric melodies
4. Syncopated rhythms, cross rhythms, triplets

1. Romantic
2. Norway, was influenced by folk music of the region
3. Germany
4. Peer Gynt Suite and Piano Concerto

Page 95

1. His wife, Clara Wieck

Level 6, Pages 84-95

Page 96

2. Piano
3. Album for the Young
4. A musical journal; Schumann edited it
5. German
6. Romantic
7. Chopin, Schubert (other names are possible)

LESSON 16: THE 20th & 21st CENTURIES (CONTEMPORARY) (Pages 97-100)

Page 98

1. a. Bitonality
   b. Quartal Harmony
   c. Atonality
   d. Polytonality

Page 99

2. They are avoided
3. Irregular or changing (or complex)
4. Polyphonic
5. Classical forms (such as Sonata form)

Page 100

1. St. Petersburg, Russia
2. At age 18
3. Folk music, patriotic songs
4. Teacher, administrator, writer

1. Used untraditional sounds
2. Hungarian; influenced by folk music of this country
3. A set of beginning piano pieces
4. 20th & 21st Centuries (Contemporary)
5. Shostakovich, Copland (other names are possible)

REVIEW: LESSONS 8-16 (Pages 101-104)

Page 101

1.a.

b.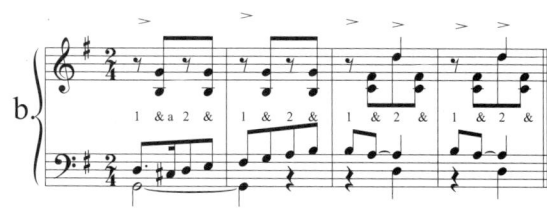

Page 102, No. 1, cont.

c.

2. a. Loud followed immediately by soft
   b. Sorrowfully
   c. System of classifying a composer's works
   d. Contradiction of meter, often by changing strong and weak beats in a measure
   e. Robustly
   f. Playfully
   g. Sustained
   h. Marked, stressed
   i. Continue in the same style
   j. Double sharp: raise the note a whole step
   k. Double flat: lower the note a whole step

3. a. Repetition

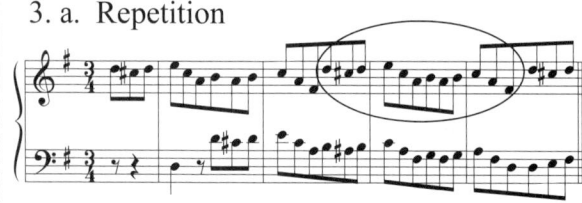

Page 103

b. Sequence

c. Imitation

4. Modulation

5.

Page 104

6. Baroque: 1600-1750
   Classical: 1750-1830
   Romantic: 1830-1900
   20th & 21st Centuries (Contemporary):
       1900-present

7. T, F, T, T, T, F, T, F, F

REVIEW TEST (Pages 105-111)

Page 105

1. D Major, b minor
   D♭ Major, b♭ minor
   A Major, f♯ minor
   A♭ Major, f minor

Page 105, cont.

2.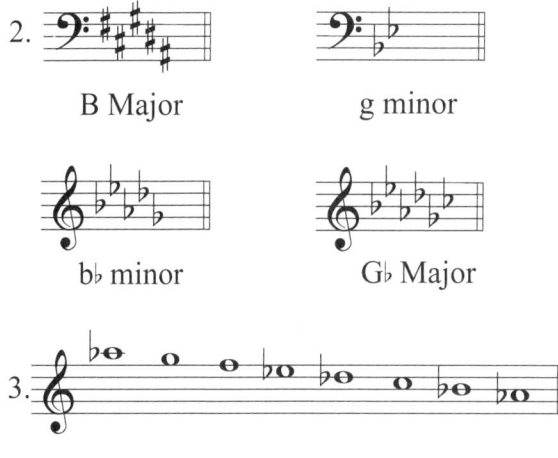

   B Major   g minor

   b♭ minor   G♭ Major

3.

Page 106

4. a.

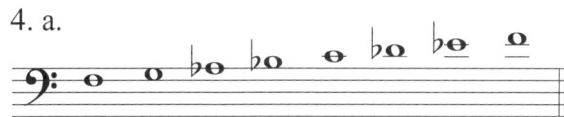

4. b.

5. Ex. 1: E♭ Augmented   Ex. 2: C♯ Major
   Ex. 3: f♯ minor   Ex. 4: B Augmented
   Ex. 5: a minor   Ex. 6: b♭ diminished

6.

   Key of: AM   em   DM   gm   E♭M   cm

Page 107

7. a. d minor
   b. A Major; $\underline{V}$
   c. d minor; i⁶
   d. $\frac{2}{4}$; first beat in each measure
   e. a minor; $\underline{V}$
   f. Phrase
   g. Baroque

Level 6, Pages 103-107

Page 108

8. a. Sorrowfully
   b. Sustained
   c. Marked, stressed
   d. Robustly
   e. With brilliance
   f. Continue in the same style
   g. Playfully
   h. Lightly

9. a. D Major
   b. Sequence
   c. 3/8
   d. 1. m3 2. m2 3. P5 4. m7
      5. m2 6. M6
   e. Chromatic
   f. 20th & 21st Centuries (Contemporary)

Page 109

10.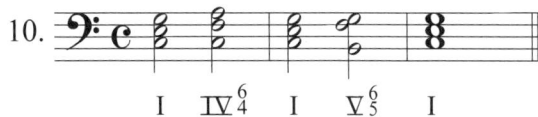

11. a. C Major
    b. V⁶, I, vi
    c.
    d. Walking tempo with motion
    e. 1. m3 2. m6 3. M2
       4. m3 5. m2
    f. Classical (or transitional, between Classical and Romantic)

Page 110

12. a. c minor
    b. i, V
    c. 4/4
    d. Fast and lively
    e. First and third in each measure
    f. Classical; Clementi, Haydn, Beethoven etc.

Page 111

13. a. 2/2
    b. First in each measure
    c. F Major; no
    d. i, iv
    e. Very fast
    f. Romantic

LEVEL 7

LESSON 1: MAJOR AND MINOR KEY SIGNATURES (Pages 1-12)

Page 4

1. A Major, B♭ Major, G Major, F♯ Major, C♭ Major

   C♯ Major, G♭ Major, B Major, E♭ Major, F Major

   A♭ Major, E Major, D Major, C Major, D♭ Major

2.

Page 5, No. 2, cont.

Page 6

3. e minor   f♯ minor
    c minor   c♯ minor
    a minor   b♭ minor
    d minor   g♯ minor
    g minor   a♭ minor
    b minor   e♭ minor
    f minor

Page 6, cont.

4. F Major   D Major
    G Major   E Major
    A♭ Major   D♭ Major
    E♭ Major   B Major
    C Major   G♭ Major
    A Major   C♭ Major
    B♭ Major

Page 7

5. b minor, a minor, b♭ minor, c minor, d minor, e♭ minor

    f♯ minor, g minor, e minor, f minor, c♯ minor, g♯ minor

6.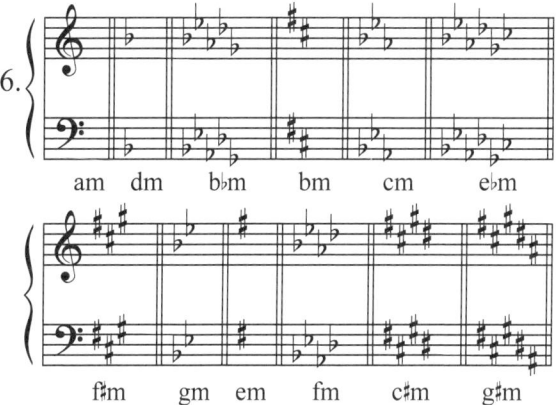

Page 8

7. a. A Major
    b. E♭ Major
    c. g minor

Page 9, No. 7, cont.

   d. B♭ Major
   e. b minor
   f. c minor

Page 10, No. 7, cont.

   g. d minor
   h. E Major

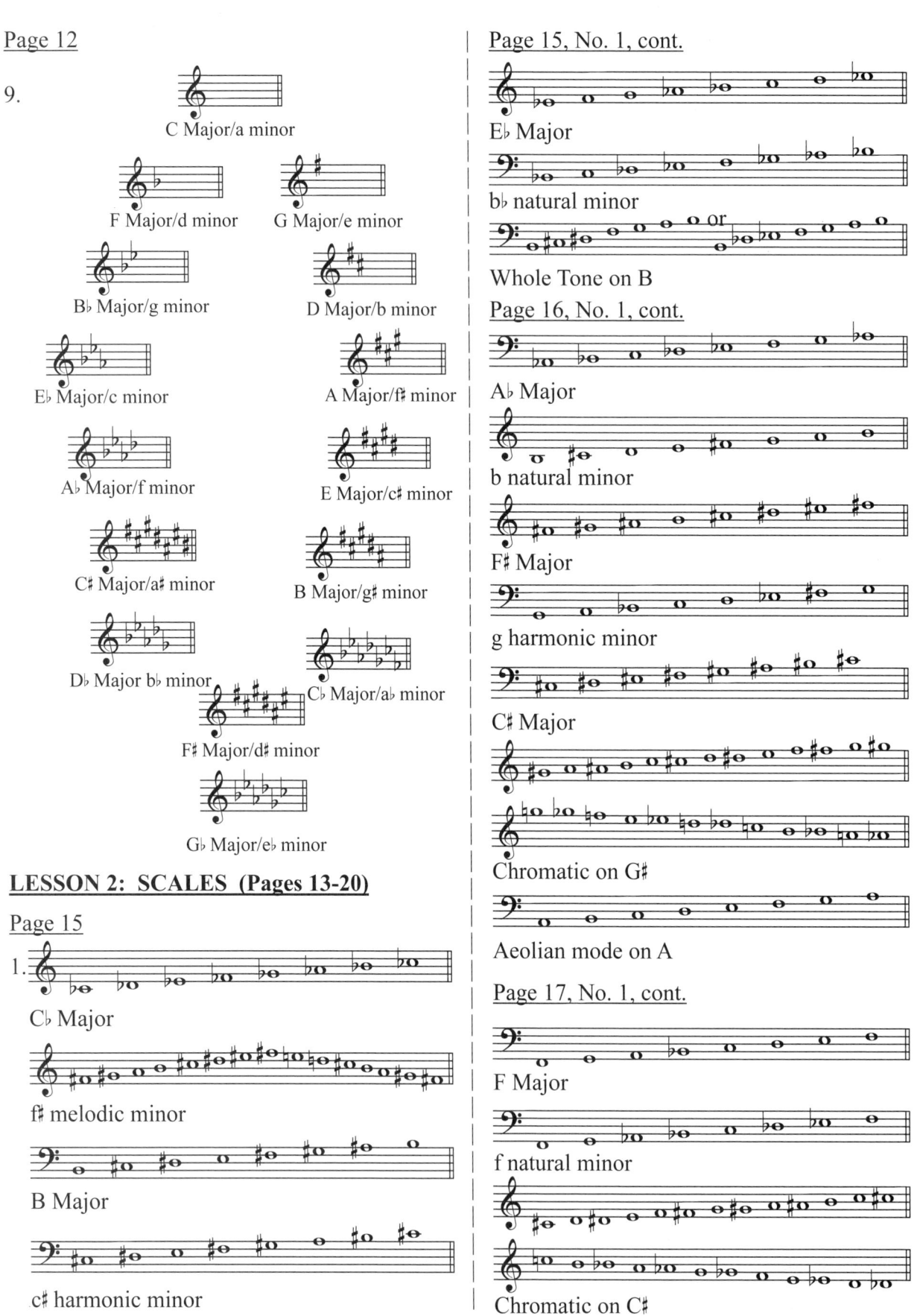

Page 17, No. 1, cont.

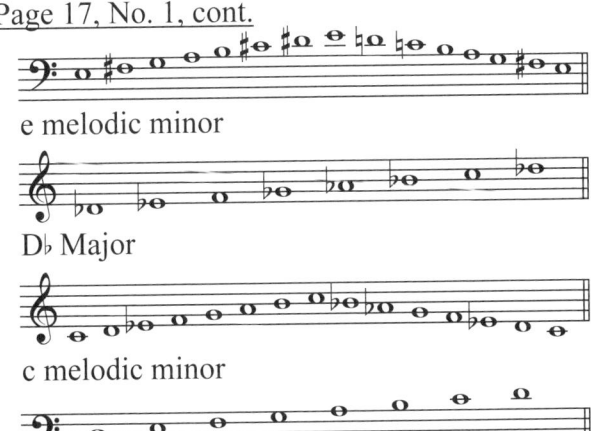

e melodic minor

D♭ Major

c melodic minor

Dorian mode on D

Page 18, No. 1, cont.

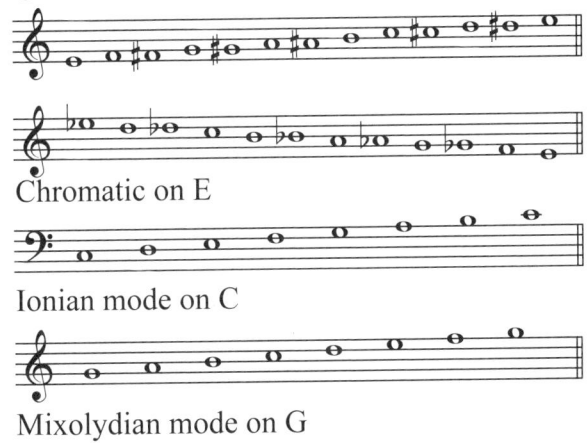

Chromatic on E

Ionian mode on C

Mixolydian mode on G

2. a. G Major
   b. Chromatic

Page 19

   c. C Major
   d. Chromatic
   e. F Major

Page 20

   f. f harmonic minor
   g. g natural minor
   h. d natural minor

LESSON 3: INTERVALS (Pages 21-24)

Page 23

1. m3, d5, A6, P8, d2, d7, A4, P5
   P4, M6, A2, d8, P5, M3, M7, m6

Page 23, cont.

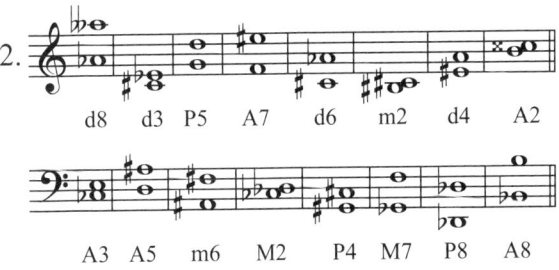

2. d8 d3 P5 A7 d6 m2 d4 A2

   A3 A5 m6 M2 P4 M7 P8 A8

Page 24

3. a. P4, m3, A2, m3, A4, P5

   b. m3, P4, m2, P5, m3, M2, M3

   c. P8, m2, m3, m6, m2, m7

LESSON 4: MAJOR, MINOR, AUGMENTED AND DIMINISHED TRIADS AND INVERSIONS (Pages 25-32)

Page 26

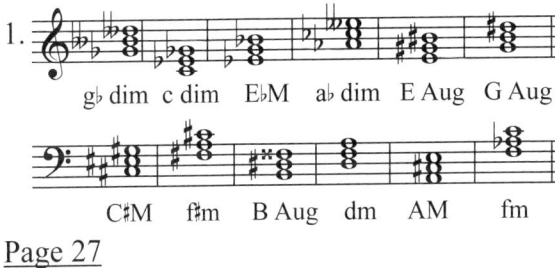

1. g♭ dim c dim E♭M a♭ dim E Aug G Aug

   C♯M f♯m B Aug dm AM fm

Page 27

2. g diminished, D Major, c♭ diminished, e♭ minor, c minor, A♭ Major

   E Major, F♯ Augmented, b♭ diminished, d♭ minor, A Augmented, G♭ Augmented

Page 29

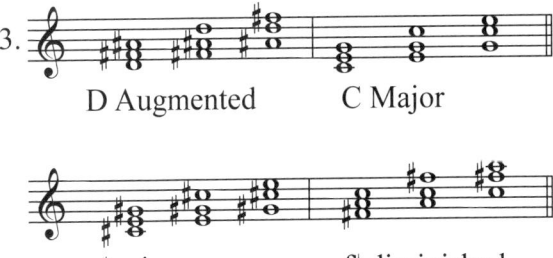

3. D Augmented   C Major

   c♯ minor   f♯ diminished

Page 29, No. 3, cont.

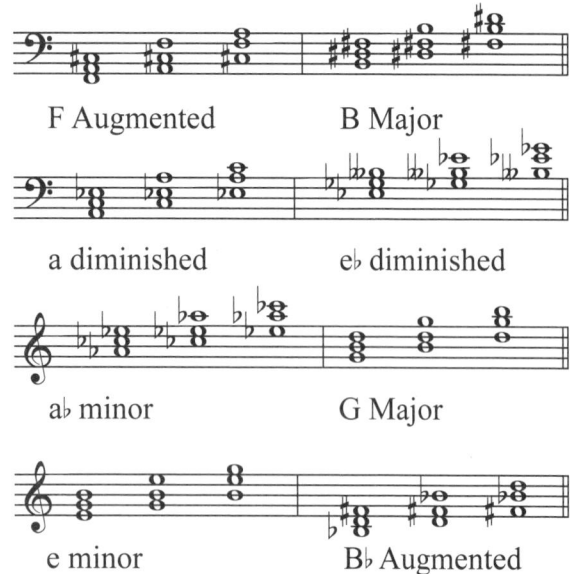

F Augmented   B Major

a diminished   e♭ diminished

a♭ minor   G Major

e minor   B♭ Augmented

Page 30*

4. G♭ Major $^6_4$, f diminished ^{6}, D♭ Major,
A Major ^{6}, E♭ Augmented $^6_4$, B♭ Major ^{6}

    f♯ minor ^{6}, b diminished, C♯ Augmented $^6_4$,
e minor, a minor ^{6}, B Major $^6_4$

    d diminished ^{6}, A♭ Augmented $^6_4$, g minor,
C Augmented $^6_4$, C♭ Augmented,
e diminished ^{6}

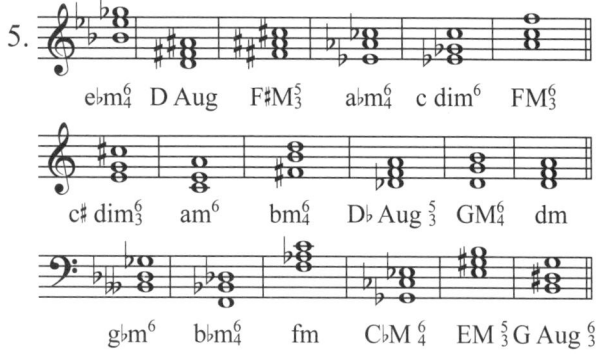

5.

e♭m$^6_4$ D Aug   F♯M$^5_3$ a♭m$^6_4$ c dim^6 FM$^6_3$

c♯ dim$^6_3$ am^6 bm$^6_4$ D♭ Aug$^5_3$ GM$^6_4$ dm

g♭m^6 b♭m$^6_4$ fm   C♭M$^6_4$ EM$^5_3$ G Aug$^6_3$

Page 31

6. a. A Major, b minor ^{6}, E Major, A Major,
D Major, b minor ^{6}

* $^5_3$ for root position and $^6_3$ for first inversion are acceptable

Level 7, Pages 29-35

Page 32, No. 6, cont.

    b. B♭ Major $^6_4$, g minor, c minor,
c minor $^6_4$, g minor $^6_4$

    c. c minor, c minor, A♭ Major, D♭ Major,
A♭ Major, c minor, G Major, G Major

LESSON 5: PRIMARY AND SECONDARY TRIADS (Pages 33-40)

Page 34**

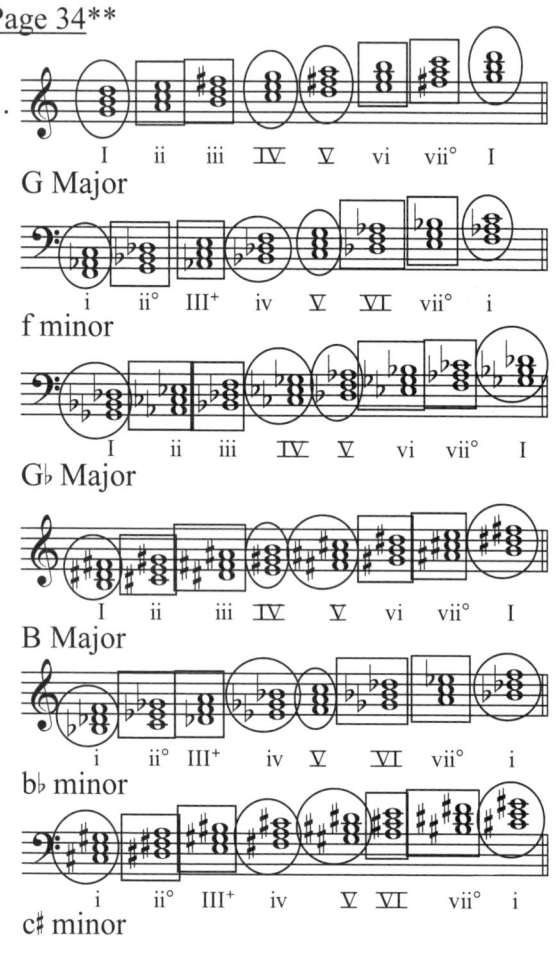

1.

    I   ii   iii   IV   V   vi   vii°   I
G Major

    i   ii°   III⁺   iv   V   VI   vii°   i
f minor

    I   ii   iii   IV   V   vi   vii°   I
G♭ Major

    I   ii   iii   IV   V   vi   vii°   I
B Major

    i   ii°   III⁺   iv   V   VI   vii°   i
b♭ minor

    i   ii°   III⁺   iv   V   VI   vii°   i
c♯ minor

Page 35

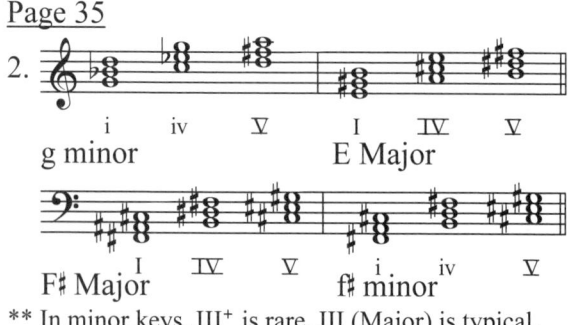

2.

    i   iv   V   I   IV   V
g minor   E Major

    I   IV   V   i   iv   V
F♯ Major   f♯ minor

** In minor keys, III⁺ is rare. III (Major) is typical.

Page 35, No. 2, cont.

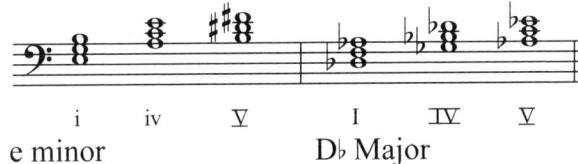
i iv V I IV V
e minor   D♭ Major

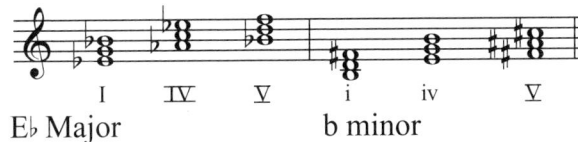
I IV V i iv V
E♭ Major   b minor

Page 36

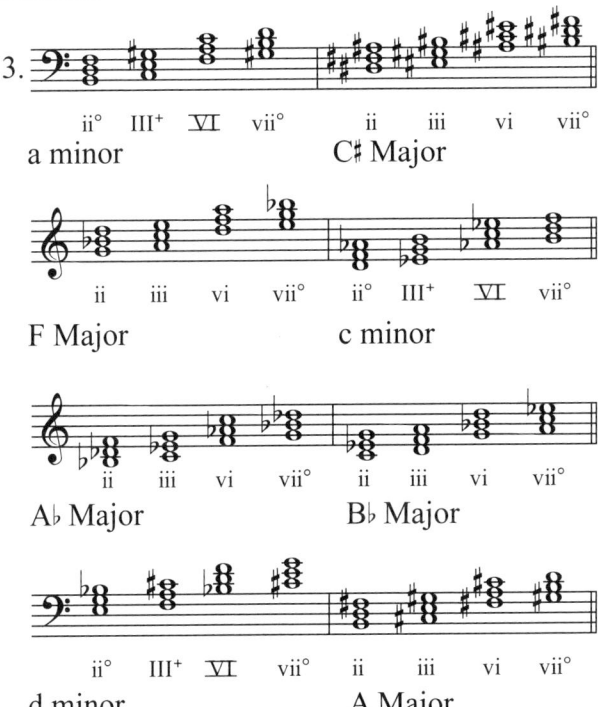
3.
ii° III+ VI vii°   ii iii vi vii°
a minor   C# Major

ii iii vi vii°   ii III+ VI vii°
F Major   c minor

ii iii vi vii°   ii iii vi vii°
A♭ Major   B♭ Major

ii° III+ VI vii°   ii iii vi vii°
d minor   A Major

Page 37

4. f, g, a, e, d, c, b

5. Tonic, Supertonic, Mediant, Subdominant, Dominant, Submediant, Leading Tone

Page 39

6. a. Key of C Major: V⁶, I, ii, V
   b. Key of G Major: I, V⁶, vi, iii⁶, IV, V, V⁶
   c. Key of D Major: I, vii°⁶, I⁶, IV

Page 40, No. 6, cont.

d. Key of B♭ Major: I, V, vi, I, vi, IV
e. Key of G Major: I, I⁶, V⁶₄, V⁶, vii°
f. Key of E Major: I, vii°⁶₄, I⁶, ii, ii, V

LESSON 6: DOMINANT AND DIMINISHED SEVENTH CHORDS (Pages 41-46)

Page 42*

1.
V⁷ V⁶₅ V⁴₃ V²   V⁷ V⁶₅ V⁴₃ V²
C# Major   f minor

V⁷ V⁶₅ V⁴₃ V²   V⁷ V⁶₅ V⁴₃ V²
F# Major   b♭ minor

V⁷ V⁶₅ V⁴₃ V²   V⁷ V⁶₅ V⁴₃ V²
C♭ Major   g minor

2.

Page 43

3.
c dim. 7th   g dim. 7th

a dim. 7th   b♭ dim. 7th

c# dim. 7th   f dim. 7th

e♭ dim. 7th   f# dim. 7th

* ⁴₂ for third inversion is also acceptable.

94

Page 44

4. a. f𝄪 dim. 7
   b. $\underline{V}^7$
   c. $\underline{V}^4_3$
   d. c♯ dim. $^6_5$
   e. f♯ dim. 7
   f. $\underline{V}^7$

Page 45, No. 4, cont.

   g. c♯ dim. 2
   h. a♯ dim. 2
   i. $\underline{V}^7$
   j. $\underline{V}^4_3$
   k. $\underline{V}^6_5$
   l. d♯ dim. 7

Page 46, No. 4, cont.

   m. c♯ dim. 7
   n. $\underline{V}^7$

LESSON 7: AUTHENTIC, HALF, PLAGAL, AND DECEPTIVE CADENCES; CHORD PROGRESSIONS (Pages 47-56)

Page 47

1.

   $\underline{V}$ I $\underline{V}^7$ i $\underline{V}^6_5$ I $\underline{V}^6$ i

   $\underline{V}$ i $\underline{V}^6_5$ I $\underline{V}^6$ I $\underline{V}^7$ i

Page 48

2.

   $\underline{IV}$ I $\underline{IV}^6_4$ I $\underline{IV}^6_4$ I   iv i

   iv$^6_4$ i $\underline{IV}$ I   iv i $\underline{IV}^6_4$ I

Page 49

3.

   I $\underline{V}$ iv$^6_4$ $\underline{V}^7$ ii^6$\underline{V}^7$ i $\underline{V}$

   i$^6_4$ $\underline{V}^6_5$ ii^6 $\underline{V}$ ii $\underline{V}$ I $\underline{V}$

Page 50

4.

   $\underline{V}$ vi $\underline{V}$ $\underline{VI}$ $\underline{V}$ $\underline{VI}$ $\underline{V}$ $\underline{VI}$

   $\underline{V}$ $\underline{VI}$ $\underline{V}$ vi $\underline{V}$ vi $\underline{IV}$ vi

5. $\underline{IV}^6_4$- I, Plagal
   i - $\underline{V}$, Half
   $\underline{V}$ - $\underline{VI}$, Deceptive
   $\underline{V}^6_5$- I, Authentic

   $\underline{V}$ - vi, Deceptive
   $\underline{V}$ - $\underline{VI}$, Deceptive
   ii^6- $\underline{V}^6_5$, Half
   iv - $\underline{VI}$, Deceptive

Page 52

6.

   I $\underline{IV}$ ii $\underline{V}^7$ I   i iv ii° $\underline{V}$ i

   i iv ii° $\underline{V}$ i   I $\underline{IV}$ ii $\underline{V}^7$ vi

Level 7, Pages 44-52

Page 52, No. 6, cont.

I IV ii V vi   i iv ii° V⁷ VI

i iv ii° V⁷ VI   I IV ii V I

Page 53

7. a. Key of D Major: V⁷- vi, Deceptive
   b. Key of G Major: IV ⁶₄ - I, Plagal

Page 54

c. Key of C Major: V⁶₅- I, Authentic
d. Key of b minor: V - i, Authentic
e. Key of F Major: IV - I, Plagal

Page 55

f. Key of b minor: V⁷- VI, Deceptive
g. Key of e minor: iv⁶- V⁷, Half
h. Key of G Major: I⁶₄ - V, Half

Page 56

i. Key of a minor: V⁶₄ - i, Authentic
j. Key of e minor: V⁷- VI, Deceptive
k. Key of C Major: I⁶₄ - V, Half

REVIEW: LESSONS 1-7 (Pages 59-66)

Page 59

1. D Major, B♭ Major, G♭ Major, C Major, A♭ Major, E Major

Page 59, cont.

2. b minor, c♯ minor, a minor, g minor, b♭ minor, d minor, e♭ minor

em GM E♭M f♯m AM D♭M a♭m

Page 60, No. 3, cont.

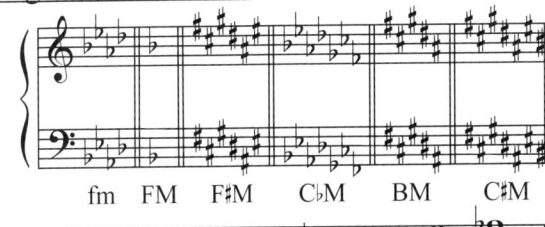

fm FM F♯M C♭M BM C♯M

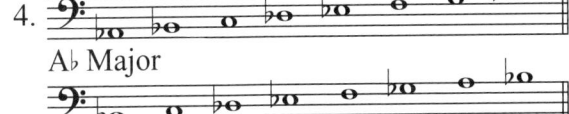

A♭ Major

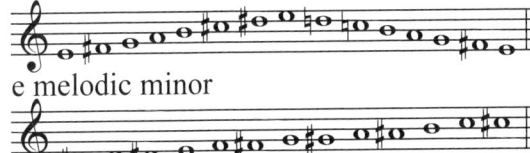

b♭ harmonic minor

e melodic minor

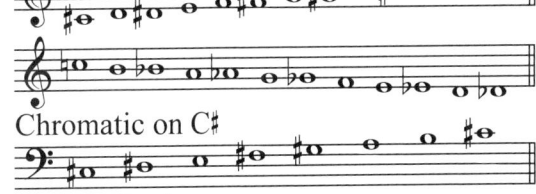

Chromatic on C♯

c♯ natural minor

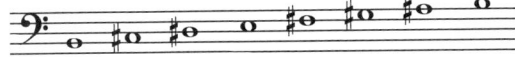

B Major

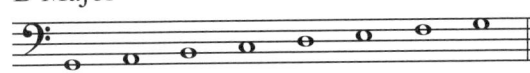

Mixolydian mode on G

Page 61

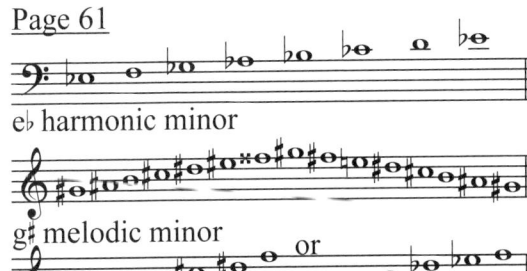

e♭ harmonic minor

g♯ melodic minor

Whole Tone on F

Page 61, cont.

5. D Major ^{6}, C Dominant ^{7}, c diminished, D♭ Dominant ^{2}, E Major, a diminished $^6_4$

   F♯ Major $^6_4$, D♭ Augmented ^{6}, G Major, g diminished ^{7}, F♯ Dominant $^6_5$, A♭ Augmented ^{6}

6.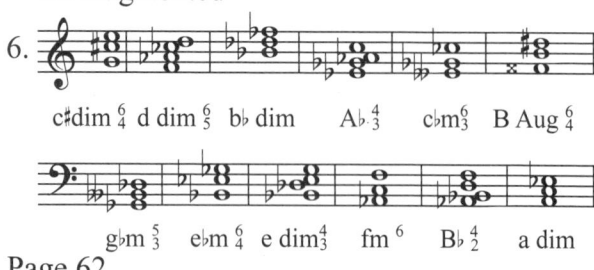

   c♯dim $^6_4$ d dim $^6_5$ b♭ dim   A♭ $^4_3$ c♭m $^6_3$ B Aug $^6_4$

   g♭m $^5_3$ e♭m $^6_4$ e dim $^4_3$ fm ^{6} B♭ $^4_2$ a dim

Page 62

7. P4, m6, A3, d5, P8, d7, M2, A5

8.

   M3   A6   m2   M7   A4   d8   P5   m3

9. B♭ Major, C♯ Major, F Major, E♭ Major, D♭ Major, A Major, G♭ Major, F♯ Major

10. a. Tonic   e. Dominant
    b. Supertonic   f. Submediant
    c. Mediant   g. Leading Tone
    d. Subdominant

11. V$^6_5$ - I: Authentic; I - V: Half;
    V - vi: Deceptive; i - V^6: Half

Page 63, No. 11, cont.

   iv$^6_4$ - i: Plagal; IV - I: Plagal;
   V^6 - i: Authentic; iv - i: Plagal

12.

   V vi   iv$^6_4$ i   I V   V^6 i

   iv VI   V$^6_5$ I   V i   V^7 I

Page 63, cont.

13.

   I IV ii V I   i iv ii° V i

   I IV ii V^7 vi   i iv ii° V^7 VI

Page 64

14. a. G Major
    b. Chromatic
    c. Triad 1: G Major, I
       Triad 2: G Major, I^6
       Triad 3: D Major, V^6
       Triad 4: f♯ diminished, vii°
    d. a. P4 b. m3 c. m2 d. P4
       e. P8 f. M6
    e. Authentic (V - I)

Page 65

15. a. B♭ Major
    b. Triad 1: B♭ Major, I$^6_4$
       Triad 2: E♭ Major, IV^6
       Triad 3: F Dominant 7, V$^4_3$
       Triad 4: B♭ Major, I
    c. a. P8 b. M3 c. m2 d. m3
       e. d5 f. M2
    d. Measure 7: V^7 (Accept V$^6_5$)
       Measure 8: I
       Authentic

Page 66

16. a. F Major
    b. <u>VI</u>
    c. Triad 1: F Major, I
       Triad 2: C Major, <u>V</u>
       Triad 3: B♭ Major, <u>IV</u>
       Triad 4: F Major, I⁶
       Triad 5: g minor, ii
    d. a. m3   b. m3   c. M3   d. P5
       e. P4   f. P8
    e. Authentic (<u>V</u> ⁷- I)

LESSON 8: TIME SIGNATURES (Pages 67-74)

Page 70

1. 2 = 2 beats per measure
   4 = Quarter note receives one beat

   3 = 3 beats per measure
   4 = Quarter note receives one beat

   3 = 3 beats per measure
   8 = Eighth note receives one beat

   ₵ = $\frac{2}{2}$ or Alla Breve

   C = $\frac{4}{4}$ or Common Time

   2 = 2 beats per measure
   2 = Quarter note receives one beat

   7 = 7 beats per measure
   4 = Quarter note receives one beat

   6 = 6 beats per measure (or 2)
   8 = Eighth note receives one beat
      (or dotted quarter)

Page 72

2. a.

Page 72, No. 2, cont.

Page 73, No. 2, cont.

Page 74, No. 2, cont.

Page 74, No. 2, cont.

g.

h.

LESSON 9: SIGNS AND TERMS (Pages 75-86)

Page 81

1. k, e, h, j, d, i, f, c, a, g, b

Page 82

2. e, f, d, a, c, b

3. d, a, b, c, g, e, f

Page 83

4. i, a, f, g, d, b, e or j, e or j, c, h

5. h, f, a, g, b, c, d, e

Page 84

6. e, g, f, q, b, m, d, n, j, s, a, k, i, l, h, c, p, r, o

Page 85

7. d, f, a, h, b, e, c, g, k, i, l, j

8. i, f, a, g, h, b, c, d, j, e

Page 86

9. b, c or i, c or i, e, j, h, a, l, g, d, k, f, n, m

Level 7, Pages 74-91

LESSON 10: COMPOSITIONAL TECHNIQUES (Pages 87-92)

Page 90

1. a. Sequence

b. Repetition

c. Canon

Page 91

d. Repetition

e. Sequence

f. Sequence

Page 92

g. Imitation

h. Canon

LESSON 11: TRANSPOSITION (Pages 93-96)

Page 95

1.

2.

Page 96

3.

LESSON 12: MODULATION (Pages 97-98)

Page 98

1. a. Modulates to B♭ Major
   b. Modulates to B♭ Major
   c. Modulates to G Major

LESSON 13: THE FOUR PERIODS OF MUSIC HISTORY; THE BAROQUE PERIOD; FRESCOBALDI AND SOLER (Pages 99-104)

Page 102

1. Baroque: 1600-1750
   Classical: 1750-1830
   Romantic: 1830-1900
   20th & 21st Centuries (Contemporary): 1900-present

2. a. Polyphonic Texture: Two or more equally important voices
   b. Ornamentation: Trills, mordents, etc.
   c. Improvisation: Cadenzas, figured bass

Page 103

   d. Keyboard music written for harpsichord, clavichord, and organ
   e. Terraced dynamics: dynamic changes by section rather than gradually

3. Frescobaldi

   - 1583-1643
   - Baroque
   - Italy
   - Organ
   - Organist of St. Trastavere, St. Peters, and Florentine Court of Ferdinando II de' Medici
   - Arie musicali, Fiori musicali
   - Skilled contrapuntal writer; influenced J.S. Bach

Level 7, Pages 92-103

Page 104

Soler

- 1729-1783
- Baroque
- Spain
- Jeronymite Monk, music director at monastery
- Sonatas
- Llave de la modulacion theory book on how to change keys quickly
- Sacred vocal works, instrumental pieces
- Scarlatti; style of upcoming Classical Period

4. J.S. Bach, Germany, 1685-1750
G.F. Handel, Germany, 1685-1760
Domenico Scarlatti, Italy, 1685-1757
Henry Purcell, England, 1659-1695
Georg Philipp Telemann, Germany, 1681-1767

LESSON 14: THE CLASSICAL PERIOD; HAYDN AND BEETHOVEN (Pages 105-110)

Page 108

1. a. Homophonic Texture: Clear melody and harmony
   b. Harmonic structure obvious
   c. Rests used to set off new sections
   d. Alberti bass
   e. Sonata and Sonatina forms: Exposition, Development, Recapitulation; 2nd movement slow, 3rd movement Rondo

2. Haydn (Pages 108-109)

   - 1732-1809
   - Classical
   - Austria
   - Vienna Choir School
   - Director of Music to Prince Esterhazy at Eisenstadt
   - Symphony; Sonata form
   - Symphonies, chamber music, sonatas
   - Farewell and Surprise Symphonies

Page 109, cont.

Beethoven

- 1770-1827
- Classical (transitioning to Romantic)
- Germany
- Teacher and composer
- Sonatas, concertos, symphonies, string quartets, choral music, opera
- Gave richness to Classical forms

Page 110

3. W.A. Mozart, Austria, 1756-1791
Muzio Clementi, Italy, 1752-1832
Frederich Kuhlau, Germany, 1786-1832
Carl Czerny, Austria, 1791-1857

4. Exposition, Development, Recapitulation

LESSON 15: THE ROMANTIC PERIOD; DVORÁK AND GRIEG (Pages 111-114)

Page 113

1. a. Music more emotional
   b. Harmonies more complicated
   c. Lyric melodies
   d. Rhythms more complicated

Page 114

2. Grieg

   - 1843-1907
   - Romantic
   - Norway
   - Germany
   - Peer Gynt Suite, Piano Concerto
   - Folk tunes of Norway
   - Music for orchestra and solo instruments

Page 114, No. 2, cont.

Dvorák

- 1841-1904
- Romantic
- Czechoslovakia
- Violist in dance band and theater orchestra, stipend from Austria, director of National Conservatory of Music in New York, professor of composition at Prague University
- Orchestral music, symphonies, chamber music, operas, cantatas
- Czech folk music

3. Robert Schumann, Germany, 1810-1856
   Frederick Chopin, Poland, 1810-1849
   Franz Schubert, Austria, 1797-1828
   Johannes Brahms, Germany, 1833-1897

LESSON 16: THE 20th & 21st CENTURIES (CONTEMPORARY); DELLO-JOIO AND PROKOFIEV (Pages 115-120)

Page 118-119

1. a. Major and minor tonalities avoided
   b. Quartal harmony (use of 4ths)
   c. Bitonality (two keys)
   d. Polytonality (many keys)
   e. Atonality (no key)
   f. Irregular and changing meters
   g. Polyphonic texture
   h. Use of Classical forms

2. Dello-Joio

   - 1913-2008
   - 20th & 21st Centuries (Contemporary)
   - U.S.A.
   - Julliard School
   - Professor at Sarah Lawrence College
   - Pulitzer Prize
   - Concerto for Harp and Orchestra, Ricercari, New York Profiles

Page 120, No. 2, cont.

Prokofiev

- 1891-1953
- 20th & 21st Centuries (Contemporary)
- Russia
- St. Petersburg Conservatory
- Dissonant, driving rhythms, neo-classic
- Piano concertos, orchestral works, solo piano works, ballets, songs
- Music for Children, Peter and the Wolf

3. Béla Bartók, Hungary, 1881-1945
   Dmitri Shostakovich, Russia, 1906-1975
   Dmitri Kabalevsky, Russia, 1904-1987
   Aaron Copland, U.S.A., 1900-1990

REVIEW: LESSONS 8-16 (Pages 121-126)

Page 121 1. a.

Page 122

2. a. broadening; gradually slower
   b. less motion
   c. more motion
   d. with fire
   e. gradually slower
   f. immediately slower
   g. without
   h. always
   i. more
   j. less
   k. slowly
   l. merrily, with humor
   m. gracefully
   n. heavily
   o. broken chord pattern: low-high-middle-high
   p. two names for same pitch
   q. suffix meaning little
   r. suffix meaning little
   s. trill with prefix from below
   t. trill with prefix from above
   u. momentary contradiction of meter, often by use of strong notes on weak beats
   v. strict imitation of an entire theme
   w. major and minor keys with same letter names
   x. major and minor keys with same key signature
   y. motive repeated a note lower or higher
   z. motive repeated in a different voice

Page 123

3. a. Repetition

b. Imitation

Page 123, No. 3, cont.

c. Canon

Page 124

d. Sequence

4. Baroque: 1600-1750
   Classical: 1750-1830
   Romantic: 1830-1900
   20th & 21st Centuries (Contemporary): 1900-present

5. T, T, F, T, T, F, F, F, T, F, T

Page 125

6. Meter: The division of beats into equal groups

7.

8. Modulation

9. Exposition, Development, Recapitulation

Level 7, Pages 122-125

REVIEW TEST (Pages 127-134)

Page 127

1.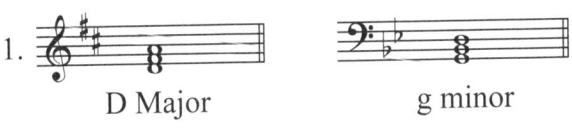
   D Major   g minor

   F♯ Major   f♯ minor

   A♭ Major   b♭ minor

   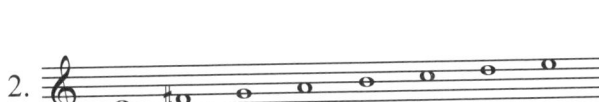
   E Major   b minor

2.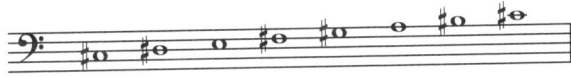
   a. e natural minor

   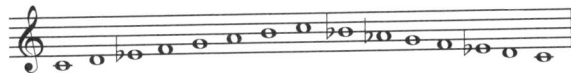
   b. c♯ harmonic minor

   c. c melodic minor

Page 128

3. M3, P4, m6, P8, d5
   M6, d4, m2, A5, A7

4.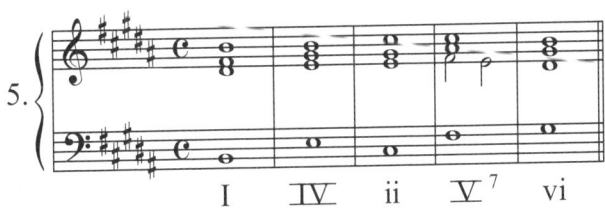
   Major   diminished   minor   Augmented   Major

5. (I, IV, ii, V⁷, vi)

Page 128, cont.

6.

Page 129

7. a. $\frac{3}{4}$ b. $\frac{6}{8}$ c. $\frac{4}{4}$ d. $\frac{5}{4}$ e. $\frac{3}{8}$

8. 4, 6, 1, 7, 3, 5, 8, 2

Page 130

9. a. E Major
   b. Turn
   c.

   d. B Major
   e. Baroque
   f. Soler, Frescobaldi (any Baroque composer acceptable)

Page 131

10. a. F Major
    b. a. F Major, I
       b. C Major, V⁶
       c. C Dominant 7, V$^4_3$
       d. e diminished, vii°$^6_4$
       e. C Major, V
    c. Authentic (V⁷ - I)
    d. Half
    e. Classical

Level 7, Pages 127-131

Page 132

11. a. F Major
    b. a. F Major, I
       b. d minor, vi
       c. a minor, iii
       d. B♭ Major, IV
       e. C Major, V
    c. Half
    d. Romantic
    e. Dvorák, Grieg (any Romantic composer accpetable)

Page 133

12. a. a minor
    b. a. a minor
       b. b minor 6/4
       c. b minor 6/4
       d. b diminished
       e. C Major 6/4
    c. Chromatic
    d. 20th & 21st Centuries (Contemporary)
    e. Dello-Joio, Prokofiev (any 20th/21st Century (Contemporary) composer acceptable)

Page 134

13. a. C Major
    b.
    c. 1. P8 2. m2 3. m3 4. P4 5. m6
       6. M3 7. M6 8. P5
    d. Classical
    e. Beethoven, Clementi (any Classical composer acceptable)

Level 7, Pages 132-134

LEVEL 8

LESSON 1: MAJOR AND MINOR KEY SIGNATURES (Pages 1-12)

Page 4

1. E Major, G Major, A♭ Major, A Major, G♭ Major

   E♭ Major, F♯ Major, F Major, C♭ Major, C♯ Major

   D Major, B♭ Major, C Major, B Major, D♭ Major

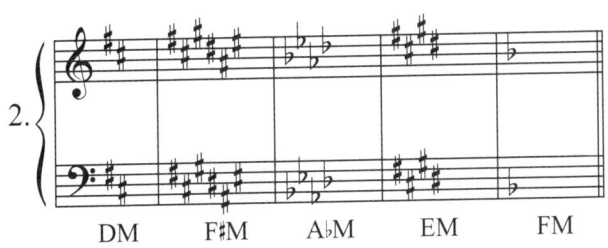

Page 5, No. 2, cont.

Page 6

3. e minor   f minor
   c minor   f♯ minor
   a minor   c♯ minor
   d minor   b♭ minor
   g minor   e♭ minor
   b minor   g♯ minor

Page 6, cont.

4. F Major   B♭ Major
   G Major   D Major
   A♭ Major   E Major
   E♭ Major   D♭ Major
   C Major   G♭ Major
   A Major   B Major

Page 7

5. D♭ Major, a minor, c minor, f♯ minor, d minor, e♭ minor

   g♯ minor, g minor, f minor, e minor, c♯ minor, b minor

Page 8

7. a. a minor
   b. E Major
   c. c minor

Page 9

   d. G♭ Major
   e. A♭ Major
   f. g minor

Page 10

   g. D Major
   h. A Major

Page 12

9.

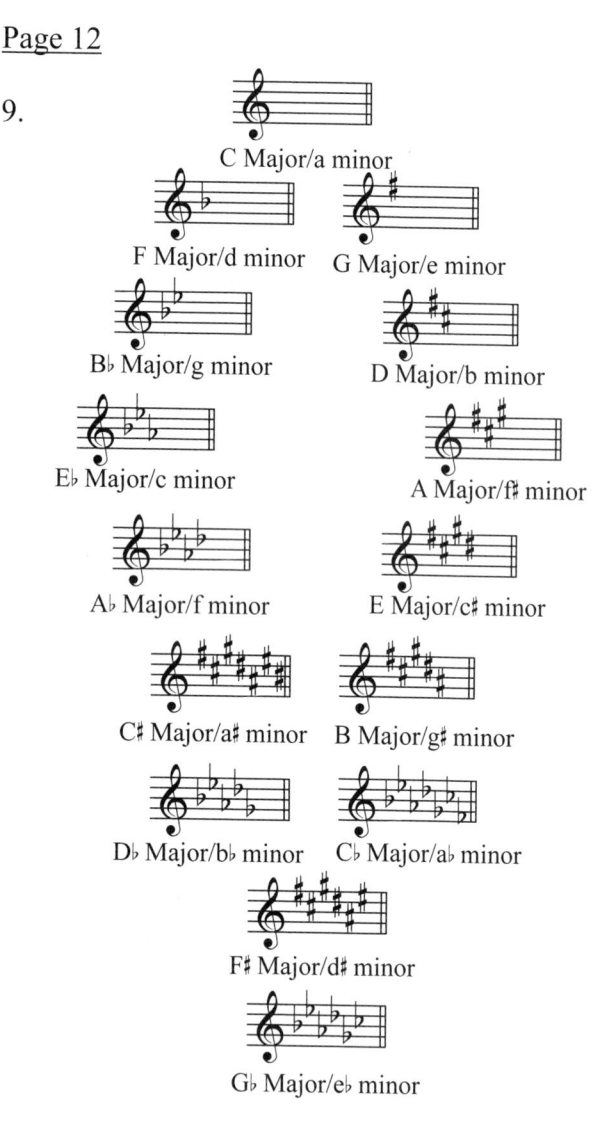

LESSON 2: SCALES (Pages 13-20)

Page 16

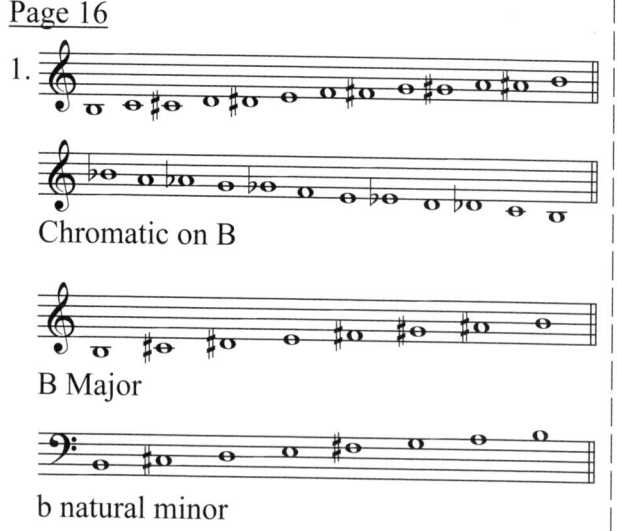

Page 16, No. 1, cont.

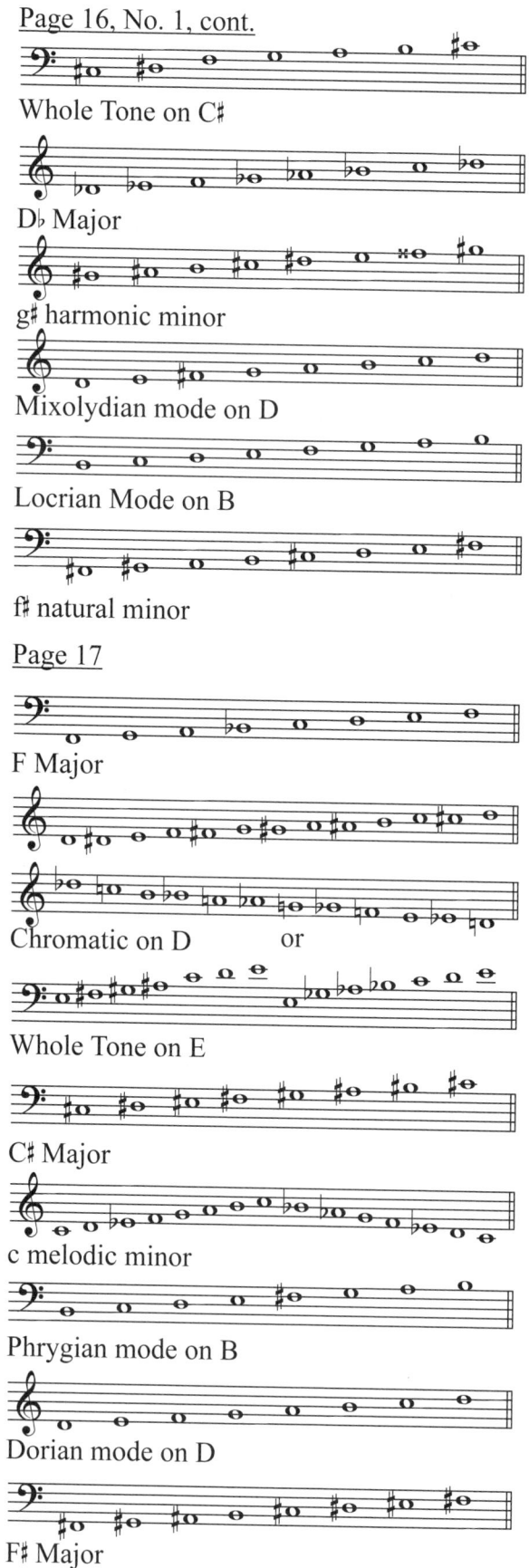

Page 17, cont.

Chromatic on A♯

Page 18

Whole Tone on G♭

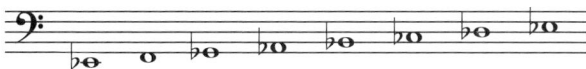
e♭ natural minor

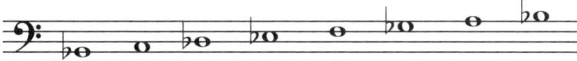
b♭ harmonic minor

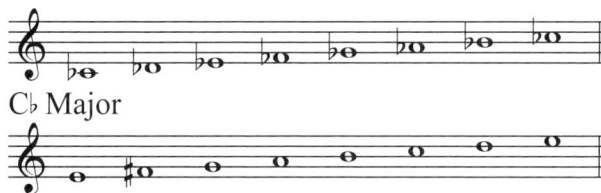
C♭ Major

Aeolian mode on E

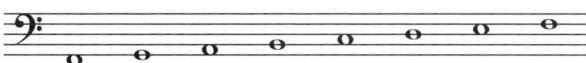
Lydian mode on F

1. a. E Major

Page 19
    b. D Major
    c. B♭ Major
    d. d natural minor (or Aeolian mode)
    e. Chromatic

Page 20
    f. A Major (or Mixolydian mode)
    g. g natural minor (or Aeolian mode)
    h. Whole Tone
    i. C Major

LESSON 3: INTERVALS (Pages 21-24)

Page 23

1. M2, M3, M6, P4, d4, A3, m7, d6
   A7, A5, m3, M2, M7, d8, P5, P8

Page 23, cont.

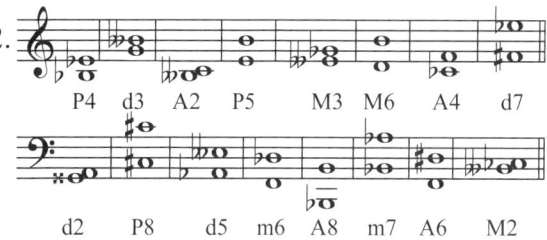

Page 24

3. a. m3, m3, M3, P4, P5, M2

   b. P4, A4, m2, M2, m2, m6, P4, M6

   c. m3, m2, m7, M3, m3, m3, m3, m2, m6, P4

LESSON 4; DIATONIC AND CHROMATIC HALF STEPS (Pages 25-28)

Page 26

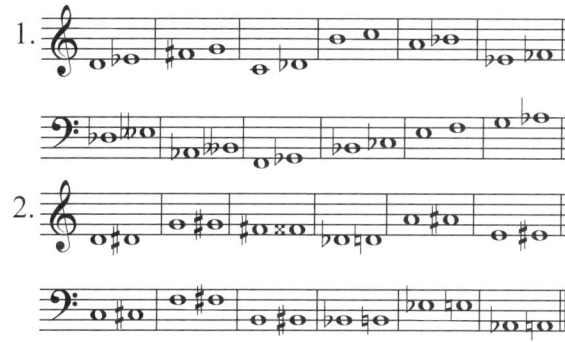

Page 27

3. a. Key of C Major (Meas. 1-2: G Major)
    Definition 1: D, C, C, D
    Definition 2: D, C, C, D

   b. Key of C Major
    Definition 1: D, D, C
    Definition 2: D, D, C

Page 28, No. 3, cont.

   c. Key of B♭ Major
    Definition 1: C, C, C, C, D, D
    Definition 2: C, D, D, C, D, D

   d. Key of c♯ minor
    Definition 1: C, C, C, D, D, D
    Definition 2: D, C, C, D, D, D

LESSON 5: MAJOR, MINOR, AUGMENTED AND DIMINISHED TRIADS AND INVERSIONS
(Pages 29-36)

Page 30

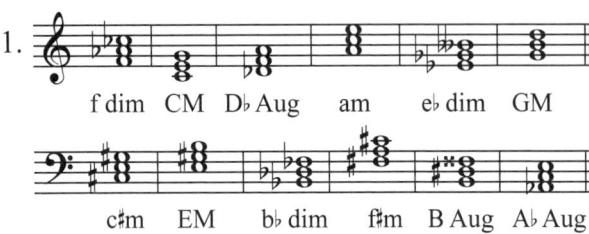

1. f dim, CM, D♭ Aug, am, e♭ dim, GM

   c♯m, EM, b♭ dim, f♯m, B Aug, A♭ Aug

2. d minor, F♯ Major, A Major, F Augmented, A♭ Major, c♯ diminished

   c♭ diminished, E♭ Augmented, g♭ diminished, b minor, B♭ Augmented, e minor

Page 32

3.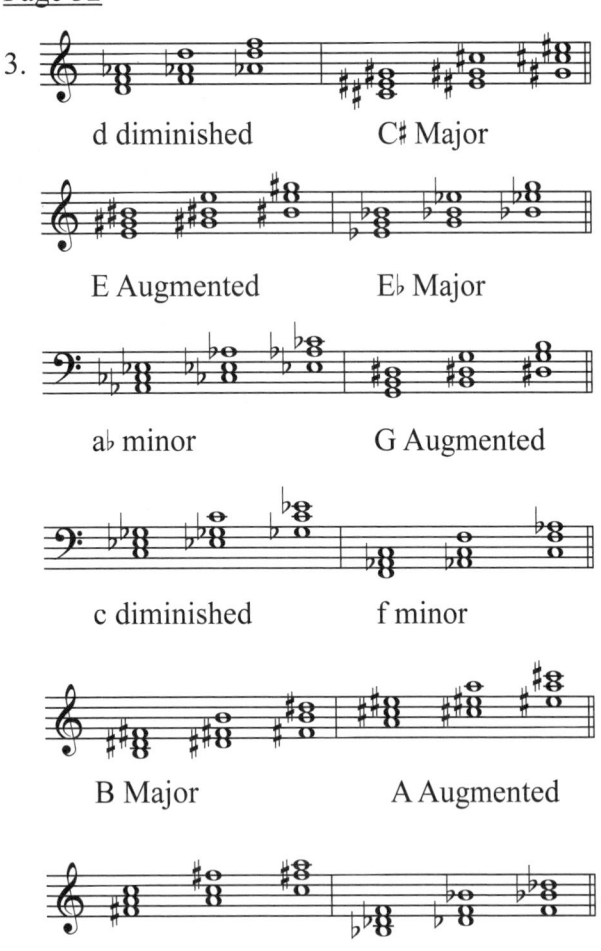

   d diminished   C♯ Major

   E Augmented   E♭ Major

   a♭ minor   G Augmented

   c diminished   f minor

   B Major   A Augmented

   f♯ diminished   b♭ minor

Page 33*

4. e♭ minor ^{6}, G Major $^6_4$, c minor ^{6}, A Augmented, E Augmented ^{6}, D♭ Augmented ^{6}

   C♯ Major $^6_4$, a♭ diminished $^6_4$, D Major, a♭ minor $^6_4$, C♭ Major, g diminished ^{6}

   G♭ Augmented, b diminished ^{6}, f diminished, b♭ minor $^6_4$, F♯ Major, b♭ minor $^6_4$

5.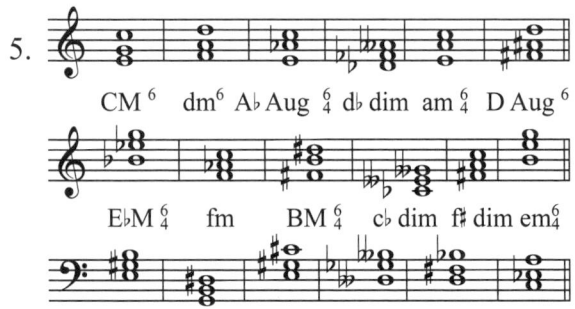

   CM ^{6} dm ^{6} A♭ Aug $^6_4$ d♭ dim am $^6_4$ D Aug ^{6}

   E♭M $^6_4$ fm BM $^6_4$ c♭ dim f♯ dim em $^6_4$

   EM G Aug c♯m ^{6} g♭ dim $^6_4$ B♭ Aug $^6_3$ a dim $^6_3$

Page 35

6. a. G♭ Major, e♭ minor, C♭ Major, G♭ Major

   b. g minor ^{6}, f♯ diminished ^{6}, c minor

   c. A Major, E Major, c♯ minor, f♯ minor ^{6}, B Major, E Major, b minor ^{6}, A Major, f♯ minor, b minor ^{6}, E Major, A Major

Page 36

   d. e minor, G Major, D Major

   e. e minor ^{6}, c♯ diminished $^6_4$, a♯ diminished, G♭ Major ^{6}, g diminished ^{6}, g minor ^{6}

   f. E Major ^{6}, A Major $^6_4$, D Major ^{6}, D Major, E Major, A Major

* $^5_3$ for root position, and $^6_3$ for first inversion are acceptable.

Level 8, Pages 30-36

LESSON 6: PRIMARY AND SECONDARY TRIADS; FIGURED BASS (Pages 37-44)

Page 38*

1.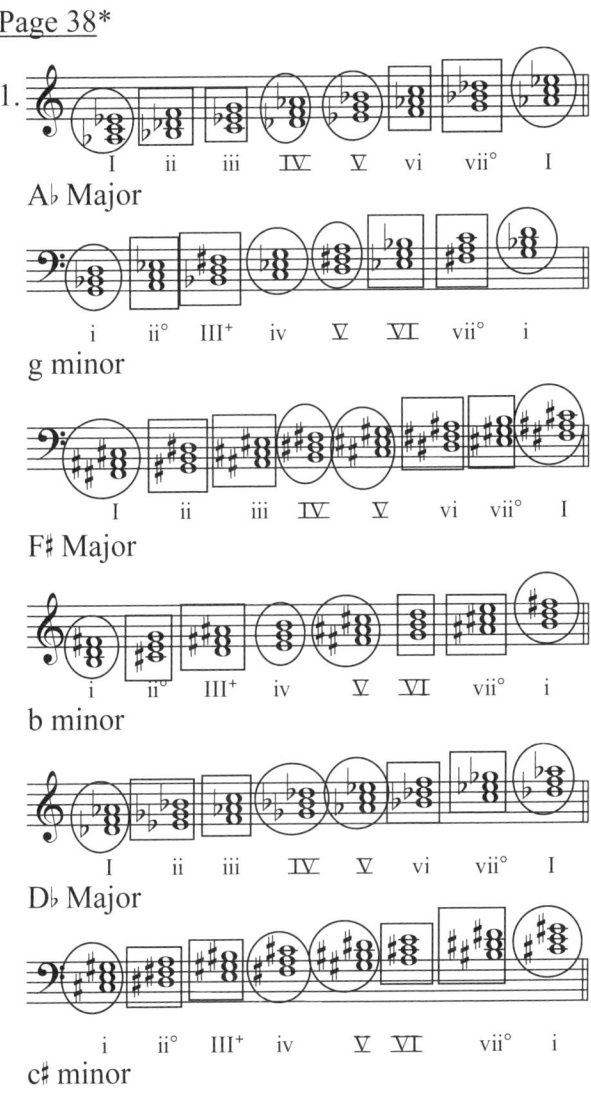

Page 39

2.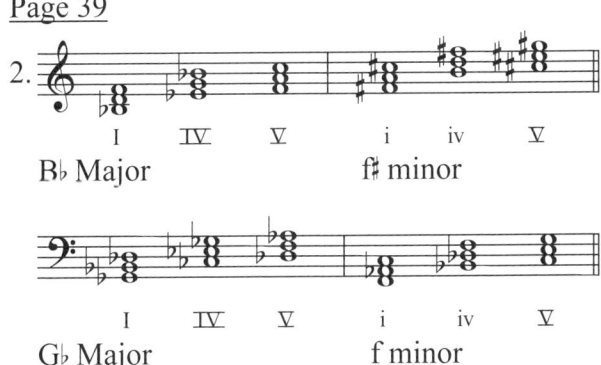

*In minor keys, III+ is rare. III (Major) is typical.

Page 39, No. 2, cont.

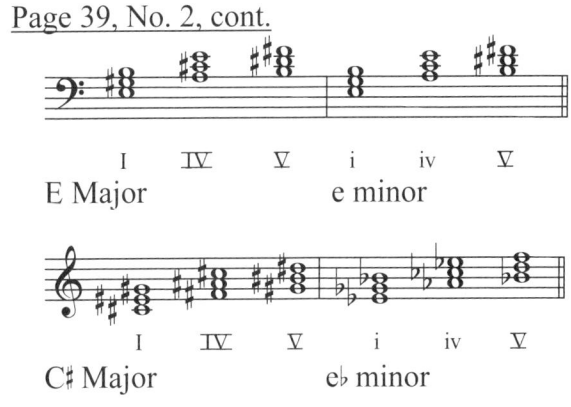

Page 40

3.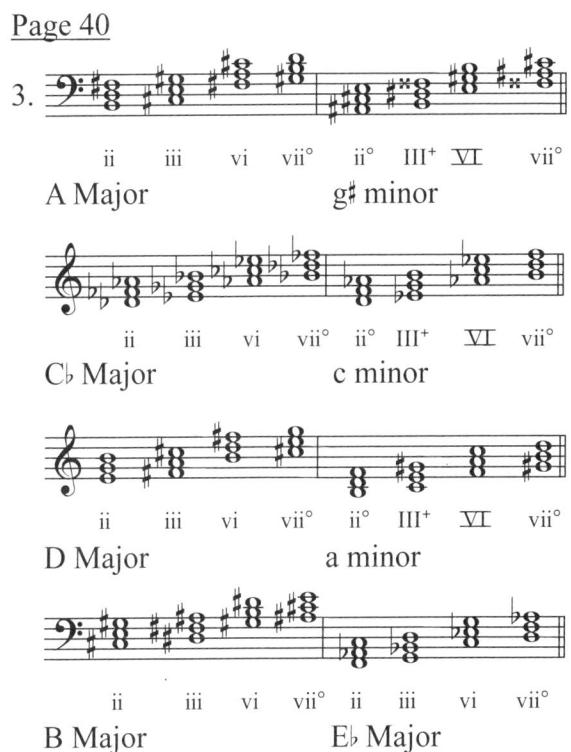

Page 41

4. f, g, a, e, d, c, b

5. Tonic, Supertonic, Mediant, Subdominant, Dominant, Submediant, Leading Tone

Page 43

6. a. Key of a minor
   V iv i⁶ ii°⁶ i⁶ i V

Page 43, No. 6, cont.

b. Key of c# minor
i iv i V i iv

Page 44

c. Key of a minor
i VI V i⁶

d. Key of D Major
vi ii V⁶ I V I⁶

e. Key of G Major
vi ii V I⁶ IV I

LESSON 7: DOMINANT AND DIMINISHED SEVENTH CHORDS (Pages 45-50)

Page 46

Page 46, cont.

Page 47

3.

c diminished 7th

f diminished 7th

bb diminished 7th

b diminished 7th

e diminished 7th

g diminished 7th

c# diminished 7th

g# diminished 7th

Level 8, Pages 43-47

Page 48

4. a. V^7
   b. V^6_5
   c. b♯ diminished ^{7}, e♯ diminished ^{7}

Page 49

d. V^2
e. V^6_5
f. c♯ diminished ^{2}, a♯ diminished ^{2}, e diminished ^{7}

Page 50

g. V^7
h. a diminished ^{7}
i. b♯ diminished $^4_3$, V^7

LESSON 8: THE SECONDARY DOMINANT (Pages 51-56)

Page 52

1.
V/ii ii$^6_4$ V^6_5/iv iv V^7/iii iii^6 V^6/V V

V^6_4/V V^6 V^2/vi vi$^6_3$ V^7/ii ii$^6_4$ V^7/IV IV$^6_4$

V^4_3/ii ii^6 V^6_4/iii iii^6 V^6_5/V V V^6_5/iii iii

V^7/ii ii$^6_4$ V^4_3/VI VI^6 V^4_2/IV IV^6 V^6_5/V V

Page 54

2. a. Key of A Major
   V^7/IV IV$^6_4$ V^7/ii ii$^6_4$
   (bass clef f♯ carries over from previous chord)

   b. Key of c♯ minor
   V of iv   iv

   c. Key of a minor
   V^6_5 of iv   iv

Page 55, No. 2, cont.

d. Key of A♭ Major
V^2/V   V

e. Key of A♭ Major
V^7/V   V V^7/vi   vi

f. Key of B Major
V^6_4/V   V

Page 56

g. Key of E Major
V of V   V

h. Key of E Major
V^4_3 of V   V

i. Key of E Major
V of ii   ii

j. Key of E Major
V of vi   vi

LESSON 9: AUTHENTIC, HALF, PLAGAL, AND DECEPTIVE CADENCES; CHORD PROGRESSIONS (Pages 57-66)

Page 57

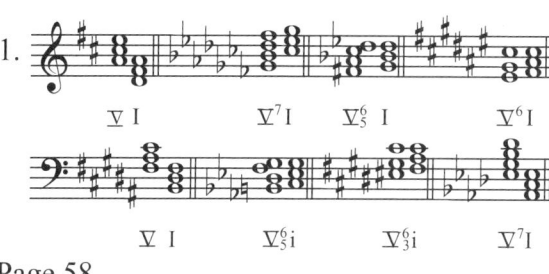

1.
V I V^7 I V^6_5 I V^6 I

V I V^6_5 i V^6_3 i V^7 I

Page 58

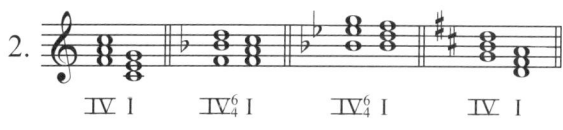

2.
IV I   IV$^6_4$ I   IV$^6_4$ I   IV I

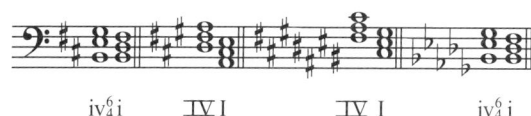

iv$^6_4$ i   IV I   IV I   iv$^6_4$ i

112

Page 59

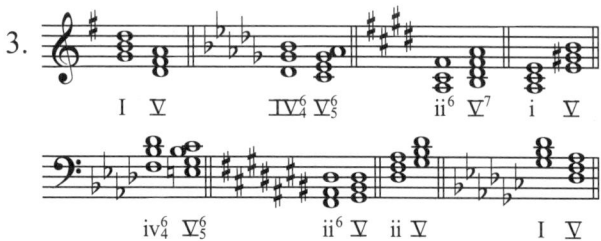

Page 60

5. IV$^6_4$ - I, Plagal
   iv - i, Plagal
   I - V, Half
   V - i, Authentic

   V - vi, Deceptive
   V - VI, Deceptive
   V$^6_5$ - I, Authentic
   I - V$^6_5$, Half

Page 62

Page 62, No. 6, cont.

Page 63

7. a. Key of G♭ Major
      IV - I, Plagal

   b. Key of A Major
      V - I, Authentic

Page 64

   c. Key of c♯ minor
      V^7 - i, Authentic

   d. Key of a minor
      i - V, Half

   e. Key of a minor
      V^7 - VI, Deceptive

Page 65

   f. Key of A♭ Major
      I - V$^6_5$, Half

   g. Key of E Major
      V/V - V, Half

   h. Key of A Major
      V^7-vi, Deceptive

Level 8, Pages 59-65

Page 66, No. 7, cont.

   i. Key of a minor
      V^7 - VI, Deceptive

   j. Key of D Major
      IV$^6_4$ - I, Plagal

   k. Key of F Major
      IV$^6_4$ - I, Plagal

LESSON 10: MODULATION (Pages 67-72)

Page 68-71

1. a. E Major, A Major
   b. A♭ Major, E♭ Major
   c. b minor, D Major
   d. c♯ minor, A Major

REVIEW: LESSONS 1-10 (Pages 75-82)

Page 75

1. C♭ Major, B Major, D Major, A♭ Major, C♯ Major, E♭ Major

2. e♭ minor, g♯ minor, f minor, b minor, d minor, a minor

G♭M   b♭m   cm   EM   c♯m   GM

F♯M   em   D♭M   B♭M   AM   f♯m

Page 76

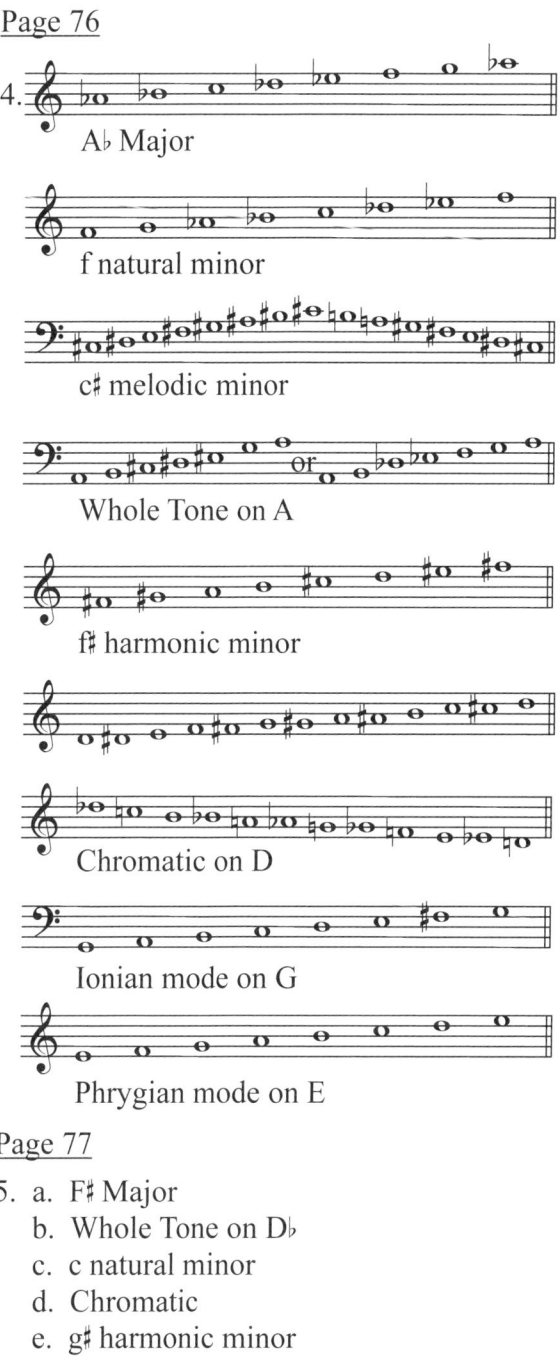

4. A♭ Major

   f natural minor

   c♯ melodic minor

   Whole Tone on A

   f♯ harmonic minor

   Chromatic on D

   Ionian mode on G

   Phrygian mode on E

Page 77

5. a. F♯ Major
   b. Whole Tone on D♭
   c. c natural minor
   d. Chromatic
   e. g♯ harmonic minor
   f. b♭ melodic minor

Page 78

6. M3, m3, m7, d5, A8, M2, P5, A4

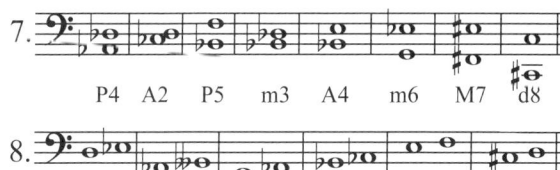

7. P4   A2   P5   m3   A4   m6   M7   d8

8.

Level 8, Pages 66-78

Page 78, cont.

9.

10. E Dominant ^{7}, a♭ diminished ^{7}, f♯ diminished, c minor ^{6}, g♭ diminished $^4_3$, D Major ^{6}

    b♭ diminished, d♭ diminished $^6_4$, C♭ Major $^6_4$, c minor, E Augmented, g minor ^{6}

Page 79

11.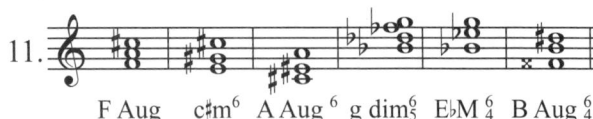
    F Aug   c♯m^6 A Aug   g dim$^6_5$ E♭M $^6_4$ B Aug $^6_4$

12. a. Tonic   e. Dominant
    b. Supertonic   f. Dominant Seventh
    c. Mediant   g. Submediant
    d. Subdominant   h. Leading Tone

13.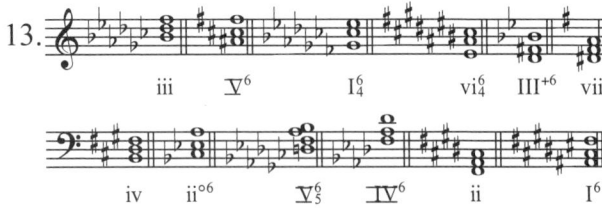
    iii V^6 I^6_4 vi$^6_4$ III^{+6} vii°
    iv   ii°^{6} V^6_5 IV^6 ii I^6

14.
    V^7 I   V VI   IV I   i V

15.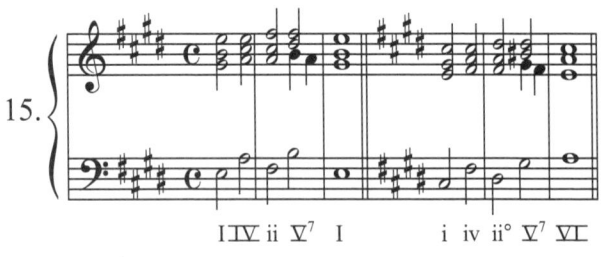
    I IV ii V^7 I   i iv ii° V^7 VI

Page 80

16. a. a minor
    b. m2, M2, m6, P4, P5, m2, P4
    c. a. d minor, iv^6
       b. E Dominant 7, V^7
       c. a minor, i$^6_4$
       d. G Dominant 7, V^6_5/ III
       e. C Major, III
    d. Secondary Dominant
    e. C Major

Page 81

17. a. A Major
    b. M2, P4, P4, P8, P5, m3, m6
    c. a. A Major, I
       b. E Dominant 7, V^7
       c. b♯ diminished 7
       d. c♯ minor, iii
       e. E Major, V^6
       f. G♯ Major, V^6/ iii
       g. c♯ minor, iii
       h. E Major, V
    d. Secondary Dominant
    e. Authentic
    f. Half

Page 82

18. a. E Major
    b. P4, P5, m6, m3, M2, m3, m6
    c. a. E Major, I^6
       b. d♯ diminished, vii°
       c. A Major, IV
       d. e♯ diminished
       e. f♯ minor, ii$^6_4$
       f. B Major, V
    d. E Major

LESSON 11: TIME SIGNATURES
(Pages 83-92)

Page 86

1. 2 = Two beats per measure
   4 = Quarter note receives one beat

   3 = Three beats per measure
   4 = Quarter note receives one beat

   3 = Three beats per measure
   8 = Eighth note receives one beat

   𝄴 = Common Time or 4/4

   𝄵 = Alla Breve or 2/2

   2 = Two beats per measure
   2 = Half note receives one beat

   7 = Seven beats per measure
   4 = Quarter note receives one beat

   6 = Six beats per measure (or 2)
   8 = Eighth note receives one beat
       (or dotted quarter)

Page 89

2. a. 2 pulses per measure

Page 89, No. 2, cont.

   b. 3 pulses per measure

3. 3 pulses per measure

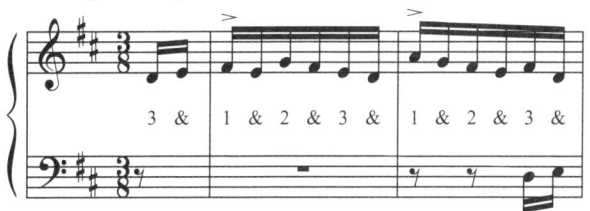

Page 90

   d. 3 pulses per measure

Page 90, cont.

e. 2 pulses per measure

f. 2 pulses per measure

Page 91

g. 4 pulses per measure

Page 91, cont.

h. 2 pulses per measure

i. 4 then 3 pulses per measure

Page 92

j. 2 pulses per measure

Level 8, Pages 90-92

Page 92, cont.

k. 3 pulses per measure

l. 4 pulses per measure

LESSON 12: SIGNS AND TERMS (Pages 93-104)

Page 99

1. d, i, j, g, b, h, f, a, e, k, c

Page 100

2. e, f, d, a, c, b

3. c, a, b, d, g, e, f

Page 101

4. i, a, f, g, d, b, e or j, e or j, c, h

5. h, f, a, g, b, c, d, e

Page 102

6. e, g, f, q, b, a, d, n, j, s, o, k, i, l, h, c, p, r, m

Page 103

7. d, f, a, h, b, e, c, g

8. i, f, a, g, h, b, c, d, j, e

Page 104

9. b, c or i, c or i, e, j, h, a, l, g, d, k, f, n, r, q, o, m, p

LESSON 13: CONTRAPUNTAL TECHNIQUES (Pages 105-112)

Page 108

1. a. Imitation

Page 109

b. Repetition

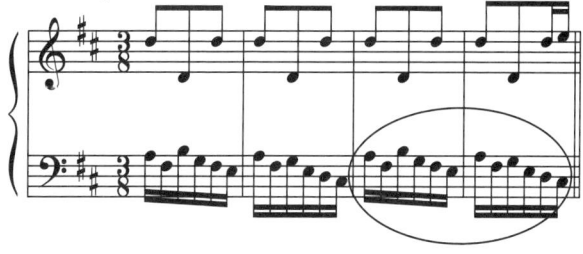

Level 8, Pages 109-111

Page 111, cont.

j. Augmentation

Page 112

k. Pedal Point

l. Sequence

m. Diminution

LESSON 14: HOMOPHONIC AND POLYPHONIC TEXTURES (Pages 113-116)

Page 114

1. a. Polyphonic
   b. Homophonic
   c. Homophonic

Page 115

   d. Polyphonic
   e. Homophonic

Page 116

   f. Polyphonic

LESSON 15: TRANSPOSITION (Pages 117-120)

Page 119

1.

2.

3.

Level 8, Pages 111-119

LESSON 16: THE FOUR PERIODS OF MUSIC HISTORY; THE BAROQUE PERIOD; KIRNBERGER, TELEMANN, AND VIVALDI (Pages 121-128)

Page 126

1. Baroque: 1600-1750
   Classical: 1750-1830
   Romantic: 1830-1900
   20th & 21st Centuries (Contemporary): 1900-present

2. a. Polyphonic texture
   b. Ornamentation (trills, etc.)
   c. Improvisation (cadenzas, figured bass)
   d. Dance Suite: Allemande, Courante or Corrente, Sarabande, Optional Dance, Gigue
   e. Harpsichord, clavichord, organ

Page 127

   f. Terraced dymanics
3. - Allemande: $\frac{4}{4}$, short upbeat, running figures
   - Courante: French, $\frac{3}{2}$ or $\frac{6}{4}$, shifting meters
   - Sarabande: Triple meter, slow, accented 2nd beats
   - Optional Dances: Minuet, Bouree, Gavotte, Passapeid, Polonaise, Anglaise, Loure, Air
   - Gigue: $\frac{6}{8}$, dotted rhythms, large intervals, fugal texture

4. a. Kirnberger
   - 1721-1783
   - Baroque
   - Germany
   - Solo instrumental music, chamber music, vocal works
   - Worked for various Polish noblemen, music director at Benedictine Convent in Reusch-Lemberg, violinist at Prussian royal chapel, chapel of Prince Heinrich of Prussia, and for Princess Anna Analia of Prussia
   - Theoretical works, taught J.A.P. Schultz

Page 128

   b. Telemann
   - 1681-1767
   - Baroque
   - Germany
   - Organist and director of Neukirche in Leipzig, musical director of Leipzig Opera, Kappelmeister of Court of Sorau, Kappelmeister at Barfusserkirche in Frankfurt, musical director and Kantor in Hamburg
   - Operas, oratorios, secular cantatas, serenades, Passions, sacred cantatas, odes, chorales, sacred canons, orchestral works, chamber music, duos, trios, keyboard music

   c. Vivaldi
   - 1678-1741
   - Baroque
   - Italy
   - Violin and choir music, Opera, concertos
   - Priest, teacher at orphanage, work for governor of Mantau, director of operas in Venice
   - Contributions to development of violin playing and the concerto

5. J.S. Bach, Germany, 1685-1750
   Frescobaldi, Italy, 1583-1643
   Handel, Germany, 1685-1760
   Purcell, England, 1659-1695
   Scarlatti, Italy, 1685-1757
   Soler, Spain, 1729-1783

LESSON 17: THE CLASSICAL PERIOD; CLEMENTI, CZERNY, AND DIABELLI (Pages 129-134)

Page 132

1. a. Homophonic texture
   b. Obvious cadence points
   c. Alberti bass
   d. Sonata form

Page 133

2. a. Clementi

   - 1752-1832
   - Classical
   - Italy
   - Piano sonatas, exercises
   - Pianist for Beckford house, teacher and performer in London, seller of pianos, publisher, conductor
   - *Gradus ad Parnassum*, exercise book

   b. Czerny

   - 1791-1857
   - Classical
   - Austria
   - Teacher
   - Sacred Masses, Graduals, Offertories, symphonies, overtures, concertos, chamber music, stage works, songs, piano sonatas, duet arrangements
   - Beethoven
   - Volumes of exercises

Page 134

   c. Diabelli

   - 1781-1858
   - Classical
   - Austria
   - Opera, sacred music, chamber music, piano sonatinas, guitar music
   - Piano and guitar teacher, proofreader, publisher
   - Beethoven's Diabelli Variations

Page 134, cont.

3. Beethoven, Germany, 1770-1827
   Haydn, Austria, 1732-1809
   Mozart, Austria, 1756-1791
   Kuhlau, Germany, 1786-1832

4. Exposition, Development, Recapitulation

LESSON 18: THE ROMANTIC PERIOD; FIELD, HELLER, AND MENDELSSOHN (Pages 135-140)

Page 138

1. a. Programme Music
   b. More complicated harmonies
   c. Lyric melodies
   d. More complicated rhythms

Page 139

2. a. Field

   - 1782-1837
   - Romantic
   - Ireland
   - Russia
   - Piano nocturnes, sonatas, concertos, fantasies, chamber music
   - Studied and traveled with Clementi, promoting pianos and publications

   b. Heller

   - 1813-1888
   - Romantic
   - Hungary
   - Vienna, Austria & Paris, France
   - Czerny, Halm
   - Correspondent to *Neue Zeitschrift für Musik*, music critic in Paris
   - Piano variations, studies, character pieces, transcriptions, sonatas, sonatinas, short pieces, violin and piano works

Level 8, Pages 132-139

Page 140

c. Mendelssohn

- 1809-1847
- Romantic
- Germany
- Gave first modern performance of Bach's *St. Matthew Passion*
- Conductor in various places, director of conservatory in Leipzig
- Chamber music, symphonies, oratorios, concertos, piano works, including *Songs Without Words*

3. Brahms, Germany, 1833-1897
   Chopin, Poland, 1810-1849
   Dvořák, Prague, 1841-1904
   Grieg, Norway, 1843-1907
   Schubert, Austria, 1797-1828
   Schumann, Germany, 1810-1856

LESSON 19: THE 20th & 21st CENTURIES (CONTEMPORARY); BRITTEN, POULENC, AND STRAVINSKY (Pages 141-146)

Page 145

1. a. Major and minor avoided
   b. Quartal harmony
   c. Bitonality
   d. Polytonality
   e. Atonality
   f. Irregular and changing meters
   g. Polyphonic texture
   h. Neo-classic writing

2. a. Britten

   - 1913-1976
   - 20th & 21st Centuries (Contemporary)
   - England
   - Studied composition with Frank Bridge, went to Royal College
   - Wrote for documentary film company, professional composer

Britten, cont.

   - Operas, song cycles, concertos, *Peter Grimes* (opera), *War Requiem* for choir and orchestra
   - Conservative style

Page 146

b. Poulenc

   - 1899-1963
   - 20th & 21st Centuries (Contemporary)
   - France
   - Piano with Ricardo Vines, self-taught composer
   - Witty, anti-conventional style
   - Song cycles, concertos, sonatas, operas, choral works
   - *Les Six*: Auric, Durey, Honneger, Milhaud, Tailleferre, Poulenc; thought music should be sparce, up-to-date, witty

c. Stravinsky

   - 1882-1971
   - 20th & 21st Centuries (Contemporary)
   - Russia
   - Studied composition with Rimsky-Korsakov
   - Neo-classic style
   - Serial music
   - Ballets, opera, concerto, Mass, cantata, orchestral forms; ballets include *Rite of Spring, Petrushka, Firebird*

3. Bartók, Hungary, 1881-1945
   Copland, United States, 1900-1990
   Dello-Joio, United States, 1913-2008
   Kabalevsky, Russia, 1904-1987
   Prokofiev, Russia, 1891-1953
   Shostakovich, Russia, 1906-1975

REVIEW: LESSONS 11-19 (Pages 147-154)

Page 147

1. a.

b.

c.

Page 148

2. a. No specific key or tonality
   b. Use of two different keys at the same time
   c. Exact copy of the theme by another voice
   d. Two different names for the same pitch
   e. Major and minor keys with the same letter names

Page 148, No. 2, cont.

   f. Use of many different keys at the same time
   g. Major and minor keys with the same key signature
   h. Immediately slower
   i. Jokingly, playfully
   j. Momentary contradiction of meter, often through use of strong notes on weak beats
   k. m.d.: *mano destra,* right hand
   l. m.s.: *mano sinistra,* left hand

3. a. Canon

Page 149

b. Imitation

c. Augmentation

Level 8, Pages 147-149

Page 149, cont.

d. Repetition

Page 150

e. Pedal Point

f. Diminution

4. a. Polyphonic

Page 151

b. Homophonic

5. a, b, d, c, b, c, d, d, a, a, b, d, c, a, b

6. Exposition, Development, Recapitulation

7. The division of beats into equal groups

Pages 152-153

8. For information on composers, see answers for Lessons 15-18, pages 120-122 in this Answer Book

Level 8, Pages 149-157

Page 154

9.

REVIEW TEST (Pages 155-161)

Page 155

1. c, d, b
   f, e, a

Page 156

2. E♭ Major, B Major, A Major, C♭ Major, G Major, G♭ Major

3. A: Augmentation
   B: Diminution

4. [music notation]

5. d, c, b, a

Page 157

6. b, c, a, d, b, d, a, c

7. Measure 1: V⁷/IV   IV
   Measure 2: V / iii   iii
   Measure 3: V⁶₅/V   V
   Measure 4: V⁶/ ii   ii
   Measure 5: V⁷/V   V
   Measure 6: V / vi   vi

8. c, e, a, d, f, b

Page 158

9.
   a. b minor
   b. Harmonic
   c. P4, m3, M2, m3
   d. Tonic
   e. Leading Tone
   f. Diatonic
   g. Half
   h. Imitation
   i. Baroque

Page 159

10.
   a. F Major
   b. Tonic, Subdominant, Tonic
   c. Chromatic
   d. Syncopation
   e. Trill
   f. Very fast
   g. Classical
   h. Accept any composer from the Classical Period

Page 160

11.
   a. a minor
   b. 3
   c. D Dominant 7, A♭ Major, D Dominant 7
   d. m7, P8, M3, d5
   e. Homophonic
   f. Walking tempo
   g. Romantic

Page 161

12.
   a. A♭ Major
   b. C Major
   c. Modulation
   d. Fast and merrily
   e. Immediately slow down greatly
   f. A♭ Major, A♭ Dominant 7, G Dominant 7
   g. $\frac{2}{4}$
   h. 20th & 21st Centuries (Contemporary)
   i. Accept any 20th & 21st Centuries (Contemporary) Composer

This page has purposely been left blank

LEVEL 9

LESSON 1: MAJOR AND MINOR KEY SIGNATURES (Pages 1-12)

Page 4

1. E Major, A♭ Major, A Major, B♭ Major, D Major

   F Major, C♯ Major, C Major, G♭ Major, F♯ Major

   G Major, E♭ Major, D♭ Major, C♭ Major, B Major

Page 5

2. DM, C♯M, GM, B♭M, EM
   CM, BM, D♭M, E♭M, G♭M
   F♯M, A♭M, AM, FM, C♭M

Page 6

3. c♯ minor, e minor, d minor, c minor, b minor, b♭ minor

Page 7

f♯ minor, g minor, a minor, g♯ minor, f minor, e♭ minor

Page 7, cont.

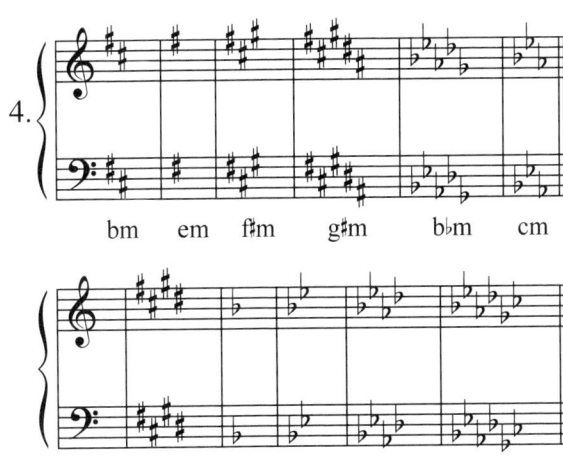

4. bm, em, f♯m, g♯m, b♭m, cm
   am, c♯m, dm, gm, fm, e♭m

Page 8

5. a. B♭ Major
   b. E Major
   c. e minor

Page 9

   d. E♭ Major
   e. D Major
   f. f minor

Page 10

   g. A Major
   h. c minor
   i. b minor

Page 17, cont.

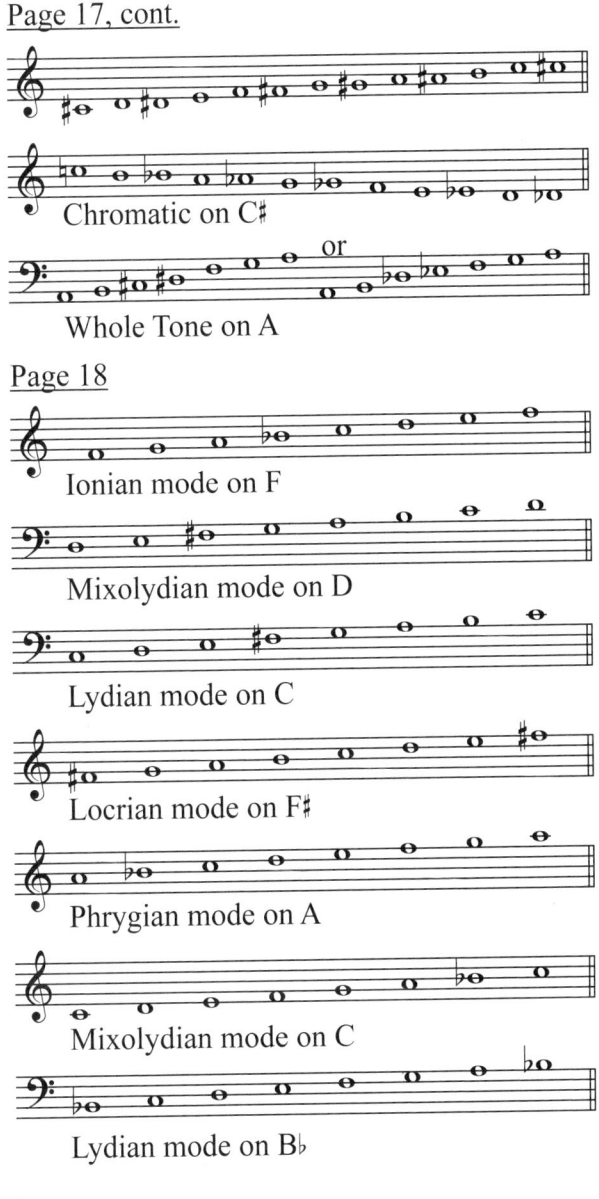

Chromatic on C♯

Whole Tone on A

Page 18

Ionian mode on F

Mixolydian mode on D

Lydian mode on C

Locrian mode on F♯

Phrygian mode on A

Mixolydian mode on C

Lydian mode on B♭

2. a. a melodic minor

Page 19

　b. G Major
　c. C Major
　d. d harmonic minor
　e. B♭ Major

Page 20

　f. a melodic minor
　g. d harmonic minor
　h. Chromatic
　i. Chromatic

LESSON 3: INTERVALS (Pages 21-24)

Page 23

1. M2, A4, P5, M3, P4, m7, M3, M7

   m3, d5, m2, A6, d6, P8, P4, P8

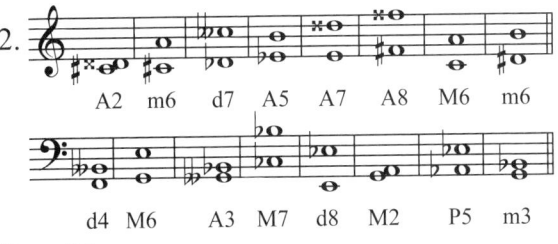

2. A2 m6 d7 A5 A7 A8 M6 m6

   d4 M6 A3 M7 d8 M2 P5 m3

Page 24

3. a. m6, P5, m2, m3, M2, m3, m6, M3

　b. M6, m2, P5, P4, m7, P4

　c. P8, m2, A4, M2, m3, P5

LESSON 4: DIATONIC AND CHROMATIC HALF STEPS (Page 25-28)

Page 26

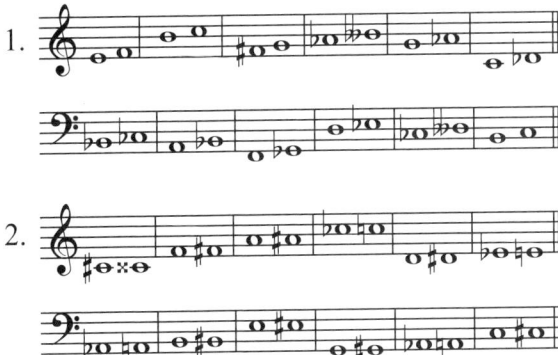

Page 27

3. a. Key of f minor
　　Def. 1: D, C, C, C, D, D, C, D, D
　　Def 2: D, C, D, C, D, D, D, D, D
　b. Key of E♭ Major
　　Def 1: C, C, D, D, C, C
　　Def 2: D, D, D, D, D, D

Page 28

　c. Key of d minor　　(Key of a minor)
　　Def 1: C, C, D, C　Def 1: D, D, D, D
　　Def 2: D, D, D, D
　d. Key of G Major
　　Def 1: D, C, C, D, C, D
　　Def 1: D, C, D, D, D, D

Level 9, Pages 17-28

LESSON 5: MAJOR, MINOR, AUGMENTED, AND DIMINISHED TRIADS AND INVERSIONS (Pages 29-36)

Page 32

1. Ab Major   c minor
   G Major   eb diminished
   E Augmented   bb diminished
   A Augmented   d diminished
   c# minor   F Major
   F# Augmented   B Major

Page 33*

2. db minor ^{6}, F Augmented $^6_4$, Gb Major ^{6}
   C Major $^6_4$, e diminished, B Major

   d diminished, ab diminished ^{6}
   Eb Augmented, a minor ^{6}, bb minor ^{6},
   Gb Major $^6_4$

   cb minor, C# Augmented $^6_4$, f# minor ^{6},
   B Augmented $^6_4$, Ab Major,
   bb diminished $^6_4$

* $^5_3$ for root position and $^6_3$ for second version are acceptable

Page 33, cont.

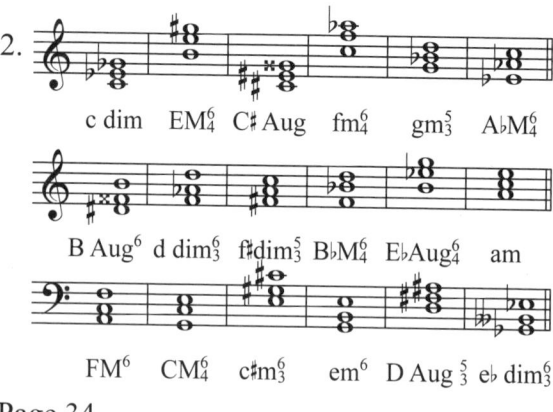

2. c dim   EM$^6_4$ C# Aug   fm$^6_4$ gm$^5_3$ AbM$^6_4$

B Aug^6 d dim$^6_3$ f#dim$^5_3$ BbM$^6_4$ EbAug$^6_4$ am

FM^6 CM$^6_4$ c#m$^6_3$ em^6 D Aug $^5_3$ eb dim$^6_3$

Page 34

4. a. E Major, A Major $^6_4$, E Major

Page 35

b. Eb Major, Bb Major, Ab Major,
   Eb Major, Bb Major,
   c minor ^{6} (accept Ab Major $^6_4$)

c. d minor ^{6}, a minor ^{6}, d minor,
   E Major

d. a minor, G Major, a minor

Page 36

e. Bb Major, Eb Major, c minor, F Major

f. d minor $^6_4$, A Major, Bb Major ^{6}

g. D Major, c# diminished ^{6}, D Major ^{6},
   e minor ^{6}

LESSON 6: PRIMARY AND SECONDARY TRIADS; FIGURED BASS (Pages 37-46)

Page 38

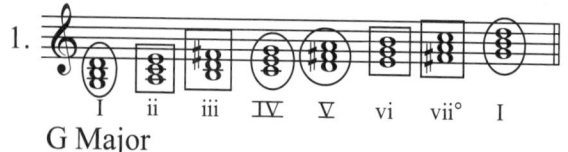

1. I   ii   iii   IV   V   vi   vii°   I

G Major

Page 38, No. 1, cont.*

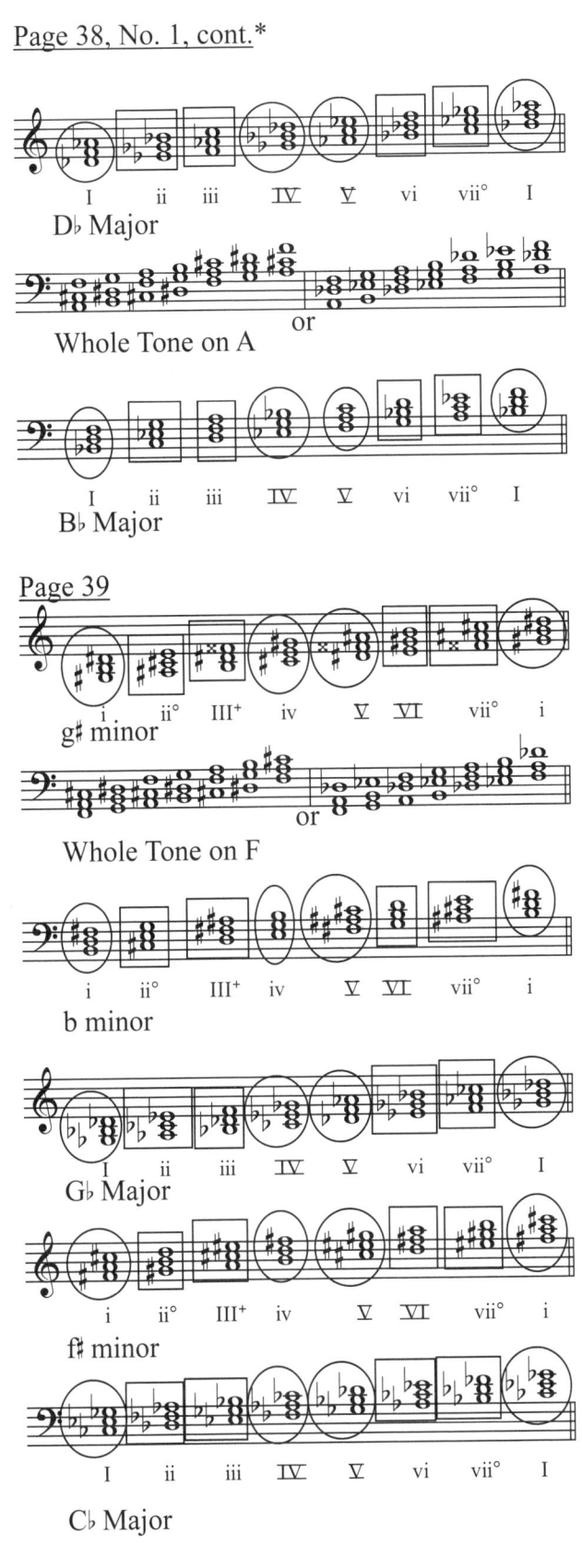

* In minor keys, III⁺ is rare. III (Major) is typical.

Page 39, cont.

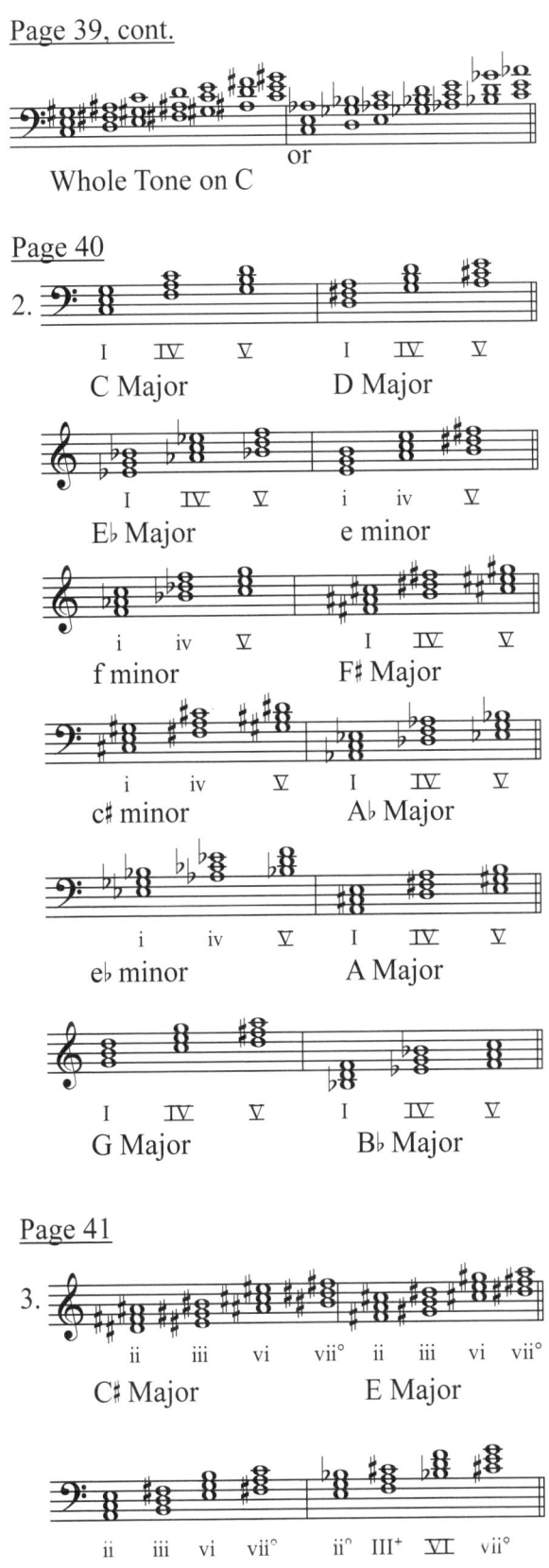

Level 9, Pages 38-41

Page 41, cont.

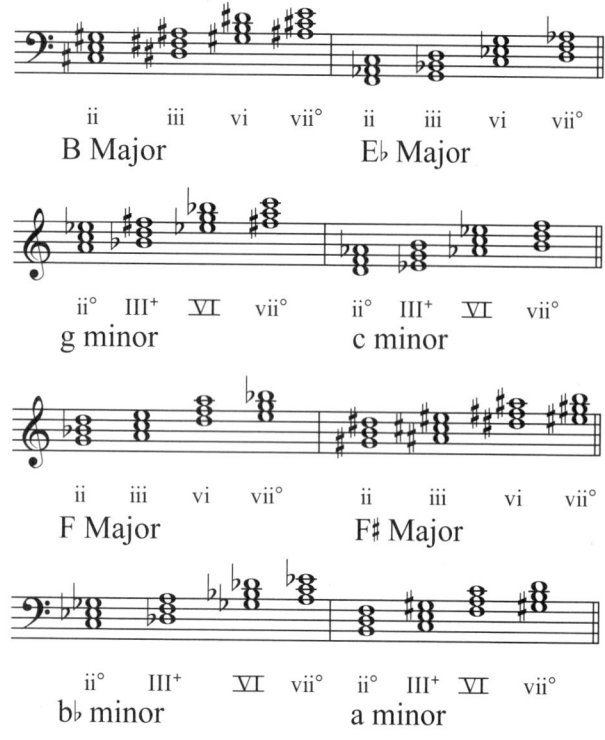

Page 42

4. f, g, a, e, d, c, b

5. Tonic, Supertonic, Mediant, Subdominant, Dominant, Submediant, Leading Tone

Page 44

6. a. Key of D Major
   I   vi   ii⁶   I   ii⁶   I⁶₄   V̲ (bass clef A carries over)

   b. Key of G Major
   I⁶   IV̲   I⁶₄   V̲   I⁶₄   IV̲⁶   I   V̲

Page 45

   c. Key of D♭ Major
   V̲   vi   ii⁶   I

   d. Key of b minor
   i   iv⁶₄ (bass clef B carries over)
   iv   iv

Page 45, No. 6, cont.

   e. Key of E♭ Major
   I⁶   IV̲   I⁶₄   vi   I⁶₄   ii⁶

Page 46

   f. Key of D Major
   ii⁶   vi   vii°   vii°⁶   I⁶   V̲ ⁶

LESSON 7: SEVENTH CHORDS
  (Pages 47-54)

Page 48*

* ⁴₂ is acceptable for third inversion

Page 49, cont.

4.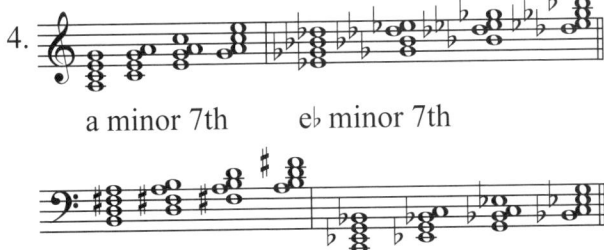

a minor 7th   eb minor 7th

b minor 7th   c minor 7th

Page 50

5.

g half- diminished 7th

eb half-diminished 7th

a half-diminished 7th

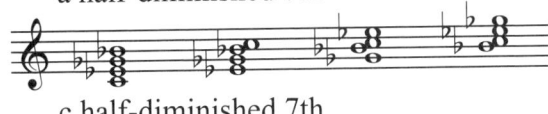

c half-diminished 7th

Page 51

6.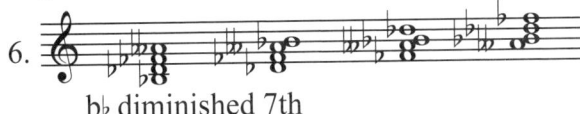

bb diminished 7th

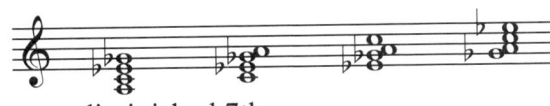

a diminished 7th

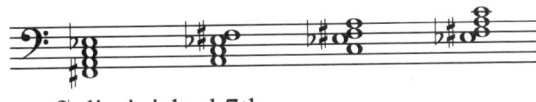

f# diminished 7th

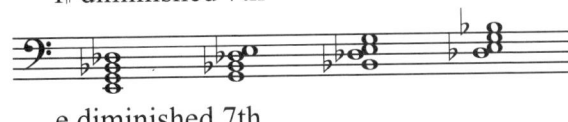

e diminished 7th

7. E Major $^6_5$, f minor $^6_5$, c diminished $^4_3$, A Dominant ^{7}, d half diminished $^6_5$, c# minor ^{7}

a minor ^{2}, C Major ^{7}, bb minor ^{2}, e diminished $^4_3$, g diminished $^4_3$, Db Major ^{7}

Page 51, No. 7, cont.

B Dominant $^4_3$, eb half diminished $^6_5$, ab diminished $^6_5$, Cb Major ^{7}, f# half diminished $^4_3$, gb minor ^{2}

Bb Major $^6_5$, E Dominant ^{7}, g half diminished ^{2}, d diminished $^4_3$, cb minor ^{7}, b half diminished $^6_5$

Page 52

8. a. Bb Dominant $^4_3$
   b. B Dominant $^4_3$
   c. f minor $^6_5$, Bb Dominant ^{7}
   d. c# diminished $^6_5$

Page 53

   e. c# diminished ^{7}
   f. A Dominant ^{7}
   g. D Dominant ^{7}, a minor ^{7}, D Dominant ^{7}
   h. C Major ^{2}, a minor ^{7}

Page 54

   i. F Dominant $^6_5$, eb minor $^6_5$, Ab Dominant ^{7}, Ab Dominant $^6_5$, f minor $^6_5$
   j. d minor ^{7}
   k. d# diminished ^{7}
   l. D Major $^4_3$

LESSON 8: THE SECONDARY DOMINANT (Pages 55-60)

Page 56

1.

V/iii   iii$^4_4$ V^7/V   V$^4_6$ V$^4_3$/vi vi^6 V^6/V V

V$^6_5$/ii ii   V^2/ii ii^6 V$^6_4$/iv iv^6 V/vi vi$^6_4$

Level 9, Pages 49-56

Page 56, No. 1, cont.

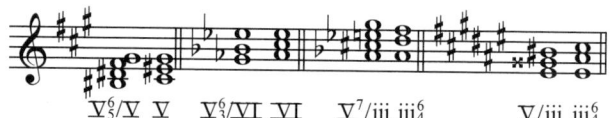

V_5^6/V V V_3^6/VI VI V^7/iii iii_4^6 V/iii iii_4^6

V_5^6/IV IV V^2/ii ii^6 V_3^4/V V^6 V^7/IV IV_4^6

Page 58

2. a. Key of d minor
   V/V V

   b. Key of G Major
   V^7/IV IV_4^6

   c. Key of G Major
   V_3^4/V V^6

Page 59

   d. Key of D♭ Major
   V_5^6/vi vi

   e. Key of b minor
   V^7/iv iv_4^6
   V_5^6/iv iv
   V/iv iv

   f. Key of F Major
   V_5^6/V V

Page 60

   g. Key of D Major
   V_3^4 of V V

   h. Key of A♭ Major
   V^7 of ii   ii

   i. Key of F Major
   V^7 of V V

LESSON 9: AUTHENTIC, HALF, PLAGAL, AND DECEPTIVE CADENCES; CHORD PROGRESSION (Pages 61-68)

Page 62

1.

$V_3^6 I$ iv i^6 $ii^6 V_2^4$ IV I^6

iv VI_4^6 V vi V_4^6 i^6 i_4^6 V

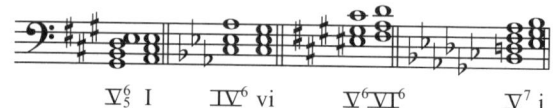

V_5^6 I IV^6 vi $V^6 VI^6$ V^7 i

iv_4^6 i V_3^6/V V IV^6 I_4^6 i V^6

Page 63

2. V^6- I, Authentic
   iv_4^6 - i, Plagal
   V_4^6- vi_4^6, Deceptive
   I - V^6, Half

   IV- I^6, Plagal
   V_4^6 - VI_4^6, Deceptive
   V- i_4^6, Authentic
   i - V_5^6, Half

   V_3^4 - i^6, Authentic
   I_4^6 - V^7, Half
   V^6- VI^6, Deceptive
   IV_4^6 -I, Plagal

   iv^6 - i_4^6, Plagal
   ii^6 - V^7, Half
   V_2^4- I^6, Authentic
   i^6 - V_4^6, Half

Page 64

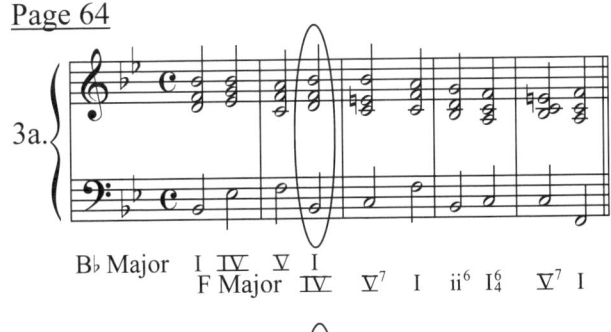

Bb Major I IV V I
F Major   IV   V⁷ I ii⁶ I⁶₄ V⁷ I

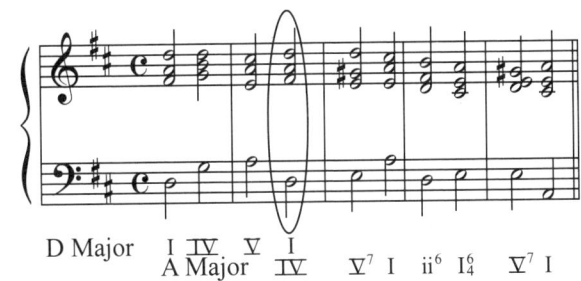

D Major   I IV V I
A Major   IV   V⁷ I ii⁶ I⁶₄ V⁷ I

Page 65

C Major I IV V I
G Major   IV   V⁷ I ii⁶ I⁶₄ V⁷ I

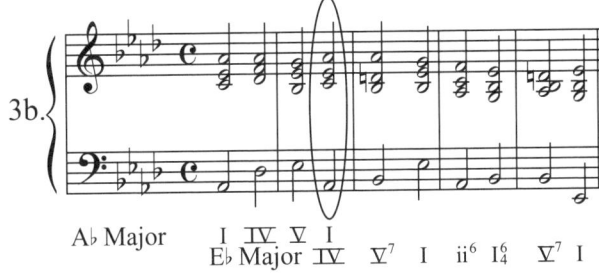

3b.
Ab Major   I IV V I
Eb Major   IV   V⁷ I ii⁶ I⁶₄ V⁷ I

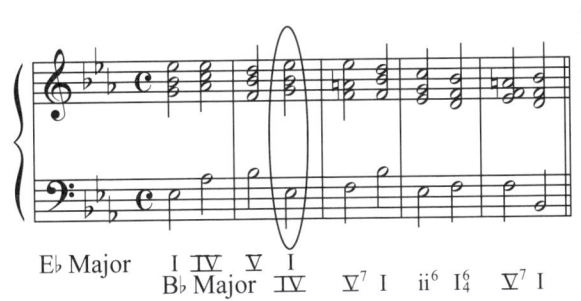

Eb Major   I IV V I
Bb Major   IV   V⁷ I ii⁶ I⁶₄ V⁷ I

Page 65, No. 3, cont.

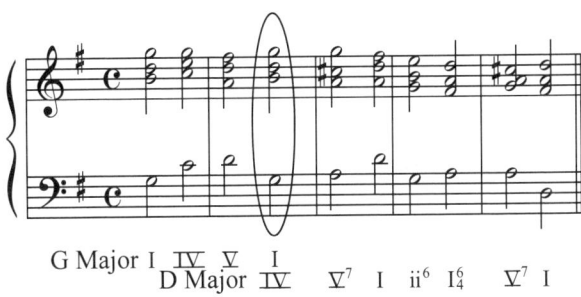

G Major I IV V I
D Major   IV   V⁷ I ii⁶ I⁶₄ V⁷ I

Page 66

4. a. Key of Eb Major
   V - vi⁶, Deceptive

  b. Key of c minor
   I - V⁴₃ , Half

Page 67

  c. Key of f minor
   iv⁶₄ - i, Plagal

  d. Key of Eb Major
   V⁷ - vi, Deceptive

  e. Key of D Major
   ii⁶ - V⁷, Half

Page 68

  f. Key of D major
   V⁷ - vi, Deceptive

  g. Key of C Major
   V - I, Authentic

  h. Key of D Major
   I⁶₄ - V, Half

Level 9, Pages 64-68

LESSON 10: MODULATION
(Pages 69-74)

Page 70

1. a. Original key: B♭ Major
   Modulates to: F Major

Page 71-72

   b. Original key: C Major
      Modulates to: G Major

Page 73

   c. Original key: A Major
      Modulates to: f♯ minor

Page 74

   d. Original key: E♭ Major
      Modulates to: B♭ Major

REVIEW: LESSONS 1-10 (Pages 77-86)

Page 77

1. D♭ Major, A Major, C♯ Major, G♭ Major, F♯ Major, A♭ Major

2. g♯ minor, c minor, f♯ minor, c♯ minor, f minor, g minor

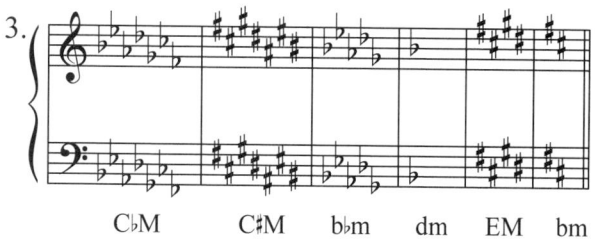
3. C♭M   C♯M   b♭m   dm   EM   bm

Page 78

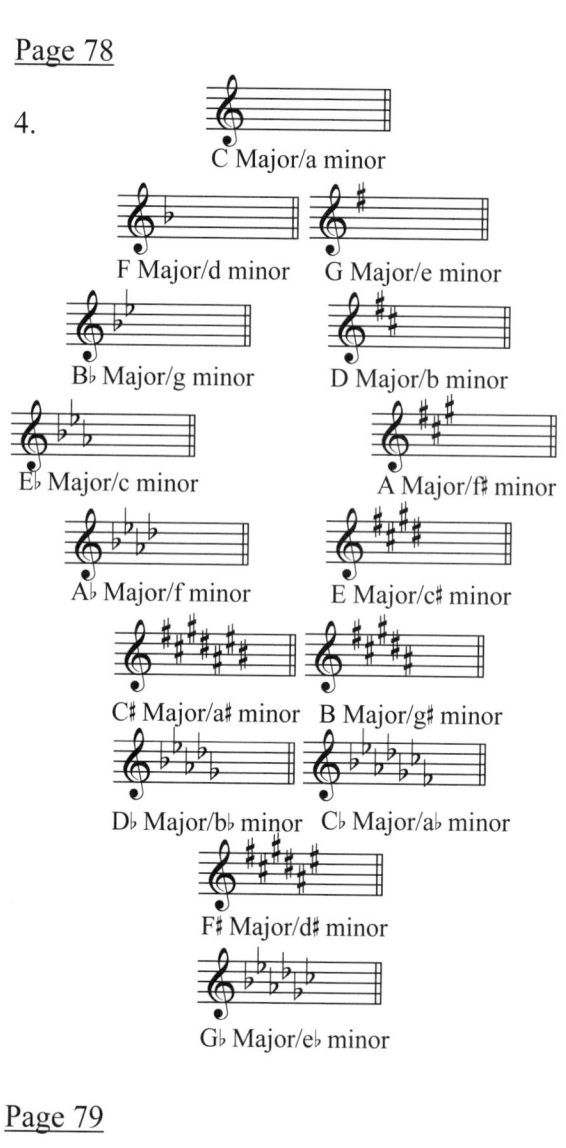
4. C Major/a minor
F Major/d minor   G Major/e minor
B♭ Major/g minor   D Major/b minor
E♭ Major/c minor   A Major/f♯ minor
A♭ Major/f minor   E Major/c♯ minor
C♯ Major/a♯ minor   B Major/g♯ minor
D♭ Major/b♭ minor   C♭ Major/a♭ minor
F♯ Major/d♯ minor
G♭ Major/e♭ minor

Page 79

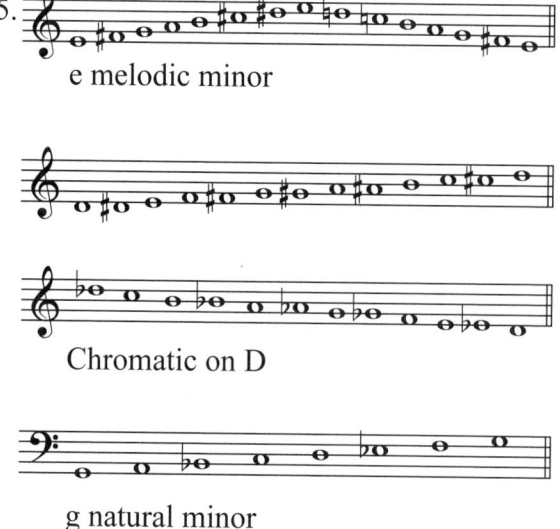
5. e melodic minor

Chromatic on D

g natural minor

Page 79, No. 5, cont.

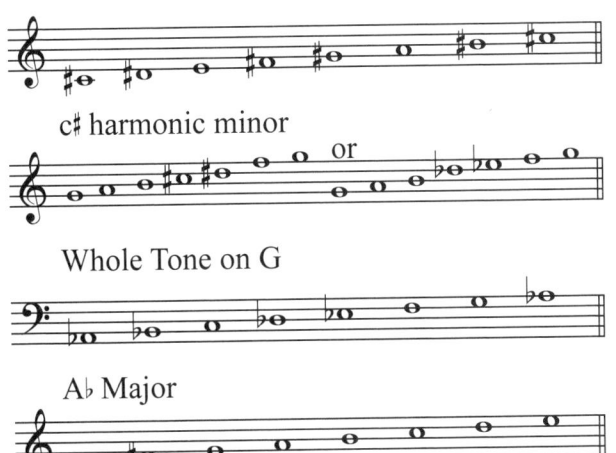

c# harmonic minor

Whole Tone on G

A♭ Major

Aeolian mode on E

Locrian mode on F#

Page 80

6. A4, M2, P5, M7, M3, P4, m6, A8

7.

8.

9.

10. c# diminished $^6_4$, F Augmented, a minor $^6_4$,
    d diminished, G Augmented ^{6}, B♭ Major $^6_4$

11.

    D♭M ^{6} f# dim $^6_4$ BM $^6_4$ e♭m A♭ Aug $^6_3$ cm $^5_3$

Page 81

12.

    i iv V   I   IV V
    a minor   G Major

    I IV V   i iv V
    A♭ Major   c# minor

Page 81, cont.

13.

    ii iii vi vii° ii° III+ VI vii°
    F# Major   g minor

    ii° III+ VI vii° ii iii vi vii°
    b minor   D Major

14.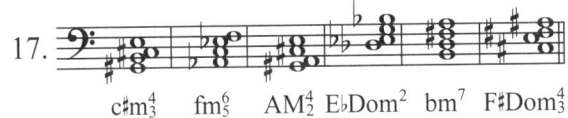

    Whole Tone on C#

    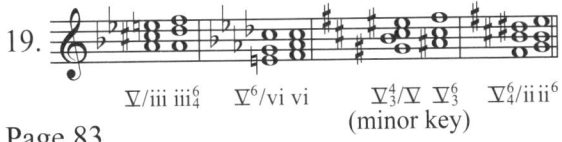

    Whole Tone on A♭

15. a. Tonic   e. Dominant
    b. Supertonic   f. Dominant 7th
    c. Mediant   g. Submediant
    d. Subdominant   h. Leading Tone

Page 82

16. D Major ^{7}, A♭ Dominant $^6_5$,
    c half-diminished ^{7}, g diminished $^4_3$,
    e half-diminished ^{2}, b♭ diminished $^6_5$

17.

    c#m$^4_3$ fm$^6_5$ AM$^4_2$ E♭Dom^2 bm^7 F#Dom$^4_3$

18. V/ii   ii   V^7/ii   ii
    V/V   V   V/vi   vi

19.

    V/iii iii$^6_4$ V^6/vi vi   V$^4_3$/V V^6 V^6/iii iii^6
                                    (minor key)

Page 83

20. IV$^6_4$ - I, Plagal
    V - I$^6_4$, Authentic
    i - V$^6_5$, Half
    V - VI, Deceptive

21.

    V$^6_4$ i^6 iv i^6 V vi   I V^6

Page 83, cont.

Page 84

23. a. c minor
    b. Melodic
    c. 1. m3 2. m2 3. P8 4. P5 5. d7
    d. a. c minor, i
       b. G Dominant 7, V^7
       c. f minor, iv

Page 85

24. a. B Major
    b. 1. m2 2. A4 3. M3 4. P4
       5. A2 6. m7 7. A4
    c. a. A# Dominant 7, V^7/iii
       b. d# minor, iii
       c. c# minor ^{6}, ii^6
       d. F# Dominant 7, V^7
       e. B Major, I
    d. Secondary Dominant
    e. Authentic

Page 86

25. a. D Major
    b. 1. m3 2. m2 3. P8 4. M3
       5. m3
    c. a. D Major, I
       b. b minor 7
       c. A Major, V
       d. D Major $^6_4$, I^6_4
       e. A Major, V

LESSON 11: TIME SIGNATURES (Pages 87-96)

Page 90

1. 2 = 2 beats per measure
   4 = Quarter note receives one beat

   3 = 3 beats per measure
   4 = Quarter note receives one beat

   3 = 3 beats per measure
   8 = Eighth note receives one beat

   ₵ = Alla breve or $\frac{2}{2}$

   C = Common Time or $\frac{4}{4}$

   2 = 2 beats per measure
   2 = Half note receives one beat

   7 = 7 beats per measure
   4 = Quarter note receives one beat

   6 = 6 beats per measure (or 2)
   8 = Eighth note receives one beat (or dotted quarter)

Page 93

2. a. 4 pulses per measure

Page 93, No. 2, cont.

b. 2 pulses per measure

c. 4 pulses per measure

Page 94

d. 2 pulses per measure

e. 3 pulses per measure

Page 94, cont.

f. 3 pulses per measure

Page 95

g. 2 pulses per measure

h. 2 pulses per measure

Page 95, cont.

i. 3 pulses per measure

Page 96

j. 3 pulses

k. 3 pulses

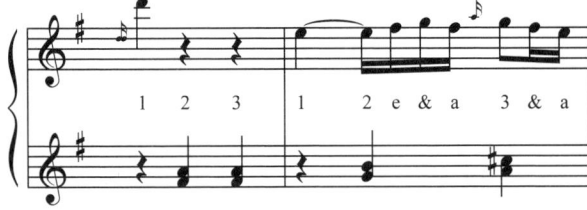

Page 96, cont.

l. 2 pulses per measure

3. a. Meter: The division of beats into equal groups
   b. Syncopation: Contradiction of the meter or pulse, often by placing strong notes on weak beats
   c. Hemiola: Changing of the meter from two to three pulses per measure

LESSON 12: HOMOPHONIC AND POLYPHONIC TEXTURES (Pages 97-100)

Page 98

1. a. Homophonic
   b. Polyphonic
   c. Homophonic

Page 99

   d. Homophonic
   e. Polyphonic

Page 100

   f. Polyphonic

LESSON 13: CONTRAPUNTAL TECHNIQUES (Pages 101-110)

Page 105

a. Sequence

b. Imitation

c. Repetition

Page 106

d. Augmentation

Page 106, cont.

e. Repetition

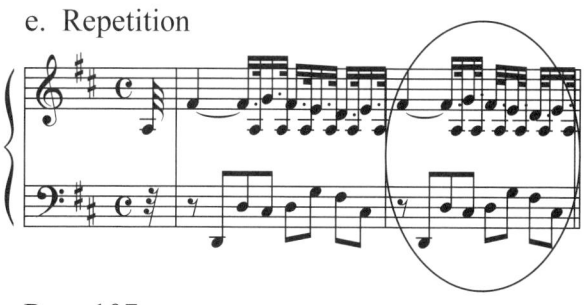

Page 107

f. Pedal Point

g. Imitation

Page 108

h. Repetition and Pedal Point

Level 9, Pages 105-108

Page 108, cont.

i. Sequence

j. Augmentation

Page 109

k. Diminution

Page 109, cont.

l. Imitation

Page 110

m. Pedal Point

n. Canon

Level 9, Pages 108-110

LESSON 14: THE FUGUE (Pages 111-118)

Pages 115-118

2.

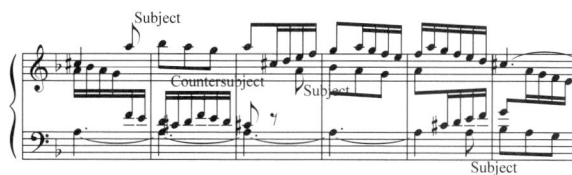

LESSON 15: THE DANCES OF THE BAROQUE SUITE (Pages 119-124)

Page 124

1. b, d, a, e, f, c

2. Allemande
   Courante or Corrente
   Sarabande
   Optional Dances (Minuet, Bouree, Gavotte, Passapied, Polonaise, Anglaise, Loure, Air)
   Gigue

LESSON 16: SONATA FORM (Pages 125-134)

Page 131-134

1. Exposition: Measures 1-54
   Theme 1: Measures 1-11, G Major, I
   Theme 2: Measures 24-31, D Major, V
   Development: Measures 55-73
   Recapitulation: Measures 73, beat 3 - end
   Theme 1: Measure 73, beat 3, G Major, I
   Theme 2: Measure 92, G Major, I

Level 9, Pages 115-134

LESSON 17: SIGNS AND TERMS
(Pages 135-146)

Page 141

1. d, i, j, g, b, h, f, a, e, k, c

Page 142

2. b, e, f, c, a, d

3. d, a, b, c, g, e, f

Page 143

4. i, a, f, g, d, b, e or j, e or j, c, h

5. h, f, a, g, b, c, d, e

Page 144

6. e, g, f, q, b, a, d, n, j, c, s, k, i, l, h, m, p, r, o

Page 145

7. d, f, a, h, b, e, c, g

8. i, f, a, g, h, b, c, d, j, e

Page 146

9. b, c or i, c or i, e, j, h, a, l, g, d, k, f, q, n, o, p, m

10. b, g, a, i, h, e, c, f, d, j

LESSON 18: TRANSPOSITION
(Pages 147-150)

Page 149

Page 150

LESSON 19: THE FOUR PERIODS OF MUSIC HISTORY; THE BAROQUE PERIOD; CORELLI, PURCELL, AND RAMEAU
(Pages 151-156)

Page 154-155

1. Baroque: 1600-1750
   Classical: 1750-1830
   Romantic: 1830-1900
   20th & 21st Centuries (Contemporary): 1900-present

2. a. Polyphonic Texture
   b. Use of ornamentation
   c. Improvisation
   d. Dance Suite
   e. Harpsichord, Clavichord, Organ
   f. Terraced Dynamics

3. a. Corelli

- 1653-1713
- Baroque
- Italy
- Director of music to Cardinal Pamphili and Cardinal Pietro Ottoboni
- Chamber music, trio sonatas, solo violin sonatas, Christmas Concerto
- Key changes, dissonance

Page 155, No. 3, cont.

b. Purcell

- 1659-1695
- Baroque
- England
- Care of instruments, copying, and organist at Westminster Abbey; organist of Chapel Royal
- Music for James II coronation and funeral of Queen Mary; instrumental music, choral anthems, four operas, longer choral works with orchestra

Page 156

c. Rameau

- 1683-1764
- Baroque
- France
- Organist at various places; opened school of composition
- Harpsichord works, operas, ballets, stage works, instrumental chamber music
- *Traite de l'harmonic, Noveau systeme de musique*

4. J.S. Bach, 1685-1750, Germany
   Frescobaldi, 1583-1643, Italy
   Handel, 1685-1760, Germany
   Kirnberger, 1721-1783, Germany
   Scarlatti, 1685-1757, Italy
   Soler, 1729-1783, Spain
   Telemann, 1681-1767, Germany
   Vivaldi, 1678-1741, Italy

LESSON 20: THE CLASSICAL PERIOD; BEETHOVEN, HAYDN, AND MOZART (Page 157-162)

Page 160

1. a. Homophonic texture
   b. Obvious cadence points
   c. Alberti Bass
   d. Sonata form

Page 161

2. a. Beethoven

- 1770-1827
- Classical
- Germany
- String quartets, piano concertos, piano sonatas, symphonies, solo instrumental works, piano trios
- Events of French Revolution
- Haydn

b. Haydn

- 1732-1809
- Classical
- Austria
- Vienna choir school
- Sonata and symphony forms
- Professional singer, music director to Prince Esterhazy
- Piano sonatas, operas, string quartets, symphonies

Page 162

c. Mozart

- 1756-1791
- Classical
- Austria
- Child prodigy, performed throughout Europe
- Piano sonatas, piano concertos, operas, symphonies, sonatas and concertos for other instruments, *Requiem*
- Music director to Archbishop of Salzburg, professional composer and teacher.

3. Clementi, Italy, 1752-1832
   Czerny, Austria, 1791-1857
   Diabelli, Austria, 1781-1858
   Kuhlau, Germany, 1786-1832

LESSON 21: THE ROMANTIC PERIOD BRAHMS, LISZT, AND TCHAIKOVSKY (Pages 163-168)

Page 166

1. a. Programme music
   b. Complicated harmonies
   c. Lyric melodies
   d. Complicated rhythms

Page 167

2. a. Brahms

- 1833-1897
- Romantic
- Germany
- Piano concertos, sonatas, piano quartets and quintets, *Requiem*, choral works, symphonies, short piano pieces, clarinet sonatas
- Robert and Clara Schumann, Franz Liszt

b. Franz Liszt

- 1811-1886
- Romantic
- Hungary
- Child prodigy, traveled and performed
- Professional performer, Kappelmeister Extraordinary in Weimar
- Sonatas, *Hungarian Rhapsodies, Consolations*, ballades, Polonaises, *Transcendental Etudes*, piano concertos, symphonic poems, songs, transcriptions, choral works, oratorios
- Hungarian music

Page 168

c. Tchaikovsky

- 1840-1893
- Romantic
- Russia
- St. Petersburg School of Jurisprudence, St. Petersburg Conservatory

Page 168, No. 2, c, cont.

- Taught at St. Petersburg & Moscow Conservatories
- Opera, symphonic poems, ballets, piano concertos, symphonies, violin concerto
- Theory textbook: *Guide to the Practical Study of Harmony*
- Russian folk music

3. Chopin, Poland, 1810-1849
   Dvorák, Prague (Czechoslovokia), 1841-1904
   Field, Ireland, 1782-1837
   Grieg, Norway, 1843-1907
   Heller, Hungary, 1813-1888
   Mendelssohn, Germany, 1809-1847
   Schubert, Austria, 1797-1828
   Schumann, Germany, 1810-1856

LESSON 22: IMPRESSIONISM IN MUSIC; DEBUSSY, RAVEL, GRIFFES (Pages 169-172)

Page 171

1. Unclear tonalities, non metric rhythms, flowing, musically blurred images, whole tone scales, pentatonic scales, parallel chords, augmented triads, ostinato figures.

2. a. Debussy

- 1862-1918
- Impressionism
- France
- Paris Conservatory
- Professional composer and conductor
- Piano preludes and etudes, opera, orchestral works, *Children's Corner Suite*

Page 172

b. Ravel

- 1875-1937
- Impressionism
- France
- Paris Conservatory
- *Bolero, Pavanne for a Dead Princess, Miroirs, Scheherazade*, ballet *Daphnes and Chloe*
- Orchestrations

c. Griffes

- 1884-1920
- Impressionism
- U.S.A.
- Piano with Mary Selena Broughton; Stern Conservatory in Berlin
- Teacher at Hackley School in New York
- Songs, chamber music, stage works, piano sonata, short pieces for piano.
- Impressionistic movement; Japanese folk songs

LESSON 23: THE 20th & 21st CENTURIES (CONTEMPORARY); COPLAND, IVES, GERSHWIN (Pages 173-178)

Page 176-177

1. a. Major and minor tonalities avoided
   b. Quartal harmony
   c. Bitonality
   d. Polytonality
   e. Atonality
   f. Irregular and changing meters
   g. Polyphonic texture
   h. Neo-Classic writing
   i. Serial or Twelve-Tone writing

Page 177, cont.

2. a. Copland

- 1900-1990
- 20th & 21st Centuries (Contemporary)
- U.S.A.
- Studied in Paris with Nadie Boulanger
- Taught at New School for Social Research in New York and Tanglewood
- Neo-classic style combined with jazz elements, American style influenced by folk music
- *El Salon Mexico*, ballets *Billy the Kid, Rodeo, Appalachian Spring*, piano concerto, works for solo instruments and piano
- *The New Music; Music and Imagination*

Page 178

b. Ives

- 1874-1954
- 20th & 21st Centuries (Contemporary)
- U.S.A.
- Father; Horatio Parker at Yale
- Bitonality, Atonality, clashing meters, quarter tones
- Songs, piano sonatas, orchestral works, chamber music

c. Gershwin

- 1898-1937
- 20th & 21st Centuries (Contemporary)
- U.S.A.
- Piano with Charles Hambitzer, composition with Henry Cowell
- Combined jazz style with classical forms
- *Rhapsody in Blue, American in Paris, Porgy and Bess,* songs, piano pieces

Page 178, cont.

3. Bartók, Hungary, 1881-1945
   Britten, England, 1913-1976
   Della Joio, U.S.A., 1913-
   Kabalevsky, Russia, 1904-1987
   Poulenc, France, 1899-1963
   Prokofiev, Russia, 1891-1953
   Shostakovich, Russia, 1906-1975
   Stravinsky, Russia, 1882-1971

REVIEW: LESSONS 11-23 (Pages 179-186)

Page 179

1. a. 4 pulses per measure

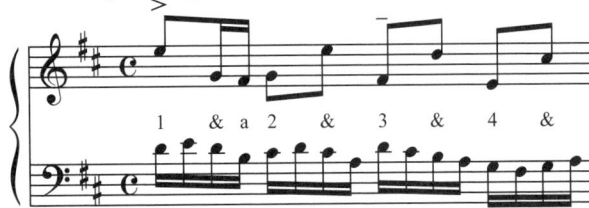

   b. 2 pulses per measure

Page 179, No. 1, cont.

   c. 4 pulses per measure

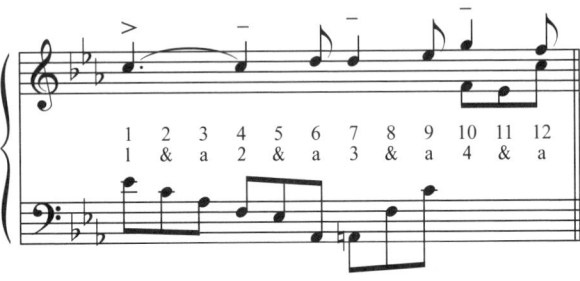

Page 180

2. a. No specific key or tonality
   b. First section of Sonata form
   c. Style of composition in which voices imitate one another
   d. Two names for the same pitch
   e. Major and minor keys with the same letter name
   f. Several different keys used at once
   g. Set of related pieces that are performed as a group
   h. Immediately slower
   i. Playfully
   j. Momentary contradiction of meter, often by the use of strong notes on weak beats
   k. Changing of meter from 2 to 3 pulses per measure
   l. Dying away
   m. Virtuoso piece common during the Baroque Period, written in free style with many scales and rapid passages
   n. In a low voice
   o. Varying the rhythm by slowing or rushing the tempo

Level 9, Pages 178-180

Page 180, cont.

3. a. Sequence

Page 181

b. Repetition

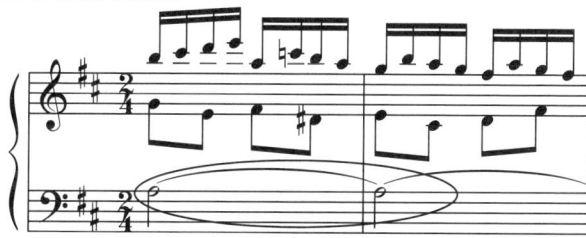

c. Pedal Point

4. a. Polyphonic

Page 182

   b. Homophonic

Page 182, cont.

5. Exposition   Theme 1 (I)
                      Theme 2 (V or other
                               related key)
   Development Motives based on theme
                        in various keys
   Recapitulation Theme 1 (I)
                        Theme 2 (I)

6. a   b   b
    b   b   a
    b   b   b
    b   a   b
    b   b   b
    b   a

Page 183

7. b, a, e, b, c, c, e, d, a, e, b, e, c, a, b

Pages 183-186

8. For information on composers, see answers for Lessons 19-23, pages 144 to 148 in this Answer Book

Page 186

9.

REVIEW TEST (Pages 187-193)

Page 187

1. M3   m2
    A4   d7
    m6   M7
    P8   d5

2. F Major   d minor
    A Major   f# minor
    G♭ Major   e♭ minor
    B Major   g# minor
    D♭ Major   b♭ minor

Page 188

3. a.

b.

c.

d.

e.

4. a. $\frac{6}{8}$ b. $\frac{2}{4}$ c. $\frac{3}{4}$ d. $\frac{5}{4}$

Page 189

5. Major 7th, Major 7th, minor 7th, minor 7th, diminished 7th, half-diminished 7th

6. D#, C♭, D♭, E

7. d, e, i, c, a, b, j, f, g, h

Page 190

8. d, b, e, a, c

9. 1. A Major, B♭ Major (or d minor), G Major, C Major, A Major, G Augmented (or B Major)
   2. More slowly
   3. No
   4. *pianissimo,* very soft
   5. Accept any 20th & 21st Centuries (Contemporary) composers

Page 191

10. a. e minor
    b. 3
    c. Polyphonic
    d. m2, P5, m3, m2
    e. A Major
    f. c# diminished
    g. Baroque
    h. Accept any Baroque composers

Page 192

11. a. E♭ Major
    b. Sequence
    c. Repetition
    d. 4
    e. Exposition, Development, Recapitulation
    f. B♭ Dominant 7
    g. V^7/IV IV_4^6
    h. Secondary Dominant
    i. Classical
    j. Accept any composers from the Classical Period

Page 193

12. a. C Major
    b. F Major 7th
    c. C Major 7th
    d. A4, A4, M6, P8
    e. Two
    f. Romantic
    g. Accept any Romantic composers

Level 9, Pages 188-193

Level 10 (Advanced Level)

LESSON 1: KEYS AND SCALES (Pages 1-4)

<u>Page 2</u> No. 1:

[Key signatures: BM, b♭m, C♯M, G♭M, a♭m, fm, DM, E♭M]

2. Chromatic on F

g♯ melodic minor

Chromatic on G

b harmonic minor

F♯ Major, ascending

B Major

Whole tone on A

A♭ Major, descending

<u>Page 3</u> No. 3

m2, P4, d8, d7, m6, M3, d6, d5

4. [notation: M6, m7, A4, M2, d4, A2, P5, m3]

<u>Page 3, cont.</u>

5. f♯ minor
6. f♯ harmonic minor
7. a. M2
   b. m3
   c. P4
   d. m2
   e. P5

<u>Page 4</u>

8. E♭ Major
9. B♭ Major
10. a. P8
    b. M3
    c. P8
    d. m2
    e. M2
11. F
12. T
13. T
14. F
15. F
16. T

LESSON 2: MODES (Pages 5-12)

<u>Page 7</u>

1. (Given)

2. a. D♯, F♯, G♯, C♯, (D♯)
   b. F♯, C♯, G♯, D♯
   c. E Major
   d. 7
   e. Locrian

3. a. B♭
   b. B♭
   c. F
   d. 1
   e. Ionian

152

Page 7, cont.

4. a. C#, F#
   b. F#, C#
   c. D Major
   d. 4
   e. Lydian

Page 8

5. a. Mixolydian
   b. Phrygian
   c. Aeolian
   d. Lydian
   e. Locrian
   f. Mixolydian
   g. Ionian
   h. Dorian

Page 10

6. (Given)

7. a. P1
   b. F# Major
   c. F#, C#, G#, D#, A#, E#

8. a. M3
   b. C Major
   c. No sharps or flats

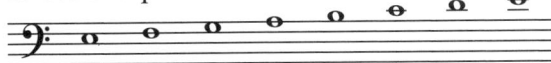

9. a. P4
   b. E♭ Major
   c. B♭, E♭, A♭

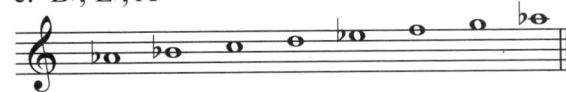

10. a. M7
    b. C♭ Major
    c. B♭, E♭, A♭, D♭, G♭, C♭, F♭

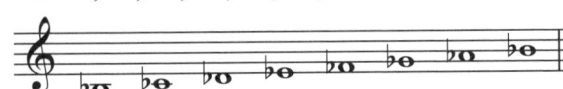

Page 11 No. 11

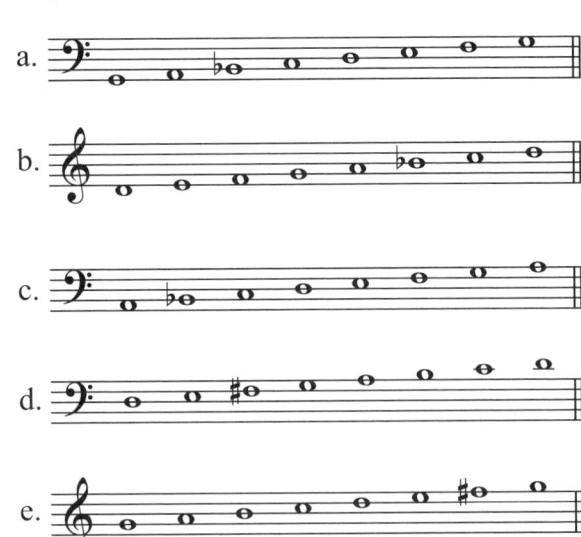

Page 12

12. a. Dorian mode
    b. Mixolydian mode
    c. Lydian mode

LESSON 3: CHORDS (Pages 13-16)

Page 13

1. c min. $^4_3$, E♭ Aug. $^6_4$, d dim. $^6_5$, A♭ Maj. $^6_3$,

   e dim. $^4_3$, D♭ Aug. $^5_3$

   F# Major $^5_3$, G♭ Dom. ^{7}, c# min. $^6_3$,

   b half dim. $^4_3$, G Maj. $^6_4$, b♭ min. $^5_3$

Level 10, Pages 7-13

Page 14, No. 2

DM $^6_5$ g♭°^{6} A+$^6_4$ a♭ m $^5_3$ E Dom$^4_3$ f♯ °^{6}

a^{ø7} C♭ M $^6_5$ f °$^6_4$ c♯ m $^4_2$ B♭ Dom$^4_3$ E♭ M^7

3. IV$^6_3$ ii$^6_3$ vi$^6_4$ V$^5_3$ iii$^5_3$ I$^6_4$
   vii°$^5_3$ V$^6_5$ iii$^6_4$ vii°$^6_3$ V$^4_3$ ii$^5_3$

Page 15, No. 4

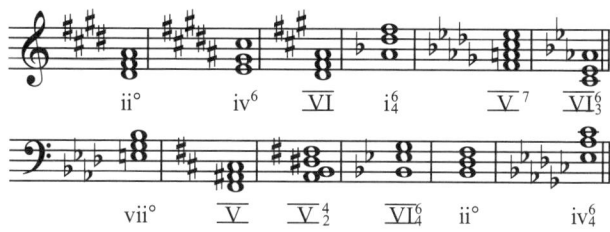

ii°   iv^6 VI   i$^6_4$ V^7 VI$^6_3$

vii°   V   V$^4_2$ VI$^6_4$ ii°   iv$^6_4$

5. E♭ Major

6. a. G Major $^5_3$
   b. G Dominant $^6_5$
   c. C Major $^6_4$
   d. A♭ Major $^6_3$
   e. E♭ Dominant $^4_2$

7. f. V^7
   g. I$^5_3$
   h. ii$^5_3$

Page 16

8. D♭ Major

9. a. I$^5_3$
   b. IV$^5_3$
   c. V^7
   d. iii$^6_3$
   e. I$^5_3$

Page 16, cont.

10. 1. d half dim. $^4_3$
    2. e dim. $^4_2$
    3. A♭ Dom. ^{7}

LESSON 4: THE SECONDARY DOMINANT (Pages 17-22)

Page 18

1. a. G♭ Major
   c. F

2. a. G Major
   c. E

3. a. c♯ minor
   c. E

4. a. b minor
   b. B

Page 19, No. 2

V$^4_3$/IV IV^6 V^7/ii ii$^6_4$ V$^4_3$/ii ii^6 V^7/IV IV$^6_4$

V$^6_5$/iv iv   V$^4_3$/vi vi   V$^6_5$/VI VI   V$^6_4$/V V^6

V^6/V V   V$^4_2$/V V^6 V^6/iii iii   V^2/VI VI^6

Page 20

3. a. g minor
   b. VI$^6_4$
   c. B♭
   d. V^7/VI

V^7/VI   VI$^6_4$

Page 20, cont.

4. a. a minor
   b. V_3^5
   c. B
   d. V_5^6/V

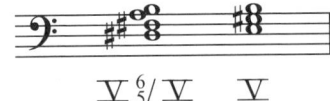
V_5^6/V V

5. a. A♭ Major
   b. IV_3^5
   c. A♭
   d. V_5^6/IV

V_5^6/IV IV

6. a. C♯ Major
   b. iii_3^6
   c. B♯
   d. V_4^6/iii

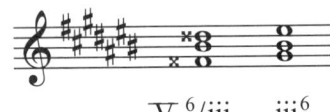
V_4^6/iii iii_3^6

7. a. F Major
   b. ii_3^5
   c. D
   d. V^7/ii

V^7/ii ii

Page 21, No. 8

a. Key of E♭ Major: V^7/ii ii_3^5;
    V/iii iii_3^5

b. Key of e minor: V^7/iv iv_3^5

Page 22

c. Key of C Major: V_5^6/V V_2^4

d. Key of E Major: V^7/V V_3^5;
    V^7/IV IV_3^5

LESSON 5: CADENCES, CHORD PROGRESSIONS, AUGMENTED SIXTH CHORDS (Pages 23-30)

Page 24

1.   I IV V I
2. A Major
3.   IV V^7 I ii^6 I_4^6 V^7 I
4. Pivot chord
5. Authentic

6. A♭ Major

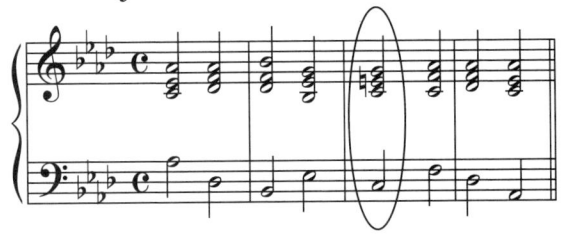

7.   I IV ii V V/vi vi IV I
8. No
9. Secondary dominant
10. Plagal

Page 25

11. C Major
12. G Major
13. a. I_4^6
    b. V_3^5
    c. V_3^5
14. Half
15. c. I_3^5
    d. I_3^5
    e. IV_4^6
    f. V_5^6
16. Chord c

Level 10, Pages 20-25

Page 26

17. G Major
18. D Major
19. I - V
20. a. I$_3^5$
    b. V$_5^6$
    c. V^7/IV
    d. IV$_4^6$
    e. V$_3^5$
21. e. I$_3^5$
    f. I$_3^5$
    g. V$_3^4$
22. Secondary dominant
23. Pivot chord

Optional: Augmented 6th Chord

Page 28

24. It.$^{+6}$ V   It.$_3^6$ V   It.^{6} V   IV$^{6\sharp}$ V

25. Fr.$^{+6}$ V   Fr.$_3^4$ V   Fr.$_{4\ 3}^{6}$ V   II$_{5\ 3}^{6\sharp}$ V

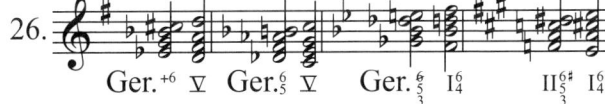

26. Ger.$^{+6}$ V   Ger.$_5^6$ V   Ger.$_3^{6}$ I$_4^6$ II$_{5\ 3}^{6\sharp}$ I$_4^6$

27. (given)

Page 29

b. F Major: Ger.$^{+6}$ V$_3^5$

c. D♭ Major: Fr.$^{+6}$ i$_4^6$

Page 30

d. d minor: It.$^{+6}$ V$_3^5$

e. A♭ Major: Ger.$^{+6}$ I$_4^6$

f. A Major: Fr.$^{+6}$ I$_4^6$

REVIEW: LESSONS 1-5 (Pages 31-32)

Page 31, No. 1

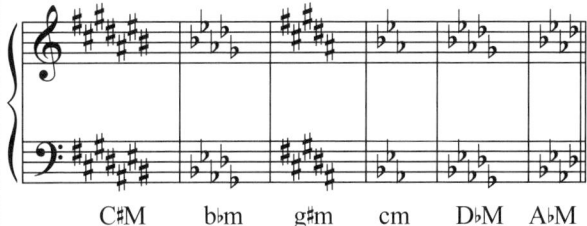

C♯M   b♭m   g♯m   cm   D♭M   A♭M

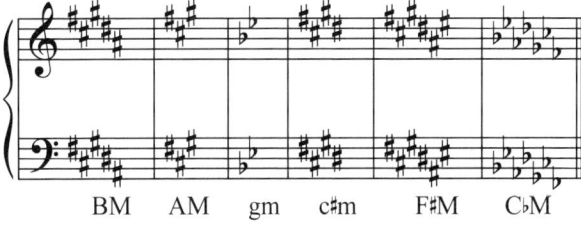

BM   AM   gm   c♯m   F♯M   C♭M

2. d melodic minor

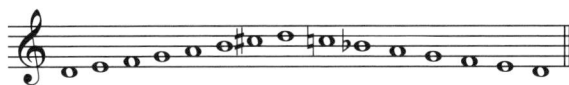

Lydian mode on B♭

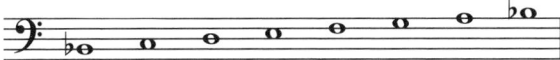

f harmonic minor

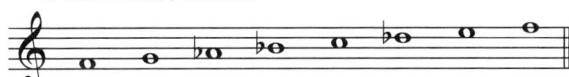

Whole tone on B

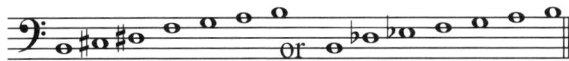

Chromatic on E

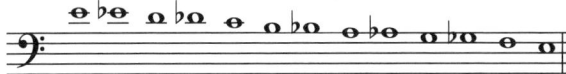

E♭ Major

Page 32, No. 3

P5   m3   M7   A4   d8   M2   m6   d7

Page 32, cont. No. 4

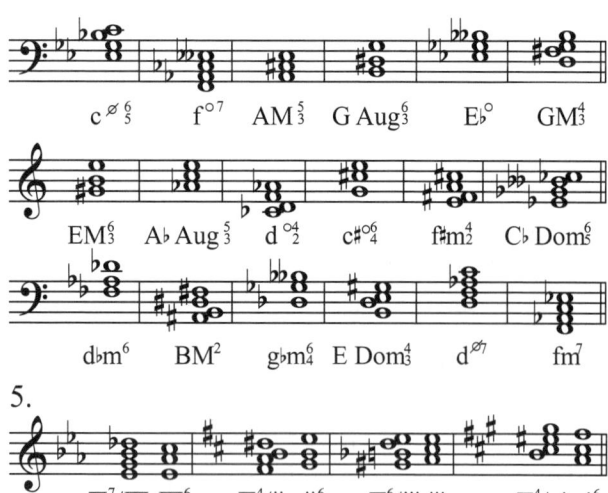

5.

6. V_3^6 ii_3^5 IV_3^6 V_3^4 iii_3^5 $vii°_3^5$

7. $ii°_4^6$ iv_3^5 $ii°_3^6$ VI_4^6 V_5^6 i_4^6

8. Authentic
   Plagal
   Half
   Deceptive

LESSON 6: TEXTURE AND COMPOSITIONAL TECHNIQUES (Pages 33-38)

Page 36

1 through 9: b, c, a, c, d, a, b, a, d

Page 37

10 through 12: a, c, d

13.

14. Theme
15. a. repetition
    b. sequence
    c. pedal point
    d. ostinato
16. No
17. Homophonic

Level 10, Pages 32-43

Page 38

18. canon
19. polyphonic
20. contrapuntal

21.

LESSON 7: NONHARMONIC TONES AND MELODIC DEVICES

Page 42

1. a. passing tone
   b. suspension
   c. anticipation
   d. neighbor tone (upper neighbor)
   e. pivot chord
   f. neighbor tone (lower neighbor)

Page 43

   g. appoggiatura
   h. acciaccatura
   i. appoggiatura

2.

Page 44

3. a. anticipation
   b. neighbor tone (lower neighbor)
   c. neighbor tone (upper neighbor)
   d. passing tone

Page 45

e. suspension
f. acciaccatura
g. appoggiatura

Page 46

4. Ger.$^{+6}$

5. Dominant
6. Harmony based on the interval of a third

LESSON 8: 20th & 21st CENTURY COMPOSITIONAL DEVICES (Pages 47-54)

Page 49

1. a. Twelve tone row
   b. Quartal harmony
   c. Atonality
   d. Bitonality (Polytonality)
   e. Polytonality

Page 50 (Enharmonics are acceptable)

(Any order acceptable)

Optional: Twelve Tone Analysis

Page 54

6. (Optional. Intervals have been simplified. enharmonics are acceptable)

7. (Optional)

REVIEW: LESSONS 6-8 (Pages 55-56)

Page 55

1. a. motive
   b. sequence
   c. canon
   d. ostinato
   e. augmentation
   f. repetition
   g. imitation
   h. diminution

Page 56

2. b, d, a, c

3.

4. anticipation, suspension, appoggiatura,
   neighbor tone (upper neighbor),
   passing tone, neighbor tone (lower neighbor)

5.

6.

7. a. polytonality
   b. atonality
   c. serialism
   d. twelve-tone row
   e. tertian harmony
   f. bitonality
   g. quartal harmony
   h. pivot chord

LESSON 4: THE FUGUE (Pages 57-66)

Assignment 1: Page 61.

1.

2. a. 2
   b. Tonal; subject begins with m2, answer begins with m3
   c. Dominant (5th); tonic is G; the tonal center of the answer is D

3. a. 5
   b. Tonic (I)

4. a. 6
   b. Dominant (5th)

5.

6. Meas. 12: B♭ Major, 3rd or relative Major

   Meas. 14: F Major, V / III (V of Relative Major)

   Meas. 16, beat 4: B♭ Major, 3rd or relative Major

   Meas. 20: c minor, iv or Subdominant

   Meas. 24: g minor, i or Tonic

Assignment 2: Page 62 (Optional)

1. a. (12)   h. 23
   b. 13   i. 28 (2nd half of beat 1)
   c. 15   j. 28 (2nd half of beat 3)
   d. 17 (2nd half of beat 1) k. 29
   e. 17 (2nd half of beat 3) l. 31
   f. 20   m. 33
   g. 21

2. a. Meas. 17 to 18
   b. Meas. 28 to 29

Page 62, cont.

3. a. 3   g. 17
    b. 5   h. 20
    c. 7   i. 22 (slightly modified)
    d. 12   j. 23 (slightly modified)
    e. 14   k. 28 (slightly modified)
    f. 15   l. 32

4. Meas. 1 to 7

5. a. Meas. 8 - 12   c. Meas. 24 - 27
    b. Meas. 18 - 20   d. Meas. 30 - 31

Page 63

6. Meas. 11-12: Key of B♭ Major
   $\underline{V}$ -I, Authentic

   Meas. 19-20: Key of c minor
   ii^{o6} - $\underline{V}$, Half

   Meas. 24, beats 2-3: Key of g minor
   $\underline{V}$ -i, Authentic

   Meas. 27-28: Key of g minor
   iv^6 - $\underline{V}$ (E♭-G-C) or It^{+6} - $\underline{V}$ (E♭-G-C♯), Half

   Meas. 34: g minor
   $\underline{V}^7$ - I, Authentic

LESSON 10: SONATA FORM (Pages 67-82)

Assignment 1, Page 73

1. Exposition: Measure 1, page 74
   Development: Measure 57, page 77
   Recapitulation: Measure 83, page 79

2. Exposition:
   Theme 1: Meas. 1, page 74
   Bridge: Meas. 13, page 74
   Theme 2: Meas. 27, page 75

   Recapitulation:
   Theme 1: Meas. 83, page 79
   Bridge: Meas. 95, page 80
   Theme 2: Meas. 109, page 81

3. Exposition: F Major
   Theme 1: F Major
   Theme 2: C Major
   Development: C Major
   Recapitulation: F Major
   Theme 1: F Major
   Theme 2: F Major

4. Exposition
   Theme 1   Theme 2
   F Major   C Major
   Tonic (I)   Dominant ($\underline{V}$)

   Development
   Begins in   Ends in
   C Major   F Major
   Dominant ($\underline{V}$) Tonic (I)

   Recapitulation
   Theme 1   Theme 2
   F Major   F Major
   Tonic (I)   Tonic (I)

Assignment 2, Page 73 (Optional)

1. Harmonic analysis (Answers are listed below to match lines in the workbook)

Page 74
I   I   I $\underline{V}^7/\underline{IV}$
$\underline{IV}^6_4$ I
$\underline{V}^6_5$ I $\underline{V}^4_3$ I^6 $\underline{IV}$ $\underline{V}$
$\underline{V}^6_5$ I vii^{o6} I^6 $\underline{IV}$ $\underline{V}$
I $\underline{V}^7$ I $\underline{V}$ I^6_4 $\underline{V}^7$ I

Page 75
$\underline{V}$ I^6_4 $\underline{V}^7$ I   vi I^6_4 b dim $^4_3$ $\underline{V}^6$
a dim $^4_3$ $\underline{IV}^6$ I^6 g♯ dim $^4_3$ A Maj ^{6}
(cont) f♯ dim $^4_3$ G Maj ^{6} $\underline{IV}^6_4$
e dim $^4_3$ I^6 ii^6
I^6_4 $\underline{V}$ New key: C Major: I
$\underline{V}^4_3$ I^6_4 $\underline{V}^6$

Page 76
$\underline{V}$ $\underline{V}^4_3$ I
$\underline{V}^7$ I I^6 ii^6
$\underline{V}^6_5/\underline{V}$ $\underline{V}$ $\underline{V}^6_5/vi$
vi I^6_4 ii^6 I^6 ii^6 I^6_4 $\underline{V}^7$
I vii^{o6} I^6

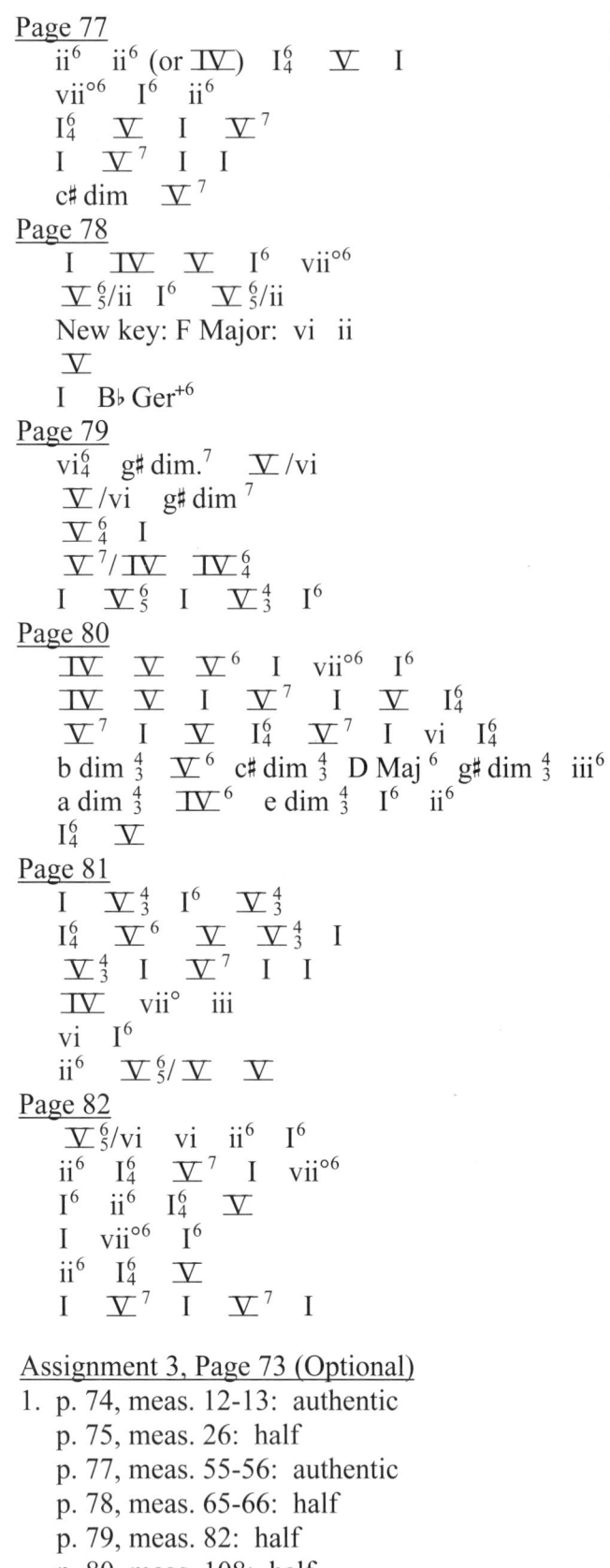

Sequence, page 78, meas. 68-71

Repetition and Pedal Point, page 79, meas. 78-79

Sequence, page 79, meas. 80-81

Syncopation, page 79-80, meas. 90 and 93

Sequence, page 81, meas. 110-115

Imitation, page 81, meas. 117-120

Sequence, page 81, meas. 123-126

Sequence, page 82, meas. 131-132 and 136-139

3. The Exposition and Recaptitulation are the same until measure 100. In measure 100 (during the Bridge) the music changes to accomodate staying in tonic key. Measure 109 (Theme 2) is in the tonic key. The music is an exact transposition until measure 117, when sixteenths are used instead of triplets. Triplets then return in measure 123, which is a transposition of the Exposition until the end of the composition.

4. Measure 6: Appoggiatura
   Measure 64: Appoggiatura

Level 10, Page 73

LESSON 11: RONDO FORM
(Pages 83-106)

Assignment 1, page 96

1a and 1b.

A: B♭ Major, I, page 97, upbeat to meas. 1
B: B♭ & F Majors, I & $\underline{V}$, page 98, meas. 18
A: B♭ Major, I, page 99, upbeat to meas. 44
C: g minor, vi (or relative minor), page 100, meas. 52
A: B♭ Major, I, page 101, upbeat to meas. 72
D: E♭ Major, $\underline{IV}$, page 102, meas. 90
A: B♭ Major, I, page 103, upbeat to meas. 115
B: B♭ Major, I, page 104, meas. 124 (This is the second theme of the B section; the first theme of the section of omitted)
A: B♭ Major, I, page 105, upbeat to meas. 143

Assignment 2, page 96

1. First repetition of A (measure 44): Only first half is repeated, exactly as beginning.

   Second repetition of A (measure 72): Exactly like beginning

   Third repetition of A (measure 115): Left hand has melody at beginning, then transfers to right hand. Only first half of A occurs.

   Fourth repetition of A (measure 143): Exactly as beginning, followed by coda

2. First time, B is in B♭ Major, then F Major
   Second time, B stays in B♭ Major

3. Measure 3: Appoggiatura
   Measure 12: Appoggiatura
   Measure 38: Suspension
   Measure 55: Appoggiatura
   Measure 59: Anticipation
   Measure 91: Upper Neighbor

4. It.+6

Assignment 3, page 97 (Optional)

1. Harmonic analysis. Answers are listed to match staff systems in the workbook.

Page 97
$\underline{V}^6$/ii ii $\underline{V}^6$ I I^6
$\underline{IV}$ I^6 $\underline{V}^4_3$ I I^6_4 $\underline{V}$ $\underline{V}^6$/ii ii ii^6 V^6_5
I I^6 I^6 $\underline{IV}$ I^6_4 $\underline{V}$ I I ii vii°
I I^6 ii^6 vii°/$\underline{V}$ $\underline{V}$ I ii vii° I $\underline{IV}$ $\underline{V}$ $\underline{V}^7$

Page 98
I $\underline{IV}$ $\underline{IV}$ I^6_4 $\underline{V}^7$ I $\underline{IV}$
$\underline{IV}$ I^6_4 $\underline{V}^7$ I $\underline{V}^7$ I $\underline{V}^7$ I
I $\underline{V}^6$ in B♭ Major, I^6 in F Major
F Major (2 beats per chord): $\underline{V}^6_5$ I $\underline{V}^4_3$ I
$\underline{V}^6_5$ I $\underline{V}^4_3$ I^6 ii^6
I^6_4 $\underline{V}^7$ I $\underline{V}^6_5$ $\underline{V}^4_3$ I^6

Page 99
I $\underline{V}^6_5$ $\underline{V}^4_3$ I I^6
$\underline{IV}$ I^6 vi ii^6 $\underline{V}$ I^6
$\underline{IV}$ $\underline{V}$
I $\underline{V}^7$/$\underline{IV}$ IV^6_4 vii°6 I $\underline{V}^7$/$\underline{IV}$ IV^6_4 vii°6
I vii° I vii° I in F, $\underline{V}$ in B♭; B♭ M: $\underline{V}^6$/ii ii $\underline{V}^6$
I I^6 $\underline{IV}$ I^6 $\underline{V}^4_3$ I I^6_4 $\underline{V}$ $\underline{V}^6$/ ii

Page 100
ii ii^6 $\underline{V}^6_5$ I I^6 I^6 $\underline{IV}$ $\underline{IV}^6$ I^6_4 $\underline{V}$
I g minor: i ii° (or vii°$^4_3$ or f♯ dim $^4_3$)
vii°$_3$ i^6 $\underline{V}^6$ i ii^6 i^6 $\underline{V}^6$/ iv
iv $\underline{VI}$ (or Ger+6) i^6_4 $\underline{V}$
$\underline{V}$ vii°6 i vii°$^6_4$ i^6
i^6_4 $\underline{V}$ i^6 $\underline{V}^6_5$/iv iv vii°$^4_3$ (or f♯ dim $^4_3$)

Page 101
i^6_4 $\underline{V}^7$ i b dim $^4_3$ C Maj ^{6}
$\underline{V}$ B♭ Major: $\underline{V}^4_3$ $\underline{V}^6$/ii
ii $\underline{V}^6$ I I^6 $\underline{IV}$ I^6 $\underline{V}^4_3$ I
I^6_4 $\underline{V}$ $\underline{V}^6$/ ii ii ii^6 $\underline{V}^6_5$ I I^6 I^6
$\underline{IV}$ $\underline{IV}^6$ I^6_4 $\underline{V}$ I ii vii° I I^6 ii^6 vii°/ $\underline{V}$
$\underline{V}$ I ii vii° I $\underline{IV}$ $\underline{V}$ $\underline{V}^7$ I $\underline{IV}$

Page 102
$\underline{IV}$ I^6_4 $\underline{V}^7$ I $\underline{IV}$ $\underline{IV}$ I^6_4 $\underline{V}^7$
I $\underline{V}^7$ I $\underline{V}^7$ I
E♭ Major: I $\underline{V}^6_5$ I
$\underline{V}^6_5$ I $\underline{IV}$
I ii $\underline{V}^7$ I^6 I
$\underline{IV}$ I ii $\underline{V}$ I

Level 10, Pages 83-97

Page 103
viiº7/vi   vi   viiº7/V
V6   V6   vi6   viiº6   I   V7
I in E♭   IV in B♭   B♭ Maj: ii6   I64   V   V43/V
V   V43/V   V
I6   V65/ii   ii   V6   I
V64   V6   V64/V   V   V42/ii

Page 104
V7   V   I64   V   V   V6/V
V   I   V65   V43   I6
I   V65   V42   I6   I
IV   I6   vi   ii6   V   I6
IV   IV
I6   ii6   V   I   IV64   viiº6

Page 105
I6   V7/IV   IV   viiº6   I6   V6
I   viiº6   I6   V6/ii   ii   V6
I   I6   IV   I6   V43   I   I64   V   V6/ii
ii   ii6   V65   I   I6   I6   IV   IV6   I64   V
I   I   ii   viiº   I   I6   ii6   viiº/V   V   I   ii   viiº
I   IV   V   V7   I   IV   V   I64   V7

Page 106
I   IV   IV   I64   V7   I   V7   I   V7
I   V7   I   V7   I

Assignment 4, page 97 (Optional)

1. p. 98, meas. 17-18: authentic
    p. 100, meas. 50-51: authentic
    p. 100, meas. 59: half
    p. 100, meas. 62-63: half
    p. 101, meas. 66-67: authentic
    p. 102, meas. 100-101: authentic
    p. 103, meas. 108-109: half
    p. 106, meas. 160-161: authentic

2. Sequence, page 97, meas. 1-2, page 99, meas. 43-45, page 101, meas. 71-73, page 103, meas. 114-116, page 105, meas. 142-144

Sequence, page 97, meas. 4-6, page 99-100, meas. 48-49, page 101, meas. 75-77, page 105, meas. 146-148

Repetition, page 98, meas. 12-16, page 101-102, meas. 83-87, page 105-106, meas. 154-158

Repetition, page 98, meas. 16-17, page 102, meas. 87-88, page 106, meas. 158-159

Repetition, page 98-99, meas. 28-31

Sequence, page 100, meas. 60-61

Sequence, page 100-101, meas. 65-66

Level 10, Page 97

Repetition and Sequence, page 103,
    meas. 106-107

Repetition, page 106, meas. 159-161

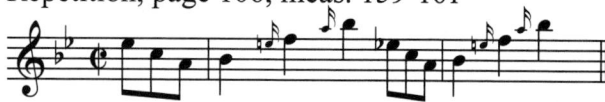

LESSON 12: THEME AND VARIATIONS
(Pages 107-122)

Page 115
1. F: I vii°⁶ V⁶₅ I ii⁶ V⁴₂ I⁶ V⁶₅ I V

Page 116
V⁴₃ V⁴₂ I⁶ IV I⁶ IV I⁶₄ V⁷ I
C: V⁴₂ I⁶ I IV⁶ V I V⁴₂ I⁶ I V⁶ V
I F: V⁴₂ I⁶ V⁶ I IV I⁶ IV I⁶₄ V⁷ I

2. Sixteenths, stepwise motion
    No
    No
3. Ties, suspensions
    No
    No
4. Chordal, many appoggiaturas,
    eighth note rhythm
    No
    No
5. Sixteenths with upbeats
    No
    Yes
6. Suspensions
    Yes, to minor
    No, but uses minor key
7. 32nd note rhythm
    No
    No
8. Dotted rhythms and 32nd notes
9. Measure 1: Appoggiatura
    Measure 2: Appoggiatura
    Measure 4: Appoggiatura
    Measure 10: Appoggiatura
    Measure 32-33: Suspension
    Measure 33-34: Suspension
    Measure 81: Suspension

LESSON 13: MUSIC HISTORY OVERVIEW AND TERMINOLOGY
(Pages 123-128)

Page 124, No. 1

a. 20th/21st Cent.
b. Baroque
c. Romantic
d. Classical
e. 20th/21st Cent.
f. Classical
g. Romantic
h. Romantic
i. Baroque
j. Classical
k. 20th/21st Cent.
l. 20th/21st Cent.
m. 20th/21st Cent.
n. Baroque
o. 20th/21st Cent.
p. Romantic
q. 20th/21st Cent.
r. Baroque
s. Romantic
t. Classical
u. 20th/21st Cent.
v. 20th/21st Cent.
w. Classical
x. Baroque
y. 20th/21st Cent.
z. Romantic

Page 128, No. 2

a. manner in which notes are executed, e.g. *staccato*
b. sharps, flats, naturals written before notes
c. shift of rhythm's pulse from 2 to 3
d. lightly
e. slight variation in rhythm
f. playfully
g. a sudden, sharp accent
h. dying away
i. half voice
j. contradiction of the meter: ♪ ♩ ♪
k. virtuosic piece with scales, rapid passages
l. without

REVIEW: LESSONS 9-13
(Pages 129-130)

Page 129

1. a. subject
   b. theme and variations
   c. exposition
   d. answer
   e. episode
   f. recapitulation
   g. theme 1 and theme 2
   h. real answer
   i. countersubject
   j. *stretto*
   k. development
   l. tonal answer
   m. rondo form

Page 129, No. 2. Allegro
                Andante
                Vivace

Page 130, No. 3 (Other composers and characteristics are possible)

Baroque composers:
    J.S. Bach
    Corelli
    Handel
    Rameau
    Scarlatti
    Telemann
    Vivaldi

Baroque characteristics:
    Polyphonic texture
    Use of ornamentation
    Improvisation
    Use of figured bass
    Dance Suite
    Keyboard instruments: Harpsichord, Clavichord, Organ
    Terraced Dynamics (*p mp mf f*)

Classical composers:
    Beethoven
    Clementi
    Czerny
    Diabelli
    Haydn
    Kuhlau
    Mozart

Classical characteristics:
    Homophonic texture
    Obvious cadence points
    Alberti bass
    Sonata form

Romantic composers:
    Brahms   Mendelssohn
    Chopin   Schubert
    Dvořák   Schumann
    Grieg   Tchaikovsky
    Liszt

Romantic characteristics:
    Programme music
    Descriptive titles
    Colorful harmonies and chromaticism
    Lyric melodies
    Complex rhythm patterns

Impressionism composers:
    Debussy
    Griffes
    Ravel

Impressionism characteristics:
    Unresolved dissonances
    Nonharmonic tones added to triads
    Parallel motion
    Whole-tone and pentatonic scales
    Irregular phrasing

20th/21st Century (Contemporary) composers:
    Bartók   Kabalevsky
    Britten   Poulenc
    Copland   Prokofiev
    Dello Joio   Shostakovich

20th/21st Century (Contemporary) characteristics:
    Less use of major and minor tonalities
    Quartal harmony
    Bitonality, Polytonality, Atonality
    Irregular and changing meters
    Polyphonic texture
    Neo-Classic writing
    Serial music
    Twelve-tone music

4. a. hold the note for its full value
   b. sustained
   c. immediately slower
   d. gradually slower
   e. chronological classification of a composer's music
   f. merrily, with humor

FINAL TEST (Pages 131-138)

Page 131, No. 1

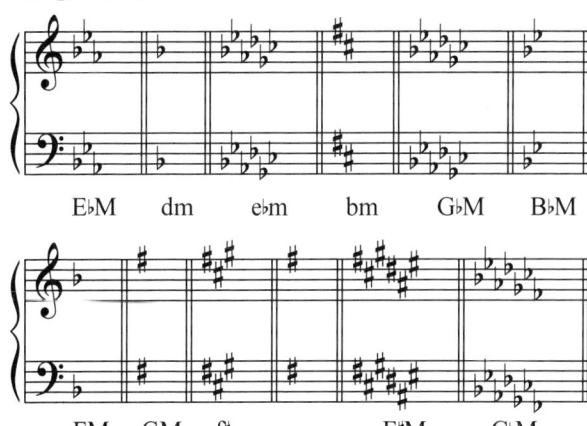

Level 10, Pages 129-131

Page 131, No. 2

f melodic minor

Mixolydian mode on C

c harmonic minor

whole tone on G

or

chromatic on D

C♭ Major

Page 132, No. 3

M2 P8 m6 d5 A8 d7 M3 P4

4. eø7 d m 6/4 e dim 6 F Aug 6/4 d♭° f♯ d 4/2

D M 6/3 C♯ Aug 5/3 E♭ Dom 6/5 A♭ M 6 C M 6/4 b dim

G♭ Dom 7 b♭ m 6/4 F M 4/3 c♭ m 7 a °4/3 g ø7

5. V 4/3 / V   V 6   V 7 /ii   ii 6/4

V 4/2 /iv   iv 6   V 6/5 /VI   VI

6. IV 6/3   vi 5/3   iii 6/4   V 6/3   ii 6/4   vii° 5/3

7. V 4/3   ii° 5/3   ii° 6/3   iv 5/3   i 6/4   VI 6/4

8. Half, Authentic, Plagal, Deceptive

Page 133

9. a. Serialism
    b. Pivot chord
    c. Homophonic texture
    d. Pedal point
    e. Augmentation
    f. Quartal harmony
    g. Motive
    h. Twelve-tone row
    i. Tertian harmony
    j. Ostinato
    k. Theme
    l. Polytonality
    m. Polyphonic texture
    n. Diminution
    o. Atonality
    p. Canon
    q. Bitonality

Page 134

10.

11.

12. retrograde inversion

13. neighbor tone (upper neighbor)
    passing tone
    appoggiatura
    anticipation

14. (Other composers and characteristics are possible)

   Baroque composers:
      J.S. Bach
      Corelli   Scarlatti
      Handel   Telemann
      Rameau   Vivaldi

Level 10, Pages 131-134

Page 134, cont.

Baroque characteristics:

    Polyphonic texture
    Use of ornamentation
    Improvisation
    Use of figured bass
    Dance Suite
    Keyboard instruments: Harpsichord, Clavichord, Organ
    Terraced Dynamics (*p mp mf f*)

Classical composers:

    Beethoven
    Clementi
    Czerny
    Diabelli
    Haydn
    Kuhlau
    Mozart

Classical characteristics:

    Homophonic texture
    Obvious cadence points
    Alberti bass
    Sonata form

Romantic composers:

    Brahms   Mendelssohn
    Chopin   Schubert
    Dvořák   Schumann
    Grieg   Tchaikovsky
    Liszt

Romantic characteristics:

    Programme music
    Descriptive titles
    Colorful harmonies and chromaticism
    Lyric melodies
    Complex rhythm patterns

Impressionism composers:

    Debussy
    Griffes
    Ravel

Impressionism characteristics:

    Unresolved dissonances
    Nonharmonic tones added to triads
    Parallel motion
    Whole-tone and pentatonic scales
    Irregular phrasing

20th/21st Century (Contemp.) composers:

    Bartók
    Britten
    Copland
    Dello Joio
    Kabalevsky
    Poulenc
    Prokofiev
    Shostakovich

20th/21st Century (Contemp.) characteristics:

    Less use of major and minor tonalities
    Quartal harmony
    Bitonality, Polytonality, Atonality
    Irregular and changing meters
    Polyphonic texture
    Neo-Classic writing
    Serial music
    Twelve-tone music

Page 135

15. E Major

16. a. IV_4^6

    b. V_3^5/vi

    c. vi_4^6

    d. I_4^6

    e. V_3^5

    f. vi_4^6

    g. iii_3^5

    h. IV_4^6

    i. I_3^5

Page 135, cont.

17. Plagal
18. syncopation
19. sequence
20. A♯ and C♮
21. Homophonic
22. Romantic

Page 137

23. F♯ Major
24. 3

25.

26. 3
27. Dominant (5th)
28. Tonal (Subject begins with 4th; answer begins with 5th)
29. 5
30. Tonic
31. Expositon
32. Episode
33. *stretto*
34. countersubject

Page 138

35. Walking tempo
36. D Major
37. A Major
38. a. D Major $_3^5$
    b. A Dominant $_5^6$
    c. a♯ diminished $_5^6$
    d. b minor $_3^6$
    e. A Major $_4^6$
    f. E Dominant $_5^6$
39. Chord e
40. Exposition
    Development
    Recapitulation
41. fast tempo

Level 10, Pages 135-138